D0820085

WILLIAMS-SONOMA

COOKING from the
farmers' market

Foreword Jennifer Maiser

Recipes Tasha De Serio & Jodi Liano

Photographs Maren Caruso

weldon**owen**

CONTENTS

VEGETABLES

FRUITS

DISCOVER THE PLEASURES OF EATING SEASONALLY, ORGANICALLY, AND LOCALLY

Today, more and more people are realizing the joys of shopping, cooking, and eating from the farmers' market. Straight from the farm, bountiful and colorful displays of produce make it easy to prepare healthy, flavorful meals using the freshest fruits and vegetables at the peak of their season.

The benefits of shopping and mingling at your local market are many: meeting the rancher who brings juicy, organic steaks; sampling the season's first sweet peaches or corn; purchasing creamy goat's cheese from a local cheesemonger for a special meal; or holding a loaf of still-warm bread fresh from the baker's oven—each is an experience that will enable you to eat the best foods available. And as an added benefit, by choosing seasonal, organic food, you are not only supporting local producers, you are eating whole foods that are good for your health, and you are guaranteed that the food you eat is impeccably fresh.

This book will show you delicious ways to use farmers' market produce for every course of the meal. The recipes are arranged by fruits or vegetables, and each is designed to be simple enough for busy home cooks to prepare any time of the week. Each mouthwatering recipe lets the featured ingredient shine. A salad of small new potatoes with a piquant mustard vinaigrette, a side dish of fresh beans tossed in olive oil and lemon, and a homemade strawberry-rhubarb pie elevate ingredients from the simple to the inspired when the produce was harvested just before you purchased it at the market. With this book as your guide, you'll discover that fresh ingredients at their peak of ripeness require little effort to be transformed into satisfying, nourishing meals—something to be enjoyed that much more when you sit down to eat.

Jennifer Maiser

THE FARMERS' MARKET

The farmers' market is becoming the town square of modern times. Not only can you shop there for impeccably fresh foods, you can catch up with your friends as you browse; you can introduce your children to the pleasures of fresh food; you can ask the apple grower about the best way to cook his prized fruits. In short, regular visits to the farmers' market help make your whole life more vibrant.

What's in Season

Do you remember the joy of eating cherries as a child? I used to anticipate the summer months when sweet, juicy cherries would be available, and then I'd eat them until I couldn't possibly eat another. Cherries were a special treat because they came around only once a year, and I knew I'd have to wait an entire year to eat them again.

Cooking in concert with the seasons is an age-old idea. Before mass transportation, people ate only what was growing in gardens, nearby farms, or orchards. Today, however, produce is transported from all corners of the world. And while these items may appear beautiful, the flavor of out-of-season produce cannot compare with that of fruits or vegetables harvested at their peak.

Seasonality may initially make you feel like you have to deprive yourself, but once you incorporate it into your meal planning, you'll see that it offers abundance. Blueberry season gives way to apricot season, which merges into corn season, and on it goes. My menus are constantly changing as they reflect the time of year. It's an exciting way to eat.

Of the many reasons to eat seasonally, one of the best is that the food simply tastes amazing. As you move toward eating this way, you may re-discover the flavors of your childhood. You'll notice that an in-season tomato is almost a different fruit than a tomato purchased in January and shipped from a distant grower. As you enjoy a pear so juicy that you have to eat it over the sink, you'll understand that buying in-season produce is a gift to yourself and your family.

An added bonus of eating in-season fruits and vegetables is that they often cost less than foods that are brought in from far away places. When farmers have a generous supply of a particular item, the price is usually very fair, making it a sensible way to help manage your food budget.

Why Organic

In the United States, the selling of organic produce is tightly controlled and regulated. Labeling that certifies organic produce is a great asset for consumers. When you see the certified organic label on produce, you can be assured that farmers have followed strict guidelines. For example, they do not use chemical pesticides and they must grow their produce in soil that has been free from chemical input. This means that all you taste in that just-picked carrot is pure, true, carrot flavor. Additionally, by buying organic produce, you can be assured that you and your family are protected from harmful chemicals.

Some certified organic products can be expensive, so if you are watching your wallet, you can prioritize these items by deciding which ones are the best to buy. Vegetables and

Tips for the Market

BUY SOMETHING NEW

Shopping at a farmers' market opens your
eyes to new varieties of vegetables and fruits.
Each time you go, don't be afraid to choose one
or two produce items that you've never cooked
with before. This book will show you at least
three delicious ways to prepare them.

BE FLEXIBLE

While you may head to the market with the
outline of a meal and a general list, be ready to
change your plan if the items you need are not
in season. For example, if your recipe calls for
spinach and it's not at the market that day, but
you see big, beautiful bunches of kale or chard,
snap them up. You can also ask vendors for
cooking suggestions. You'll find they can be very
knowledgeable about preparing and cooking
their beloved products.

TASTE BEFORE YOU BUY

Many farmers' market vendors offer samples
of their products and encourage you to taste.
Peaches, for example, can vary from highly
acidic to super sweet. You won't know what you
prefer until you try what's available. Sampling
is also a great way to learn more about the
different varieties of produce within a family
or new hybrids or heirlooms that are specially
suited to your climate.

BRING YOUR OWN BAGS

You can lessen your impact on the environment
by bringing your own bags to the market. A
couple of canvas bags, a few plastic produce
bags, and containers for delicate items will help
you to bring all your market treasures home
safely. If you're not returning home right away,
bring a small ice chest for perishables.

fruits that have an edible peel or skin—such as bell peppers, strawberries, potatoes, or apples—or a lot of surface area—such as celery, lettuces, and fresh herbs—should preferably be organic. If you're opting for conventionally grown fruits and vegetables in some cases, choose those with peels that you can remove. For example, when my budget is tight, I buy nonorganic avocados, citrus, and bananas from vendors I trust.

Buying Local

"Sorry about the broccoli," a farmer said to me one morning at the farmers' market. I looked down at the broccoli, which still had ice crystals. "We just picked it, and it was an icy morning." It was 10 a.m. The broccoli had been out of the ground for just four hours and had travelled about fifty miles to get to me. I simply smiled and thought about how delicious the just-picked vegetable would taste in the stir-fry that I would make with it that same evening.

Local food is good because it tends to be more flavorful than food that has been transported from afar. The faster a bunch of broccoli can get from the ground to your plate, the fresher it will taste, and the more likely you and your family will want to eat it. Buying local food also simplifies the cooking process. When food is fresh, the addition of only a few bright flavorings is all you need to help the dish shine. If you think of freshness as the most important ingredient in your cooking, your dishes will only get better from there.

Buying local foods gives you the opportunity to purchase directly from the farmer. By doing this, you can establish a relationship with the people who are growing your food, and then help support their business, knowing that you are buying quality products, and you know where your food comes from.

Also at the Market

The farmers' market has far more to offer than just produce. Here are some examples of other items that are likely made in your community.

MEAT & POULTRY

Ranchers selling locally raised, free-range meats and poultry are also often at the farmers' market. Look for those who feed their animals a well-rounded diet and allow them to roam free, which contributes to great flavor.

SEAFOOD

If you live close to water, you are likely to find a local fishmonger selling fresh fish and shellfish. While no organic standards have been set for seafood, the fish or shellfish will likely have been caught or harvested just before arriving at the farmstand.

DAIRY

Cheese is a staple at the farmers' market and dairy farmers or cheese makers from every region will boast their own type depending on whether sheep, cows, or goats are raised in the area. You can often substitute locally grown cheeses for the more traditional, imported varieties of cheese called for in a recipe. For example, a locally produced firm (or aged) sheep's milk or dry jack cheese could stand in for an Italian romano or Parmesan cheese.

OTHER PRODUCTS

Look for other edible items sold by artisans who use local ingredients in their products. You'll often see bread, olive oil, nuts, jams and preserves, honey, and confections among the produce vendors.

SEASONAL VEGETABLES

All vegetables have a peak season where they flourish and taste best. Most are available during certain times of the year while others, such as cauliflower, carrots, fennel, and avocados, can be found over the course of a few seasons. Use the chart to the right as a guide to determine seasonality and as a key for when certain vegetables should appear at the market. You can then find ways to use those vegetables by looking up recipes in this book.

INGREDIENTS	SPRING	SUMMER	AUTUMN	WINTER
BEANS & PEAS				
shell beans		■	■	
fava beans	■			
green beans		■		
long beans		■	■	
wax beans		■		
english peas	■			
snow peas	■	■		
sugar snap peas	■	■		
pea shoots	■	■		
CABBAGES & OTHER CRUCIFERS				
broccoli	■		■	■
cauliflower		■	■	■
brussels sprouts			■	■
broccoli rabe			■	■
green cabbage			■	■
red cabbage				■
LEAFY GREENS				
delicate lettuces	■		■	
sturdy lettuces				■
arugula	■	■	■	
spinach	■		■	
chicories	■			■
chard			■	■
kale			■	■

INGREDIENTS	SPRING	SUMMER	AUTUMN	WINTER
ROOTS & TUBERS				
starchy potatoes		▪		
waxy potatoes	▪	▪		
new potatoes	▪	▪		
sweet potatoes			▪	▪
beets		▪	▪	
carrots	▪			▪
parsnips	▪			▪
celery root	▪		▪	▪
turnips			▪	▪
rutabagas			▪	▪
radishes	▪	▪	▪	
SQUASHES				
zucchini		▪		
squash blossoms	▪			
yellow squash		▪		
pattypan squash		▪		
acorn squash				▪
butternut squash				▪
pumpkin			▪	▪
kabocha squash			▪	
STALKS, SHOOTS & BULBS				
celery				▪
fennel			▪	▪
asparagus	▪			

INGREDIENTS	SPRING	SUMMER	AUTUMN	WINTER
ONIONS & COUSINS				
onions		▪		
sweet onions	▪	▪		
garlic		▪		
green garlic	▪			
leeks	▪		▪	
green onions	▪	▪	▪	▪
VEGETABLE FRUITS				
tomatoes		▪	▪	
heirloom tomatoes		▪		
cucumbers		▪		
pickling cucumbers		▪		
sweet peppers		▪		
padrón peppers		▪		
chiles		▪	▪	
dried chiles			▪	
avocados	▪	▪	▪	
eggplants		▪		
OTHER VEGETABLES				
mushrooms	▪		▪	
sweet corn		▪		
artichokes	▪		▪	▪

SEASONAL FRUITS

Like vegetables, fruits also have peak season where they flourish and taste best. While most are available for just one season, others, such as oranges, plums, and rhubarb, can be grown and harvested a few times throughout the year. Use the chart to the right to determine seasonality and as a key for when certain fruits appear at the farmers' market. Then, choose a recipe in the book to prepare using that ingredient.

INGREDIENTS	SPRING	SUMMER	AUTUMN	WINTER
BERRIES				
strawberries	■	■		
fraises des bois	■			
blackberries	■	■	■	
raspberries	■	■	■	
blueberries		■		
huckleberries		■		
cranberries			■	■
CITRUS				
lemons	■			■
meyer lemons	■			■
limes		■	■	
key limes		■		
oranges	■			■
blood oranges	■		■	■
tangerines	■			■
mandarins	■			■
grapefruits				■
pomelos				■
MELONS				
cantaloupe		■		
honeydew		■		
galia melons		■		
watermelon		■		

INGREDIENTS	SPRING	SUMMER	AUTUMN	WINTER
STONE FRUITS				
apricots		■		
pluots		■		
cherries	■	■		
sour cherries		■		
nectarines		■		
peaches		■		
plums		■		
apriums		■		
TREE FRUITS				
apples			■	■
pears			■	■
asian pears		■	■	
pomegranates			■	■
quinces			■	■
figs		■	■	
persimmons			■	■
hachiya persimmons			■	
OTHER FRUIT				
rhubarb	■	■		
grapes	■	■	■	

Beans & Peas

The many varieties of beans and peas belong to the legume botanical group. With some exceptions, beans are generally mild in flavor and have a texture that ranges from creamy to crisp. Peas, on the other hand, are similarly varied in taste, from sweet to pleasantly subtle with a sweet texture. Among the world's oldest foods, legumes have been grown in parts of the Americas, Asia, and Europe for millennia.

Fresh beans fall into two broad categories: pod beans and shell beans. Pod beans, such as green beans and romano beans, are eaten whole with the pods. For shell beans, such as fresh fava (broad) beans, only the inner seeds can be consumed.

Like pod beans, snow peas (also known as *mangetouts*) and sugar snap peas are eaten whole. English peas, a type of shelling pea, must be removed from their pods.

A spring garden staple, peas such as English peas are harvested when young and tender. Other types of fresh beans and peas mature in spring and summer. In most cases, the younger they are, the better the legume will be.

BUYING SHELL BEANS

Look for beans that are still slightly moist. If they are in the pods, you should be able to feel round beans inside and the pods should be pliable, not crisp. Store the pods in a plastic bag in the refrigerator for up to 3 days. If the beans are shelled and you are not using them right away, blanch them (page 264), place them in an airtight container, and refrigerate for up to 5 days.

Shell Beans

Beans are among the first foods domesticated, and archaeologists have found evidence of their widespread use in the Mediterranean and Americas from as early as 9,000 B.C. Shell beans are any of the 500 varieties of beans grown around the world whose pods are removed and typically not eaten. Popular varieties include fava (broad) beans, cranberry (borlotti) beans, lima beans, chickpeas (garbanzo beans), black beans, and scarlet runner beans. Fresh shell beans, available in late summer and early autumn, have a sweet and creamy taste that cannot be matched by dried beans.

Fresh shell beans should be eaten within a few days of purchase, before they dry out. These beans need to be removed from their pods but can be prepared in the same ways as their dried counterparts, but take less time to cook. They taste great on their own alongside poultry and fish, in soups, or puréed to make a spread.

WORKING WITH SHELL BEANS

If you have purchased shell beans still in the pod, remove the beans from the pod just before cooking. Fresh shell beans tend to cook much faster than dried shell beans, so be sure to pay attention to cooking times; remove shell beans from the heat as soon as they become tender.

Fava Beans

Pale green, flat fava beans, also known as broad beans, English beans, or horse beans, grow in pods on bushy flowering plants 2 to 3 feet (60 cm to 1 m) tall. Their pods resemble very large, thick pea pods. Available briefly in the spring months, they are best harvested while still young and tender.

With their pleasantly bitter flavor, fava beans have been popular in Mediterranean and Middle Eastern cuisines for many centuries. Although these beans take time to prepare—they must be blanched to remove their tough outer skin—they are well worth the effort, as their delicious flavor can be enjoyed in a variety of dishes such as salads, soups, and pasta. They are excellent blanched whole and served simply topped with olive oil, sea salt, and shaved hard cheese, or puréed into a smooth and creamy spread to eat with flat bread.

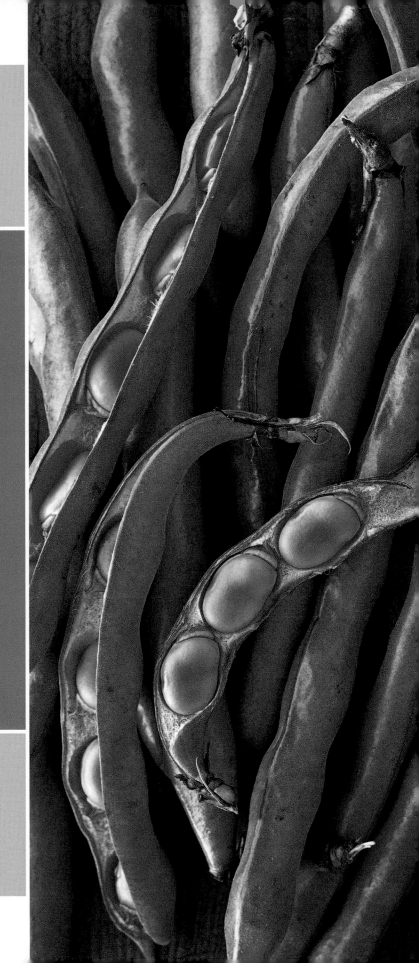

Cranberry Bean, Broccoli Rabe & Bacon Salad

MAKES 4 SERVINGS

4 cups (2 lb/1 kg) fresh cranberry (borlotti) beans, shelled

Salt and freshly ground pepper

1 bay leaf

2 fresh thyme sprigs

1 lb (500 g) broccoli rabe, stems removed

2 cloves garlic, minced

⅓ cup (3 fl oz/80 ml) extra-virgin olive oil

¼ lb (125 g) thinly sliced bacon, cut into 1-inch (2.5-cm) pieces

3–4 Tbsp red wine vinegar

Place the beans in a saucepan with water to cover by 2 inches (5 cm). Add ½ tsp salt, the bay leaf, and thyme and bring to a boil. Reduce the heat to a simmer and cook until tender, 15–25 minutes.

Chop the tender portions of the broccoli rabe. In a large frying pan over medium-high heat, sauté the garlic in the olive oil until fragrant, 2–3 minutes. Add the broccoli rabe, ¼ tsp salt, and ½ tsp pepper. Cook, stirring often, until the greens are tender, 4–5 minutes. Remove from the heat and cover.

In a small frying pan, cook the bacon until the fat is translucent, 3–4 minutes. Drain the beans and place in a serving bowl. Add the broccoli rabe and the bacon and any of its rendered fat. Add vinegar to taste and toss to mix. Serve right away.

Roasted Chicken Breasts with Fresh Beans & Sage

MAKES 4 SERVINGS

4 cups (2 lb/1 kg) fresh shelling beans, shelled

5 Tbsp (3 fl oz/80 ml) olive oil

3 cloves garlic, peeled

1 bay leaf

3 fresh sage leaves

Salt and freshly ground pepper

4 skin-on boneless chicken breasts, tenders removed

Preheat the oven to 400°F (200°C). Place the beans in a heavy pot and add water to cover by 1 inch (2.5 cm). Add 1 Tbsp of the olive oil, the garlic, bay leaf, sage, and 1 tsp salt. Bring to a boil, reduce to a simmer, and cook until tender, about 30 minutes. Add more water to cover the beans, if needed. Season to taste with salt and set aside.

Season the chicken with salt and pepper. In a large ovenproof frying pan over medium-high heat, sear the chicken on one side in 2 Tbsp of the oil, 3–4 minutes. Turn the chicken over and put the pan in the oven. Roast until cooked through, 5–8 minutes. Transfer to a plate, pour any pan drippings around the chicken and let rest for 3–4 minutes. Spoon the beans and a little of their cooking liquid on the side of the chicken and drizzle with the remaining 2 Tbsp olive oil. Serve right away.

Cannellini Bean Soup with Ham & Pasta

MAKES 8 SERVINGS

1½ lb (750 g) smoked ham hock

4 cups (2 lb/1 kg) fresh cannellini beans, shelled

Pinch of red pepper flakes

1 bay leaf

Salt

3 yellow onions, finely diced

¾ lb (375 g) tomatoes, peeled, seeded, and chopped

4 cloves garlic, thinly sliced

2 tsp chopped fresh rosemary

1 cup (3½ oz/105 g) small pasta shells

Extra-virgin olive oil for drizzling

In a large pot over medium heat, bring the ham hock and 3 quarts (3 l) water to a boil. Skim off any foam, reduce the heat to low, and cook, uncovered, for 30 minutes. Add the beans, pepper flakes, bay leaf, and a pinch of salt. Return to a boil, reduce the heat to low, and simmer for 15 minutes. Add the onions, tomatoes, garlic, and rosemary and return to a boil. Reduce the heat to low and cook until the vegetables are tender, about 30 minutes. Remove the ham hock and let cool slightly. Cut the meat away from the bone and into small pieces.

Purée 1 cup (8 fl oz/250 ml) of the soup base in a blender and return to the pot. Add the ham, season with salt, and let cool to room temperature. Refrigerate for 4–6 hours to develop the flavors.

To serve, bring the soup to a boil, add the pasta shells, and cook at a low boil until the pasta is tender, 12–15 minutes. The soup should be fairly thick; if it is too thick, thin with boiling water. Season with salt. Ladle into bowls, drizzle with olive oil, and serve right away.

EDAMAME

The Japanese name *edamame* refers to baby soybeans that have been enjoyed in many Asian cuisines for centuries. They have recently caught on just about everywhere. *Edamame* are usually boiled in water or steamed, sprinkled with salt, and served whole in the pod. They can also be substituted for shell beans in many recipes.

EDAMAME WITH SEA SALT

Cook ¾ lb (375 g) *edamame* pods in a large saucepan of salted boiling water until just tender, 2–3 minutes (3–4 minutes if frozen). Remove the beans with a slotted spoon and plunge into a bowl of ice water. Drain and sprinkle with sea salt. To eat, use your fingers to split the pods to reveal the edible seeds inside. Makes 4 servings.

ROASTED CHICKEN BREASTS WITH FRESH BEANS & SAGE

FAVA BEANS WITH OLIVE OIL & LEMON

Crostini with Fava Bean Spread

MAKES 10–12 SERVINGS

1 large baguette, cut into slices
¼ inch (6 mm) thick

5 Tbsp (3 fl oz/80 ml) extra-virgin olive oil,
plus extra for brushing

2 lb (1 kg) fresh fava (broad) beans

Salt and freshly ground pepper

3 Tbsp (3 fl oz/90 ml) heavy
(double) cream, plus more if needed

4 Tbsp chopped mint

Shaved aged hard cheese,
such as Parmesan, for garnish

Preheat the oven to 350°F (180°C).

Brush the baguette slices on both sides with
2 Tbsp of the olive oil and bake in a single
layer on a rimmed baking sheet until lightly
golden, about 10 minutes. Turn the slices
over and bake, about 10 minutes more.
Set aside to cool.

Remove the fava beans from their pods and
discard the pods. Bring a large pot of salted
water to a boil. Add the beans and cook
until tender, 2–3 minutes (the amount of
time required will depend on the freshness
of the beans). Drain the beans and then
immediately plunge into a bowl of ice water.
When cool enough to handle, slip off the
skins and discard.

In a food processor, process the beans,
the remaining 3 Tbsp oil, 3 Tbsp of the cream,
2 tsp salt, 1 tsp pepper, and the mint until
a creamy purée forms. If the mixture seems
too dry, add up to 3 Tbsp more cream. Taste
and adjust the seasoning.

Spread the purée on the baguette slices
and arrange on a platter. Sprinkle with the
cheese and serve right away.

Pasta with Fava Beans, Green Garlic & Prosciutto

MAKES 6 SERVINGS

2 lb (1 kg) fresh fava (broad) beans

2 Tbsp extra-virgin olive oil,
plus extra for drizzling

2 Tbsp thinly sliced green garlic,
white and light green parts only

Salt and freshly ground pepper

1 lb (500 g) shell-shaped pasta,
such as *conchiglie* or *lumache*

2 oz (60 g) prosciutto, cut into thin strips

½ cup (2 oz/60 g) grated aged hard
cheese, such as Pecorino

Remove the fava beans from their pods and
discard the pods. Bring a large pot of salted
water to a boil. Add the beans and cook
until tender, 2–3 minutes (the amount of
time required will depend on the freshness
of the beans). Using a slotted spoon, drain
the beans and then immediately plunge into
a bowl of ice water. Reserve the cooking
water. When cool enough to handle, slip
off the skins and discard.

In a large frying pan over medium heat, warm
the 2 Tbsp oil. Add the green garlic and
a pinch each of salt and pepper and sauté
until the garlic has softened, 2–3 minutes.
Stir in the fava beans and cook until warm,
1–2 minutes more.

Add a pinch of salt to the water and return
to a boil. Add the pasta and cook until al
dente, 9–11 minutes or according to the
package directions. Reserve 1 cup (8 fl oz/
250 ml) of the pasta cooking water and
drain the pasta.

Stir the pasta into the beans. Add enough
of the pasta water to moisten the pasta. Stir
in the prosciutto and half of the cheese.

Transfer to a serving dish and drizzle with
oil. Sprinkle with the remaining cheese and
serve right away.

Fava Beans with Olive Oil & Lemon

MAKES 6 SERVINGS

4 lb (2 kg) fresh fava (broad) beans

Salt and freshly ground pepper

3 Tbsp extra-virgin olive oil

2 Tbsp fresh lemon juice

1 clove garlic, minced

1 Tbsp chopped fresh flat-leaf
(Italian) parsley

½ tsp grated lemon zest

¾ cup (3 oz/90 g) shaved aged hard
cheese, such as Pecorino

Remove the fava beans from their pods and
discard the pods. Bring a large pot of salted
water to a boil. Add the beans and cook
until tender, 2–3 minutes (the amount of
time required will depend on the freshness
of the beans). Using a slotted spoon, drain
the beans and then immediately plunge
into a bowl of ice water.

When cool enough to handle, slip off the
skins and discard. Transfer to a serving bowl.

Whisk together the olive oil, lemon juice,
garlic, parsley, and lemon zest and season
with salt and pepper. Drizzle on top of the
beans and toss. Sprinkle the cheese over
the top and toss gently. Serve right away.

Green Beans

Also called snap beans, string beans, or runner beans, green beans can be eaten whole. Both the tender pod and the small seeds within have a mild, fresh, sweet taste. Most green beans have thin, cylindrical pods about 4 inches (10 cm) long with pointed tips. Popular varieties found at the market are Blue Lake, Kentucky Wonder, Roma, and young scarlet runner beans. Haricots verts are slim, delicate green beans much loved in France and now increasingly available locally at farmers' markets.

Green beans are at their best from early to mid-summer. They take well to a variety of cooking techniques from boiling to steaming, sautéing to deep-frying. Added to soups, they provide contrast and color to other vegetables. Green beans are ideal for canning and pickling. They are also excellent raw on crudités platters, in composed salads, or served alone, blanched, then chilled with vinaigrette.

BUYING WAX BEANS

Purchasing wax beans is much like purchasing green beans. Look for beans that are evenly colored, free of brown spots, and snap when broken. The skin of their pods will be thinner and more velvety, and depending on their variety, choose ones that are light to deep yellow or dark purple. Wrap them in dry paper towels and refrigerate in a plastic bag for up to 3 days.

Wax Beans

Closely related to green beans, wax beans differ in their color, which can be vibrant yellow or dark purple and, as their name suggests, in that their texture is slightly waxier. Like green beans, wax beans are enjoyed whole with pod and seeds, and they taste mild and fresh with sweet, grassy overtones. The most common variety is 4 inches (10 cm) long, with a cylindrical pod and tapered tips.

Also like green beans, wax beans appear at markets during the early to mid-summer. Wax beans make a colorful side dish steamed or sautéed with butter or olive oil. They are ideal in vegetable salads, pairing well with potatoes, beets, corn, and peas. They can be added to, or substituted for, green beans in recipes.

WORKING WITH WAX BEANS

Rinse the beans under cold running water. Snap off the pointy stem ends and remove any tough strings that run along the length of the bean. Yellow wax beans retain their color best when cooked whole at a high temperature for a short period of time. The color of purple beans will fade slightly when cooked.

Tempura String Beans with Aioli

1 cup (8 fl oz/250 ml) ice water

1 large egg, beaten

¾ cup (3 oz/90 g) sifted all-purpose (plain) flour, plus extra for dusting

2 or 3 ice cubes

Peanut or vegetable oil for frying

1 lb (500 g) green beans

Salt

Aioli (page 139)

In a bowl, whisk together the ice water and egg. Whisk in the ¾ cup flour; the batter should be quite lumpy. Add the ice cubes.

Pour enough oil into a wok or deep fryer to reach halfway up the sides and heat to 350°F (180°C) on a deep-frying thermometer. Working in batches, lightly dust the beans with flour, then dip in the batter, shaking off the excess. Fry, stirring occasionally, until crisp, about 3 minutes. Drain on paper towels and season with salt.

Serve right away with the Aioli for dipping.

Stewed Green Beans with Tomatoes

2 Tbsp olive oil

1 small yellow onion, chopped

4 cloves garlic, thinly sliced

1 lb (500 g) green beans

2 cups (12 oz/375 g) peeled, seeded, and chopped tomatoes

Salt and freshly ground pepper

In a large frying pan over medium heat, warm the olive oil. Add the onion and cook until soft, about 7 minutes. Add the garlic and cook, stirring, for 1 minute. Raise the heat to high and add the beans and tomatoes. Bring to a simmer, reduce the heat to low, cover, and cook until the beans are tender, about 30 minutes. Uncover, raise the heat to medium, and continue to cook until most of the liquid has evaporated, about 10 minutes more. Season with salt and pepper.

Transfer to a serving plate and serve hot or at room temperature.

Green Beans with Toasted Walnuts

2 Tbsp toasted walnuts (page 264)

1–1¼ lb (500–625 g) green beans

2–3 Tbsp extra-virgin olive oil

Salt

Chop the walnuts into small pieces and set aside.

Bring a large saucepan of salted water to a boil. Add the green beans and cook until tender, about 5 minutes.

Drain the beans and place in a shallow dish. Toss with the olive oil and sprinkle with 1 tsp salt. Scatter the walnuts over the beans. Serve warm or at room temperature.

LONG BEANS

Also called yard-long beans, these very long, rounded pod beans are similar to green beans and are commonly used in Asian cooking. They typically grow in subtropical climates such as Southeast Asia, Thailand, and southern China, but they can now be found throughout the world during late summer and early fall. Choose light green beans that are flexible but not limp or dry looking.

LONG BEANS WITH SESAME SEEDS

Toast 1½ Tbsp sesame seeds in a small frying pan over medium heat, stirring often, for 5 minutes, set aside. Cook 1 lb (500 g) long beans, cut into 3-inch (7.5-cm) lengths, in a large saucepan of salted boiling water until tender, about 5 minutes. Drain, rinse with cold running water, and pat dry. Heat 1½ Tbsp peanut oil in a large frying pan over medium-high heat. Add 2 Tbsp peeled and minced ginger, 1 minced garlic clove, and 1 minced serrano chile and sauté for 30 seconds. Add the beans and salt to taste, toss to coat, and cook until heated through. Stir in the toasted sesame seeds. Remove from the heat and add 1 tsp Asian sesame oil and ⅓ cup (½ oz/15 g) chopped fresh cilantro (fresh coriander). Makes 4 servings.

TEMPURA STRING BEANS WITH AIOLI

MIXED GARDEN BEAN SALAD WITH SHALLOTS

Mixed Garden Bean Salad with Shallots

MAKES 6–8 SERVINGS

½ lb (250 g) fresh shelling beans such as fava (broad) beans, shelled

1 lb (500 g) *each* wax beans, trimmed and cut into 2-inch (5-cm) lengths, and haricots verts

¼ cup (2 fl oz/60 ml) fresh lemon juice

2 Tbsp white wine vinegar

2 shallots, minced

¾ cup (6 fl oz/180 ml) canola oil

1 tsp grated lemon zest

1 tsp ground coriander, toasted

Salt and freshly ground pepper

Bring a large saucepan of salted water to a boil. Add the shelling beans and boil until tender, 2–3 minutes. Remove with a slotted spoon, plunge into a bowl of ice water, then drain. Repeat with the wax beans and haricots verts, cooking the wax beans for 7–8 minutes and the haricots verts about 5 minutes until tender. Drain and set aside.

In a small bowl, whisk together the lemon juice, vinegar, and shallots. Drizzle in the canola oil and whisk continuously. Stir in the lemon zest and coriander, and season with salt and pepper to taste.

Combine all the beans in a large bowl. Add the vinaigrette and toss. Let stand for at least 1 hour, or refrigerate for up to 3 hours. Serve at room temperature or chilled.

Warm Beans with Lemon Vinaigrette

MAKES 6 SERVINGS

2½ lb (1.25 kg) green beans

1½ Tbsp fresh lemon juice

Salt and freshly ground pepper

⅓ cup (3 fl oz/80 ml) extra-virgin olive oil

1 tsp grated lemon zest

2 Tbsp unsalted butter

1 shallot, finely chopped

2 plum (Roma) tomatoes, cored, seeded, and cut into small dice

Bring a large pot of salted water to a boil. Add the beans and boil until tender, about 4 minutes. Drain the beans and plunge into a bowl of ice water. When cool, remove from the ice water and set aside.

In a small bowl, whisk together the lemon juice, ¼ tsp salt, and ¼ tsp pepper. Whisk in the olive oil until blended. Stir in the lemon zest.

Just before serving, in a large frying pan over medium heat, melt the butter. Add the shallot and tomatoes and cook, stirring, until softened, about 3 minutes. Add the beans and cook just until heated through.

Transfer to a platter and drizzle with the vinaigrette. Serve right away.

Sautéed Wax Beans with Tapenade

MAKES 4–6 SERVINGS

1½ lb (750 g) wax beans

2 Tbsp olive oil

1 shallot, minced

1 tsp minced lemon zest

Tapenade (page 262)

Salt and freshly ground pepper

Bring a large saucepan of salted water to a boil. Add the beans and cook until tender, 5–7 minutes. Drain and then plunge into a bowl of ice water. Drain and set aside.

In a frying pan over medium heat, heat the olive oil. Add the shallot and sauté until softened, about 2 minutes. Raise the heat to medium-high, add the green beans, and sauté just until the beans begin to brown, about 2 minutes. Stir in the lemon zest and cook until fragrant, 20–60 seconds more. Remove from the heat, stir in the tapenade, and season with salt and pepper. Transfer to a serving dish and serve right away.

ROMANO BEANS

Also referred to as Italian-style green beans, romano beans are a variety of broad green beans with flat edible pods. They can be cooked in the same ways as green beans. Look for romano beans at the farmers' market during the summer months.

ROMANO BEANS WITH BACON & BREAD CRUMBS

Add 1 lb (500 g) trimmed romano beans to a large saucepan of salted boiling water and cook until almost tender, about 5 minutes (the amount of time will depend upon the thickness of the beans). Drain the beans and rinse under cold running water. Pat dry with paper towels. In a large frying pan over medium heat, warm ¼ cup (2 fl oz/60 ml) olive oil. Sauté 1 clove garlic, chopped, and 1½ Tbsp chopped fresh thyme until fragrant, about 1 minute. Add ¼ cup (1 oz/30 g) dried bread crumbs and cook, stirring, until crisp and browned, about 3 minutes longer. Add the beans and stir until coated with the crumbs and heated through. Stir in 2 slices cooked and crumbled bacon. Transfer to a serving dish and serve warm or at room temperature. Makes 6 servings.

English Peas

One of the sweetest and most delicate members of the legume botanical group, English peas—sometimes called garden peas or pod peas—have a fresh, slightly grassy flavor that is the essence of spring. Unlike their crunchy cousins, sugar snap peas and snow peas (*mangetouts*), English peas have a tough, inedible pod and must be shelled before use. Harvested young, the tiny peas can be smaller than pearls; these miniature gems are often called by their French name, *petits pois*.

So-called early or June peas are larger (up to the size of a fingertip) and have more starch. English peas are wonderful puréed and made into a creamy soup or spread. They add bright points of color and flavor to pilafs, risotto, fried rice, pasta, and soups. Steamed and sprinkled with fresh mint or parsley, they make a wonderful side dish.

Snow & Sugar Snap Peas

Flat, crisp snow peas and plump, shiny sugar snap peas are both eaten whole. The former are also called *mangetouts*, a name derived from the French for "eat it all." Snow peas originated in Asia more than 10,000 years ago. Snap peas, of more recent origin, were developed as a cross between snow peas and a strain of shell peas. Both are 2 to 3 inches (5 to 7.5 cm) long and have a sweet flavor and an appealing, crunchy texture.

Snow peas and sugar snap peas are at their best flavor when the weather is still cool. The sweetest and crispest ones will come to market during the early spring but are often available through mid-summer. Stir-fry them with other thinly cut vegetables, or serve them raw with flavorful dips or dressings.

Pea Soup with Crème Fraîche & Chives

MAKES 4 SERVINGS

3 cups (24 fl oz/750 ml) chicken broth

2 lb (1 kg) English peas, shelled

Salt and ground white pepper

4 Tbsp crème fraîche

2 Tbsp minced fresh chives

In a saucepan over medium-high heat, combine the chicken broth, peas, 1 tsp salt, and ½ tsp pepper. Bring to a boil, reduce the heat to low, and simmer until the peas are soft, 10–20 minutes. (The amount of time will depend upon the size and maturity of the peas.)

Transfer to a blender or food processor and purée until smooth. Return the purée to the saucepan, place over medium heat, and heat through.

Ladle the soup into warmed bowls. Add 1 Tbsp of the crème fraîche to each serving and garnish with the chives. Serve right away.

English Pea & Ricotta Tart

MAKES 4–6 SERVINGS

8-by-10-inch (20-by-25-cm) rectangle of frozen puff pastry, thawed in the refrigerator

1⅓ cups (6½ oz/200 g) shelled English peas

1 cup (8 oz/250 g) fresh whole-milk ricotta, drained

3 Tbsp finely chopped fresh mint, plus small whole leaves for garnish

1 tsp minced lemon zest

Salt and freshly ground pepper

¼ cup (¼ oz/7 g) fresh flat-leaf (Italian) parsley leaves

2 green (spring) onions, trimmed and very thinly sliced on the diagonal

Fresh lemon juice

Pea shoots for garnish, optional

Preheat the oven to 400°F (200°C). Place the puff pastry on a baking sheet lined with parchment (baking) paper and bake until puffed, 10–13 minutes. Remove from the oven and top with a sheet of parchment paper and another baking sheet, and bake until golden and crisp, 10–13 minutes. Remove the top baking sheet and parchment paper and let cool.

Bring a pot of salted water to a boil. Add the peas and cook until tender, 2–3 minutes. Drain and rinse briefly under cold running water. Reserve ⅓ cup (1½ oz/15 g) of the peas and set aside. In a food processor, process the remaining peas, the ricotta, and 1 Tbsp of the chopped mint to make a chunky purée. Stir in the lemon zest and season with salt and pepper.

In a small bowl, combine the parsley, the remaining 2 Tbsp mint, the green onions, and the reserved peas. Season with salt and lemon juice. Spread the ricotta mixture evenly over the pastry and top with the parsley mixture. Garnish with whole mint leaves and pea shoots, if desired. Cut into pieces and serve right away.

English Peas with Prosciutto

MAKES 6 SERVINGS

Salt and freshly ground pepper

1½ Tbsp olive oil

2 slices prosciutto, cut into strips ⅛ inch (3 mm) wide

3 cups (15 oz/470 g) shelled English peas

Bring a large pot of salted water to a boil.

Meanwhile, in a large frying pan over low heat, warm the olive oil. Add the prosciutto and cook slowly, stirring often, until just heated through and slightly darker in color, 2–3 minutes. Set aside.

Add the peas to the boiling water and cook until just tender, about 1 minute. Drain immediately in a fine-mesh sieve and add to the pan with the prosciutto. Raise the heat to medium and toss gently. Season with salt and pepper.

Transfer to a warmed serving dish and serve right away.

ENGLISH PEA & RICOTTA TART

CHICKEN & SUGAR SNAP PEA STIR-FRY

Sugar Snap Pea Risotto

MAKES 4 SERVINGS

3 Tbsp unsalted butter

1 small yellow onion, finely diced

Salt

5 cups (40 fl oz/1.25 l) chicken broth

1½ cups (10½ oz/330 g) short-grain rice, such as Arborio, Carnaroli, or Vialone Nano

1 tsp finely grated lemon zest

½ cup (4 fl oz/125 ml) dry white wine

10 oz (330 g) sugar snap peas, halved crosswise

⅓ cup (1 oz/30 g) freshly grated hard cheese, such as Parmesan, plus extra for sprinkling

Melt 2 Tbsp of the butter in a large, heavy pot over medium heat. Add the onion and a pinch of salt and sauté until the onion is soft, about 8 minutes. Meanwhile, in a saucepan, bring the broth and 1 tsp salt to a simmer over low heat.

Stir the rice into the onions until translucent, about 3 minutes. Add the lemon zest and wine and cook, stirring, until the wine is absorbed. Add ¾ cup (6 fl oz/185 ml) of the broth and simmer, stirring frequently, until the liquid is almost absorbed. Add another portion of the broth. Continue simmering, stirring and adding broth until the liquid is almost all absorbed, about 15 minutes. Do not let the rice dry out. Add the snap peas and continue to cook until the rice is tender but still lightly firm to the bite, about 10 minutes longer. Turn off the heat, stir in the remaining 1 Tbsp butter and the ⅓ cup cheese, and let stand for 2 minutes.

Season with salt. Divide among shallow bowls, sprinkle with cheese, and serve.

Chicken & Sugar Snap Pea Stir-fry

MAKES 4 SERVINGS

1 lb (500 g) skinless, boneless chicken breast halves, cut crosswise into thin strips

3½ Tbsp peanut oil

1 tsp baking soda (bicarbonate of soda)

2 tsp cornstarch (cornflour)

Salt

1 Tbsp oyster sauce

¾ lb (375 g) sugar snap peas, halved crosswise on the diagonal

Cooked White Rice (page 262) for serving

Soy sauce for serving

In a bowl, toss the chicken strips with 1½ Tbsp of the peanut oil, the baking soda, and the cornstarch. Cover and let marinate in the refrigerator for 1 hour. Remove from the refrigerator 15 minutes before cooking.

Heat a wok or large frying pan over high heat. Add the remaining 2 Tbsp oil. When it is hot, add the chicken, spreading it out as much as possible. Season with salt and sear for 1 minute without stirring, then stir until opaque throughout, 2–3 minutes. Stir in the oyster sauce and cook for 30 seconds. Transfer to a bowl and set aside.

Return the wok to high heat, add the peas, and stir-fry until tender-crisp, about 1 minute. Stir in the chicken and stir-fry for 30 seconds. Transfer to a platter and serve right away with rice and soy sauce.

Snow Pea & Mint Salad

MAKES 4–6 SERVINGS

1½ lb (750 g) snow peas

1 Tbsp Champagne vinegar

1 small shallot, minced

3 Tbsp extra-virgin olive oil

Salt and freshly ground pepper

¼ cup (¼ oz/7 g) fresh mint leaves, cut into thin strips

Bring a large pot of salted water to a boil. Add the snow peas and simmer until almost tender, 1½–2 minutes. Drain and transfer to a bowl filled with ice water. Let stand for 5 minutes, then drain and set aside.

In a small bowl, whisk together the vinegar, shallot, and olive oil until blended to make a vinaigrette. Season with salt and pepper.

To serve, place the peas and mint in a serving bowl and toss with the dressing. Serve right away.

PEA SHOOTS

Pea shoots are the delicate leaves and tendrils that grow from the vines of the pea plant. Tender and sweet, they are delicious when eaten raw or sautéed, and they also make an attractive garnish. Look for them at the farmers' market in the spring and early summer.

SAUTÉED PEA SHOOTS WITH CRABMEAT

Cut 1 lb (500 g) pea shoots into 2-inch (5-cm) lengths. Melt 2 Tbsp butter with 1 Tbsp olive oil in a frying pan over medium-high heat. Sauté 2 cloves minced garlic and half of the pea shoots, raise the heat to high, and add the remaining shoots as the first batch wilts. Add ½ lb (250 g) lump crabmeat, another 1 Tbsp butter, and season with salt. Sauté, stirring, until the crab is heated through, about 2 minutes. Makes 4 servings.

Cabbages &
Other Crucifers

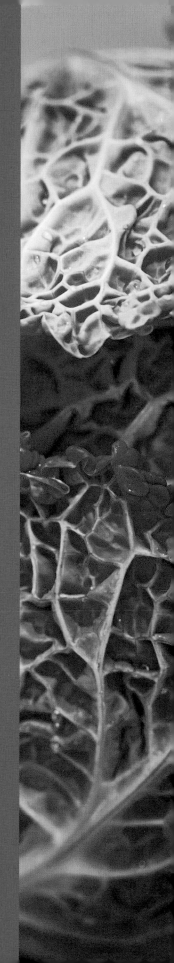

BROCCOLI

GAI LAN

CAULIFLOWER

BRUSSELS
SPROUTS

BROCCOLI RABE

GREEN CABBAGE

RED CABBAGE

From the largest cabbages to the smallest Brussels sprouts, cruciferous vegetables are known for their bold flavor. Some food historians believe that the modern cabbage and their kin are derived from related plants that grew wild centuries ago in the Mediterranean and elsewhere in Europe. Other researchers have traced cabbage-like vegetables back to ancient Egypt.

Cabbages take the form of compact heads with smooth or crinkly leaves that grow around a central core. Brussels sprouts, resembling tiny cabbages, have very tightly closed heads. The heads are often removed from their substantial stalks before being brought to market, though you can sometimes find them still attached to the long, thick stalks. Broccoli and cauliflower, also part of the cabbage family, closely resemble one another, both having clusters of florets, green or white, respectively, that grow on thick stalks.

Cabbages and their relatives are cool-weather crops, and though they can be found in many markets year round, they are at their best in autumn and winter.

Broccoli

Broccoli is one of the many members of the large and diverse Brassica group, which also includes mustard, cabbage, cauliflower, Brussels sprouts, and bok choy. Though relatively recent in its popularity, carried by Italian immigrants to England and then North America in the eighteenth century, its clusters of vivid green florets are now one of the most recognizable of vegetables.

Readily available all year long, broccoli is at its best from autumn through early spring, when the cooler weather allows its sweet, nutty flavors to develop. Its versatility and ease of cooking make it popular for a wide range of dishes. Broccoli can be eaten raw with dips, tossed into salads, roasted and topped with cheese, stirred into pasta, puréed into soup, and sautéed, steamed, or stir-fried until tender-crisp.

Cauliflower

Cauliflower's compact, creamy white florets resemble broccoli, to which it is closely related. The heads are sometimes sold at farmers' markets with their tightly enclosing, edible inner leaves, which taste similar to collard greens. Special varieties derived from older plants boast yellow, purple, or brown florets, and the popular Romanesco cauliflower from Italy has pointed florets arranged in a striking geometric pattern.

Peak season is during late summer and autumn, cauliflower can also thrive during the early winter. It has a mild, nutty flavor that marries nicely with cheese and with other vegetables such as green beans and carrots. It can also be cooked and puréed to make an excellent creamy soup, or slow-roasted with bacon. The florets are also ideal raw or lightly blanched for vegetable platters and a variety of salads.

WORKING WITH CAULIFLOWER

The easiest way to separate cauliflower into florets is to use the tip of a sharp paring knife to cut from the V of the thicker branches down to the main stem, and then continue separating these smaller bunches into bite-size pieces. If boiling cauliflower, add a few drops of lemon juice to the cooking water to help cauliflower retain its white color.

Roasted Broccoli with Red Pepper Flakes

MAKES 4 SERVINGS

2 cups (4 oz/125 g) small broccoli florets
¼ cup (2 fl oz/60 ml) olive oil
2 Tbsp red pepper flakes
Salt and freshly ground pepper

Preheat the oven to 250°F (120°C).

Place the broccoli florets in a small baking dish and drizzle evenly with the olive oil. Sprinkle with the red pepper flakes, 1 tsp salt, and 1 tsp pepper. Roast until tender, 20–25 minutes. Serve right away.

Broccoli & Cheddar Soup

MAKES 6–8 SERVINGS

1½ lb (750 g) broccoli, tough stems peeled
2 Tbsp unsalted butter
1 yellow onion, finely chopped
¼ cup (1 oz/30 g) all-purpose (plain) flour
5 cups (40 fl oz/1.25 l) chicken broth, heated
½ tsp dried thyme
1 Tbsp fresh lemon juice
2 cups (16 fl oz/500 ml) whole milk
½ lb (250 g) sharp Cheddar cheese, shredded
Salt and ground white pepper

Coarsely chop the broccoli. In a large saucepan, melt the butter over medium heat. Add the onion and sauté until soft, about 8 minutes. Sprinkle in the flour and sauté for 1 minute longer. Add the broth, broccoli, thyme, and lemon juice and bring to a boil. Reduce the heat to low, cover, and simmer until the broccoli is tender, about 20 minutes. Working in small batches, purée the soup in a blender or food processor. Return the purée to the pan, stir in the milk, and bring to a simmer over low heat.

Sprinkle half of the cheese into the soup; stir over low heat until melted. Season with salt and white pepper. Ladle the soup into bowls and top with the remaining cheese. Serve right away.

Beef, Broccoli & Crisp Garlic Sauté

MAKES 4 SERVINGS

1 lb (500 g) flank or skirt steak
1 Tbsp cornstarch (cornflour)
¼ tsp *each* salt and sugar
⅛ tsp baking soda (bicarbonate of soda)
2 Tbsp canola oil
3 cloves garlic, thinly sliced
¼ tsp red pepper flakes
2 cups (8 oz/125 g) small broccoli florets
3 Tbsp dry white wine
2 Tbsp soy sauce
Cooked White Rice (page 262) for serving

Cut the beef across the grain into strips 3 inches (7.5 cm) long and ¼ inch (6 mm) thick. In a bowl, stir together the cornstarch, salt, sugar, baking soda, and 2 Tbsp water. Add the beef and stir until well mixed. Let stand at room temperature for 30 minutes.

In a frying pan over high heat, add the canola oil. When the oil is hot, add the garlic and red pepper flakes and sauté until crisp, about 1 minute. Transfer to paper towels.

Add the beef, broccoli, and 2 Tbsp of the wine to the pan and cook until the beef is opaque and the broccoli is tender, about 5 minutes. Add the soy sauce and the remaining wine and stir for 1 minute. Transfer to warmed plates and accompany with steamed rice.

GAI LAN

Also known as Chinese broccoli, *gai lan* has a broccoli-like stalk, but it is topped with thick, flat green leaves instead of florets. It appears at the market from summer to autumn. Its leaves, stems, and flowers can all be eaten, and this versatile vegetable can be prepared in a variety of ways, such as stir-fried, added to soups, or shaved and served raw in salads.

STIR-FRIED GAI LAN WITH GINGER

Heat 2 Tbsp peanut oil in a large wok or frying pan over high heat. Add 2 thinly sliced garlic cloves, ½ tsp minced fresh ginger, and a pinch of red pepper flakes and stir-fry for about 15 seconds. Add 1½ lb (750 g) *gai lan*, cut into pieces ¼ inch (6 mm) long, and toss to coat with the oil. Add ¼ cup (2 fl oz/60 ml) water and 1½ Tbsp soy sauce, cover, and cook until the water has almost evaporated and the

gai lan stems are tender-crisp, about 3 minutes. If the wok or pan dries out, add a splash of water. Remove from the heat, add ½ tsp sugar, and toss well. Transfer the contents of the wok to a platter, pour any cooking liquid over the top, and drizzle with 1 tsp Asian sesame oil. Makes 4 servings.

BEEF, BROCCOLI & CRISP GARLIC SAUTÉ

GOLDEN CAULIFLOWER GRATIN WITH CAPERS

Cream of Cauliflower Soup

3 Tbsp olive oil, plus extra for drizzling

1 yellow onion, thinly sliced

Salt and freshly ground pepper

1½ lb (750 g) cauliflower, cored, separated into florets, and cut into slices ¼ inch (6 mm) thick

In a pot over medium-low heat, warm the 3 Tbsp olive oil. Add the onion and a pinch of salt and sauté until tender, about 12 minutes. Add the cauliflower, another pinch of salt, and 1 cup (8 fl oz/250 ml) water. Cover and simmer until the cauliflower is tender when pierced with a fork, about 10 minutes. Uncover, add another 4 cups (32 fl oz/1 l) water, raise the heat to high, and bring to a boil. Reduce the heat to maintain a low simmer and continue to cook for another 20 minutes. Let cool slightly.

Working in batches, purée the soup in a blender or food processor until smooth. Return to the pot and heat through over low heat. Thin the soup with water, if necessary, and season with salt. Ladle into serving bowls, drizzle with the olive oil, and season with pepper. Serve right away.

Golden Cauliflower Gratin with Capers

4 tsp unsalted butter, plus extra for greasing

1 medium head cauliflower

3½ Tbsp all-purpose (plain) flour

1½ cups (12 fl oz/375 ml) whole milk

Salt and freshly ground pepper

⅓ cup (⅔ oz/20 g) fresh bread crumbs

1 Tbsp capers, rinsed and drained

1 tsp red pepper flakes

Preheat the oven to 400°F (200°C). Butter a medium-sized baking dish.

In a covered steamer over boiling water, cook the whole cauliflower head until almost tender, 15–20 minutes. Transfer to a cutting board and let cool. Cut into 8 wedges and arrange in the baking dish.

In a saucepan over medium heat, melt 3 tsp of the butter. When it foams, remove it from the heat and whisk in the flour. Return to medium heat and slowly whisk in the milk. Reduce the heat to low, add 1 tsp salt and ½ tsp pepper, and cook, whisking occasionally, until the sauce is thickened and smooth, about 15 minutes.

In a small frying pan over medium heat, melt the remaining 1 tsp butter. When it foams, add the bread crumbs and cook, stirring often, until golden, 3–4 minutes.

Stir the capers and red pepper flakes into the sauce and pour over the cauliflower. Sprinkle with the bread crumbs.

Bake until the sauce is bubbling and the top is golden, about 30 minutes. Serve right away.

Pasta with Cauliflower, Anchovies & Pine Nuts

2 Tbsp olive oil, plus extra for drizzling

1 small head cauliflower, cut into 1-inch (2.5-cm) florets

Salt and freshly ground pepper

2 salt-packed anchovy fillets, mashed

1 large clove garlic, minced

½ tsp red pepper flakes

1 lb (500 g) gemelli or other curly pasta

3 Tbsp pine nuts, toasted (page 264)

¼ cup (1 oz/30 g) grated aged hard cheese, such as Parmesan

Bring a large pot of salted water to a boil.

Meanwhile, in a large saucepan over medium-high heat, add 1 Tbsp of the olive oil and, when hot, add the cauliflower florets and a pinch each of salt and pepper. Cook, stirring, until golden brown and just tender when pierced with a knife, 6–8 minutes. Remove the cauliflower from the pan. Add the remaining 1 Tbsp olive oil and reduce the heat to medium. Stir in the anchovies, garlic, and red pepper flakes. Cook, stirring, until the garlic is fragrant, about 1 minute. Return the cauliflower to the pan, stir well to combine, and remove from the heat.

Add the pasta to the boiling water. Cook until al dente, 8–10 minutes or according to the package directions. Reserve 1 cup (8 fl oz/250 ml) of the pasta cooking water and drain the pasta.

Add the pasta to the cauliflower and stir to combine. Add the pine nuts and, if needed, some of the pasta water to moisten the dish.

Transfer to a serving dish and drizzle with olive oil. Sprinkle the cheese on top and serve right away.

Brussels Sprouts

Resembling miniature green cabbages, Brussels sprouts are small buds that grow along the thick, long stalks of a large plant descended from wild cabbage. They are named for the capital of Belgium, where they were first widely cultivated, and quickly spread throughout Europe and North America. Brussels sprouts, generally sold loose or packed into small baskets, occasionally appear at farmers' markets still on their stalks.

Brussels sprouts grow best in cool coastal regions and reach their peak from autumn through mid-winter. They can be prepared in much the same way as broccoli and cauliflower, taking well to boiling, braising, steaming, and roasting. Thinly slice the heads or break off individual leaves to sauté or serve fresh as a salad or slaw.

BUYING BROCCOLI RABE

Choose broccoli rabe with bright green florets and leaves and yellow flowers that are just beginning to open. Avoid if the florets are wilted, browned or fully bloomed. The stalks should be firm and can be slightly flexible. Store broccoli rabe in a plastic bag in the refrigerator for up to 3 days.

Broccoli Rabe

Also called broccoli raab, rapini, or Italian broccoli, broccoli rabe is a relative newcomer to the vegetable section of the market. It is much loved for its long, slender stalks; abundant, tender, frilled leaves; and distinctive flower buds that resemble small florets of broccoli. Closely related to mustard, broccoli rabe has a mild, pleasantly bitter taste with overtones of sweet mustard. Varieties grown in the United States and Italy tend to be less pungent than those enjoyed in China and sold at farmers' markets serving Asian communities.

At its best in autumn and winter, broccoli rabe is popular in Italian cooking, where it may be sautéed in olive oil and garlic as an accompaniment to meat or as the basis of a pasta sauce. Similarly, in Asia, it is a favorite vegetable for stir-frying with garlic or ginger. It is excellent cooked and chilled in salads or used to top pizzas or bruschetta.

WORKING WITH BROCCOLI RABE

Trim away the ends of the stems and any wilted leaves. If any of the stems are particularly thick or tough, they can be peeled with a vegetable peeler. To reduce broccoli rabe's bitterness, it can be steamed, braised in a small amount of water, or blanched (see page 264) before serving or cooking further.

Brussels Sprouts with Chestnuts

MAKES 6 SERVINGS

½ lb (250 g) fresh chestnuts
1½ lb (750 g) brussels sprouts
Salt and freshly ground pepper
2 Tbsp unsalted butter

Using a sharp knife, make a small incision across the flat side of each chestnut. Place in a saucepan, add water to cover, and place over medium heat. Bring to a simmer, reduce the heat to low, and cook until the nutmeat can be easily pierced with a knife, 45–55 minutes. Remove the chestnuts a few at a time from the hot water. Peel away and discard the hard shells and inner sheaths. Set the chestnuts aside.

Cut the brussels sprouts in half. Bring a large saucepan of salted water to a boil. Add the brussels sprouts and simmer, uncovered, until tender, 6–8 minutes. Drain and return to the saucepan. Add the chestnuts and butter and place over medium heat until the butter melts and the chestnuts are hot, stirring often, about 1 minute. Season with salt and pepper.

Transfer to a serving dish and serve hot.

Brussels sprouts with chestnuts are delicious as a side dish alongside meat or poultry or tossed into a pasta such as fettuccine.

Pasta with Brussels Sprouts, Shallots & Asiago

MAKES 6 SERVINGS

8 shallots, peeled
1 Tbsp olive oil
Salt and freshly ground pepper
1 lb (500 g) linguine or tagliatelle pasta
1 Tbsp unsalted butter
1 lb (500 g) brussels sprouts, thinly sliced
½ tsp sugar
1 Tbsp sherry vinegar
¾ cup (6 fl oz/180 ml) heavy (double) cream
¼ cup (2 oz/60 g) grated Asiago cheese

Preheat the oven to 400°F (200°C). Place the shallots in a small baking dish and drizzle with the olive oil and a pinch each of salt and pepper. Cover the dish tightly with aluminum foil. Roast until tender, 35–40 minutes. When cool, cut the shallots into ½-inch (12-mm) slices and set aside.

Bring a large pot of salted water to a boil. Add the pasta and cook until al dente, 6–7 minutes or according to the package directions. Reserve 1 cup (8 fl oz/250 ml) of the cooking water and drain the pasta.

While the pasta is cooking, heat the butter in a large saucepan over medium-high heat until lightly browned. Stir in the brussels sprouts with a pinch of salt and the sugar. Cook, stirring often, until the brussels sprouts begin to soften, 3–4 minutes. Add the vinegar and cook, stirring, until it reduces to a syrup, about 1 minute. Reduce the heat to medium-low and add the cream and shallots. Season with salt and pepper.

Add the drained pasta to the brussels sprouts and stir to combine, adding some of the reserved pasta water if it seems dry. Transfer to a serving dish and sprinkle cheese over the top. Serve right away.

Brussels Sprout Leaves with Bacon

MAKES 6 SERVINGS

2 Tbsp red wine vinegar
½ tsp grainy mustard
1 clove garlic, minced
¼ cup (4 fl oz/125 ml) extra-virgin olive oil
Salt and freshly ground pepper
1½ lb (750 g) brussels sprouts
2 Tbsp unsalted butter
6 slices bacon, cut into ¼-inch (6-mm) pieces and cooked until crisp

In a small bowl, whisk together the vinegar, mustard, and garlic. Whisking constantly, pour in the olive oil in a slow, steady stream until well blended. Season with salt and pepper. Set aside.

Remove the outer leaves from each brussels sprout and discard any that are blemished. Continue to separate the leaves of the brussels sprouts, using a small, sharp knife to cut away the core. In a large saucepan over medium heat, melt the butter. Add the brussels sprout leaves and ½ cup (4 fl oz/125 ml) water, cover, raise the heat to high, and bring to a boil. Reduce the heat to medium-low and cook the leaves until bright green and tender, about 7 minutes, adding more water if needed. Drain and transfer to a large serving bowl.

Add the bacon to the olive oil mixture. Drizzle over the brussels sprout leaves and toss to coat. Season with salt and pepper and serve right away.

BRUSSELS SPROUT LEAVES WITH BACON

SPICY BROCCOLI RABE BRUSCHETTA

Spicy Broccoli Rabe Bruschetta

MAKES 6 SERVINGS

1½ lb (750 g) broccoli rabe

5 Tbsp (3 fl oz/80 ml) olive oil, plus extra for brushing and drizzling

3 cloves garlic, chopped

¼ tsp red pepper flakes

Salt

12 slices baguette, each ½ inch (12 mm) thick

½ cup (4 oz/125 g) ricotta cheese

Preheat the broiler (grill).

Cut the broccoli rabe stems into ¼-inch (6-mm) pieces and coarsely chop the leafy greens. Rinse and drain.

In a frying pan over medium heat, warm 3 Tbsp of the olive oil. Add the garlic and red pepper flakes and sauté until fragrant, about 30 seconds. Add as much broccoli rabe as will fit into the pan. Raise the heat to high and add the remaining broccoli rabe as the first batch wilts. Season with salt and cook until tender, 4–10 minutes. If the pan seems too dry, add a splash of water. Remove from the heat. Stir in the remaining 2 Tbsp olive oil and season with salt.

Brush the baguette slices with olive oil and broil (grill) until golden brown on both sides, about 2 minutes per side. Spread each slice with the cheese and top with the broccoli rabe. Drizzle with more olive oil and serve right away.

Orecchiette with Broccoli Rabe

MAKES 4–6 SERVINGS

⅓ cup (3 fl oz/80 ml) olive oil

8 cloves garlic, thinly sliced

¼ tsp red pepper flakes

1½ lb (750 g) broccoli rabe, stem ends trimmed

1 lb (500 g) orecchiette

Salt

1 cup (4 oz/125 g) grated hard cheese, such as Pecorino

In a large frying pan over medium heat, warm the olive oil. Add the garlic and red pepper flakes and sauté until the garlic is fragrant, 1–2 minutes. Set aside.

Bring a large pot of salted water to a boil. Add the broccoli rabe and cook until tender, 2–4 minutes. Using a slotted spoon, transfer the broccoli rabe to a bowl of ice water. Leave the pot of water over high heat. Drain the broccoli rabe and chop into 2-inch (5-cm) lengths.

Add the pasta to the boiling water and cook until al dente, about 12 minutes or according to the package directions. While the pasta is cooking, add the broccoli rabe to the frying pan with the garlic and season with salt. Sauté over medium heat until heated through, 3–5 minutes.

Drain the pasta and return to the pot. Add the broccoli rabe mixture and toss well. Divide among bowls, top with the cheese, and serve right away.

Italian Sausage with Broccoli Rabe

MAKES 4 SERVINGS

2 lb (1 kg) broccoli rabe

4 hot or mild Italian sausages, each about 5 oz (155 g)

2 tsp olive oil, plus extra as needed

4 large cloves garlic, minced

¼ tsp red pepper flakes, or to taste

Salt

½ cup (2 oz/60 g) grated hard cheese, such as Parmesan

Bring a large saucepan of salted water to a boil. Add the broccoli rabe and boil until tender, 3–4 minutes. Drain and rinse under cold running water. Drain again and chop into 2-inch (5-cm) lengths.

Preheat the oven to 250°F (120°C). Prick the sausages in several places. In a large frying pan over medium heat, sauté the sausages in the 2 tsp olive oil, turning once, until well browned and firm, about 20 minutes. Transfer to an ovenproof platter and keep warm in the oven.

Pour off all but 3 Tbsp fat from the frying pan (add olive oil if needed). Return to medium-low heat and add the garlic and red pepper flakes. Sauté until the garlic is fragrant, about 1 minute. Add the broccoli rabe and season with salt. Sauté until heated through, about 3 minutes.

Divide the sausages and broccoli rabe among individual plates, top with the cheese, and serve right away.

BUYING GREEN CABBAGE

Heads of green cabbage should be firm and heavy with tightly furled smooth or crinkled leaves, depending on variety. Color is an indication of freshness: cabbages stored too long lose their pigment and will look almost white. To ensure freshness, check that the stem end has not cracked around the base.

Green Cabbage

The most commonly available variety of cabbage has smooth, pale green leaves. Savoy cabbage, which has crinkled leaves, makes a pretty addition to coleslaws and salads. Napa cabbage, also called Chinese or celery cabbage, is elongated with wide, flat, white stems and wrinkly, pale yellow-green leaves.

A hardy plant, cabbage is sold fresh all year long but is at its best during the cooler months of autumn and early winter. Europeans and Asians depended on pickled cabbage for nutrients during long winters, sauerkraut and kimchi being the two most common recipes for preserving the vegetable. Whole leaves can be briefly boiled or steamed until pliable, stuffed with savory fillings such as beef, barley or rice, and then rolled and cooked until tender. Cut cabbage is often added to soups, braised until sweet and tender, stirred into fillings for dumplings, or tossed with dressing to make cole slaw.

WORKING WITH GREEN CABBAGE

Pull off and discard any wilted outer leaves. Remove the core, either by cutting the head into halves or quarters and slicing the core from the center, or by cutting out a cone at the base of the core. If you're shredding or slicing cabbage for salads, a mandoline or food processor fitted with the shredding disk makes quick work of the task.

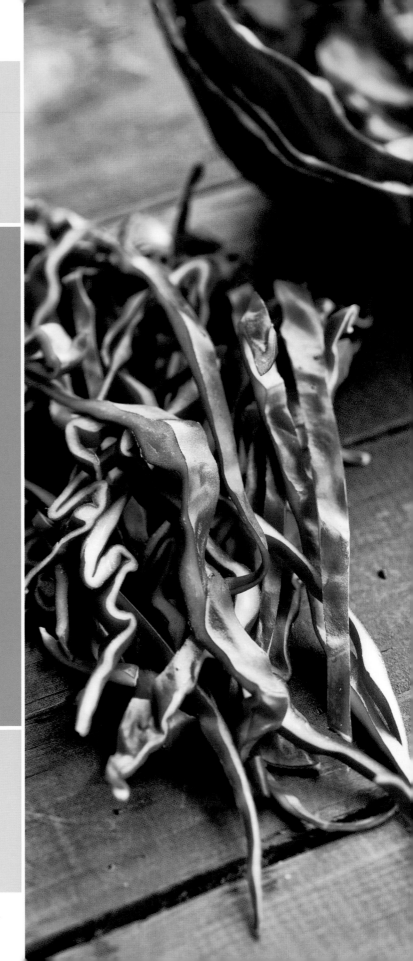

As with green cabbage, buy firm, heavy heads of red cabbage with tightly furled, smooth leaves and a vibrant purple color. Compare similarly sized heads and select the heaviest one. To ensure freshness, check that the stem end has not cracked around the base.

Red Cabbage

Similar in texture and appearance to green cabbage, red cabbage develops its deep, reddish-purple color from growing in acidic soil. With thicker leaves that have a faintly peppery taste, red cabbage tends to keep longer than its green cousin.

Thriving in humid climates with well-fertilized soil, red cabbage is primarily a winter crop. Like green cabbage, red cabbage can be used raw or cooked. Its sweet-spicy flavor and brilliant color make it delicious in cole slaw. Sliced thinly, it can also add texture to other greens in fresh salads. Holding up well to winter's heartier dishes, red cabbage is excellent braised alongside fish, pork, game, or sausage.

WORKING WITH RED CABBAGE

Red cabbage turns pale blue when heated. To retain its vibrant red color during cooking, add a small amount of vinegar or lemon juice, or cook the vegetable with acidic ingredients such as apples or wine. Work with red cabbage the same as you would with green cabbage: discard any wilted outer leaves, cut out the core, and use as directed in the recipe.

Red & Green Buttermilk Coleslaw

MAKES 6 SERVINGS

1 small head red cabbage (1 lb/500 g), quartered, cored, and thinly sliced crosswise

1 small head green cabbage (1 lb/500 g), quartered, cored, and thinly sliced crosswise

1 small red onion, very thinly sliced

Salt and freshly ground pepper

1 cup (8 fl oz/250 ml) buttermilk

½ cup (4 oz/125 g) sour cream

¼ cup (⅓ oz/10 g) chopped fresh flat-leaf (Italian) parsley or fresh cilantro (fresh coriander)

1 tsp white wine vinegar, or extra to taste

In a large bowl, toss together the cabbages, onion, and 2 tsp salt.

In a bowl, whisk together the buttermilk, sour cream, parsley, and vinegar. Pour over the cabbage, season with pepper, and toss well. Let stand for 15–30 minutes to let the flavors blend and the cabbage soften. Adjust the seasonings with salt and vinegar. Serve right away.

Stuffed Cabbage Leaves with Sausage & Onion

MAKES 4 SERVINGS

1 head savoy cabbage, outer leaves removed

2 Tbsp olive oil

1 yellow onion, finely diced

1 tsp chopped fresh thyme

Salt and freshly ground pepper

3 cloves garlic, finely chopped

½ lb (250 g) sausage, casings removed

½ cup (3½ oz/110 g) Cooked White Rice (page 262)

1 large egg, lightly beaten

¼ cup (4 oz/125 g) plus 2 Tbsp grated aged hard cheese, such as Parmesan

1½ cups (12 fl oz/375 ml) chicken broth, heated

Preheat the oven to 350°F (180°C). Bring a large pot of salted water to a boil. Remove the core from the cabbage, cut the heart into small pieces, and set aside. Put the whole leaves in the pot and boil for 1 minute, then place under cold running water and dry. Return the water to a boil, add the chopped leaves, and boil until tender, 2–3 minutes. Drain, refresh under cold running water, and drain again.

In a large frying pan over medium-low heat, warm the olive oil. Add the onion, thyme, and a pinch of salt. Sauté until the onion is tender, about 10 minutes. Add the garlic and sauté for 2 minutes. Transfer to a bowl and stir in the chopped cabbage, sausage, rice, egg, and ¼ cup cheese. Season with salt and pepper.

Without cutting through the cabbage leaves, pare down the thick rib on the outside surface to the thickness of the leaf. Spoon ¼ cup (2 oz/60 g) of the stuffing into the base of each leaf. Working from the bottom, roll the leaf one turn, fold the sides in, and finish rolling. Place the stuffed leaves, seam side down, in a baking dish. Add hot broth and cover tightly with aluminum foil. Bake for 45 minutes, top with the remaining 2 Tbsp cheese, and continue bake for 15 minutes more. Serve topped with broth.

Braised Cabbage with Apples

MAKES 4 SERVINGS

2 Tbsp unsalted butter

1 yellow onion, thinly sliced

1½ lb (750 g) tart apples, such as Granny Smith, Sierra Beauty, or pink lady, peeled, cored, and thinly sliced

1 tsp chopped fresh thyme

1 bay leaf

Salt

1 head green or red cabbage (about 2 lb/1 kg), quartered, cored, and thinly sliced crosswise

½ cup (4 fl oz/125 ml) chicken broth, plus extra as needed

In a large frying pan over medium heat, melt the butter. Add the onion, apples, thyme, and bay leaf and season with salt. Cook, stirring occasionally, until tender and golden, about 6 minutes.

Add the cabbage and the ½ cup (4 fl oz/ 125 ml) chicken broth, season with salt, and bring to a boil. Reduce the heat to medium and cover. Cook, stirring often, until the cabbage is tender, 15–20 minutes. If the pan starts to dry out, add a little broth. Serve right away or cover and keep warm in a low oven until ready to serve.

Braised cabbage is a nice accompaniment to roasted meats such as pork chops.

BRAISED CABBAGE WITH APPLES

Leafy Greens

Many plants have edible leaves, but leafy greens are those plants that are prized primarily for their leaves. This large group ranges from plants with tender leaves that are almost sweet, to sturdy greens like arugula (rocket) that have a peppery flavor, to hearty greens that have a pleasant bitterness. Historical evidence suggests that leafy greens were gathered in the wild as long ago as the time of the ancient Egyptians, Greeks, and Romans.

For cooking purposes, it is useful to divide leafy greens into four categories. Delicate lettuces include butter (Boston) lettuce, romaine (cos) lettuce, and mâche. Watercress, radicchio, and frisée, leaves with a more substantial texture, are considered sturdy lettuces. Chicory is a group to which some sturdy greens, such as radicchio, also belong. Radicchio and Belgian endive (chicory/witloof) grow as tightly packed heads; other chicories form loose heads like lettuce. Robust kale, chard, and spinach are commonly called dark greens. Dark greens, though often cooked when mature, may be harvested young for use in salads.

Leafy greens have a constant presence at the farmers' market, as different types proliferate throughout the year.

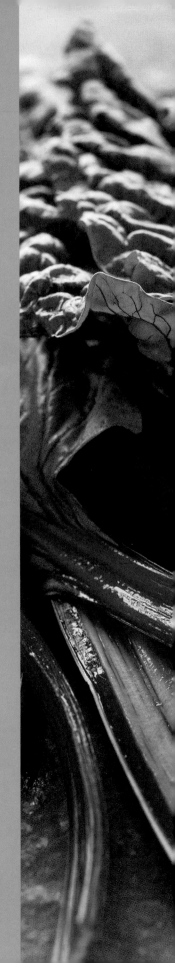

Choose heads of lettuce that are heavy for their size. Avoid any with wilted, torn, or browned leaves. Store loose greens unwashed in a plastic bag in the refrigerator for up to 4 days. Rinse the leaves just before serving and, if needed, let soak 10 minutes in cold water to refresh and crisp them.

Delicate Lettuces

Grown all over the world, the most delicate greens tend to have a sweet flavor and tender texture. From red-tinted, deeply lobed oakleaf to oval-shaped mâche, Japanese tatsoi to classic Bibb and butter (Boston) lettuce, there are many choices at local markets. *Mesclun*, which is a Provençal word for "mix," is traditionally a salad consisting of the first greens and herbs of spring. The mixes vary, but usually include a wide range of colors and textures. Some farmers also offer the tiny leaves of young plants, called baby greens, which are picked when only a few inches long.

Spring and autumn are the best times to look for young greens at the farmers' market. Experiment with different colors, textures, and flavors to make a salad that suits your palate. Less is more when showcasing sweet delicate lettuces. Milder greens star in simple salads with only a few ingredients and less acidic vinaigrettes.

WORKING WITH DELICATE LETTUCES

Wash greens by immersing them in a large bowl filled with cold water. To avoid diluting their flavor and to allow dressings to coat the leaves well, dry lettuces well in a salad spinner or shake them gently in a clean kitchen towel. Tear large leaves individually instead of cutting the heads to avoid discoloring or crushing their leaves, and dress them lightly just before serving.

Sturdy Lettuces

Often darker in color, thicker in texture, and stronger in flavor than delicate greens, sturdy lettuces such as watercress, frisée (or curly endive), chicory, and dandelion greens have become increasingly popular in recent years. Many sturdy lettuces are also considered chicories (see page 70). The shapes and flavors of sturdy lettuces are diverse, from refreshingly peppery, coin-shaped watercress to frilly, slightly bitter frisée to pungent, long, jagged dandelion leaves.

Though sturdy lettuces are available throughout the year in many areas, they have their best flavor at local markets during the winter months. Their leaves stand up to strong flavors such as bacon, olives, and anchovies in salads, pasta sauces, and side dishes. They are excellent sautéed briefly until wilted or stirred into soups during the last few minutes of simmering.

Butter Lettuce with Mustard Vinaigrette

MAKES 4–6 SERVINGS

2 heads butter lettuce

3½ Tbsp extra-virgin olive oil

1½ Tbsp red wine vinegar

1 tsp Dijon mustard

Salt and freshly ground pepper

1 Tbsp chopped fresh chives

1 Tbsp chopped fresh tarragon

1 Tbsp chopped fresh flat-leaf (Italian) parsley

Separate the lettuce leaves. Tear the largest outer leaves in half, leaving the smaller leaves whole. Wash, rinse, and dry.

In a large salad bowl, whisk together the olive oil, vinegar, mustard, and salt and pepper to taste to make a dressing. Add the lettuce, chives, tarragon, and parsley and toss well. Serve right away.

Romaine Hearts with Caesar Dressing

MAKES 4 SERVINGS

3 Tbsp mayonnaise

5–6 anchovy fillets

1 large clove garlic, chopped

⅓ cup (3 fl oz/90 ml) plus 1 Tbsp extra-virgin olive oil

2 Tbsp fresh lemon juice, plus extra if needed

Salt and freshly ground pepper

2 cups (4 oz/125 g) bread cut into ½-inch (12-mm) cubes

1½ lb (750 g) romaine (cos) lettuce hearts

1 cup (4 oz/125 g) shredded dry jack cheese

Preheat the oven to 350°F (180°C).

In a blender, combine the mayonnaise, anchovies, and garlic and blend until smooth. With the motor running, add the ⅓ cup olive oil in a slow, steady stream to make a thick dressing. Gradually blend in the 2 Tbsp lemon juice. Season with salt and pepper and blend again to combine. Transfer to a bowl and set aside.

In a large bowl, toss the bread cubes with the remaining 1 Tbsp olive oil. Transfer to a baking sheet and bake until lightly browned and crisp, about 15 minutes.

Tear the romaine leaves into bite-size pieces and place in a large salad bowl. Toss with enough of the dressing to coat the leaves lightly. Season with salt and pepper. Add the croutons and ⅔ cup (2½ oz/75 g) of the cheese and toss again.

Divide among salad plates. Top with the remaining cheese and serve right away.

Mixed Greens with Goat Cheese

MAKES 4 SERVINGS

¼ lb (125 g) fresh goat cheese

½ cup (2 oz/60 g) fine dried bread crumbs

½ tsp fresh thyme leaves

Salt and freshly ground pepper

⅓ cup (3 fl oz/80 ml) plus 1 Tbsp extra-virgin olive oil

2 Tbsp red wine vinegar

4 cups (4 oz/120 g) mixed delicate lettuce leaves such as oakleaf, mâche, and Bibb

Divide the cheese into 4 equal portions. Shape each portion into a patty about 3 inches (7.5 cm) in diameter. In a bowl, mix together the bread crumbs, the thyme, and ½ tsp each salt and pepper. Pour onto a sheet of waxed paper. Working with one cheese patty at a time, press both sides into the bread crumb mixture. Set aside.

In a large salad bowl, whisk together the ⅓ cup (3 fl oz/80 ml) olive oil, the vinegar, and salt and pepper to taste.

Add the greens to the salad bowl and toss well. Divide among plates and set aside.

In a frying pan over medium heat, warm the remaining 1 Tbsp olive oil. Add the goat cheese patties and cook until lightly browned on the bottom, 1–2 minutes. Turn and continue to cook until the cheese begins to spread slightly, about 1 minute more. Place one patty on each plate of greens and serve right away.

BUTTER LETTUCE WITH MUSTARD VINAIGRETTE

BITTER GREENS WITH PECANS & BALSAMIC VINAIGRETTE

Watercress & Grapefruit Salad

MAKES 4 SERVINGS

1½ Tbsp fresh orange juice

1 Tbsp extra-virgin olive oil

2 tsp red wine vinegar

1 tsp grated orange zest

Salt and freshly ground pepper

1 large ruby red grapefruit, segmented (page 264) with juice reserved

2 cups (2 oz/60 g) stemmed watercress leaves

2 oz (60 g) fresh goat cheese, crumbled

3 Tbsp hazelnuts (filberts), toasted (page 264) and chopped

In a bowl, whisk together the orange juice, olive oil, vinegar, orange zest and salt and pepper to taste. Add the grapefruit segments and juice to the dressing, turning the segments gently to coat.

Place the watercress in a bowl and add enough of the vinaigrette to coat the leaves. Lift the grapefruit segments from the vinaigrette and add to the salad. Add the goat cheese and hazelnuts and toss gently, adding more vinaigrette if necessary. Divide the salad among individual plates and serve right away.

Frisée Salad with Warm Bacon Vinaigrette

MAKES 4 SERVINGS

1 cup (2 oz/60 g) coarse country bread cut into 1-inch (2.5-cm) cubes

1½ Tbsp extra-virgin olive oil

Salt and freshly ground pepper

¾ lb (375 g) thick-cut bacon, cut into ½-inch (12-mm) pieces

2 shallots, finely chopped

5 Tbsp (2½ fl oz/75 ml) red wine vinegar

2 heads frisée, cored and leaves torn into 3-inch (7.5-cm) pieces

Preheat the oven to 350°F (180°C). Spread the bread cubes on a baking sheet, sprinkle with the olive oil, and season with salt and pepper. Bake, turning once or twice, until golden, about 15 minutes. Set aside.

In a frying pan over medium-high heat, cook the bacon, stirring occasionally, until crisp, 4–5 minutes. Add the shallots and sauté until softened, about 1 minute. Add the vinegar, reduce the heat to medium, and simmer until thickened, about 1 minute more. Season with salt and pepper. Set aside and keep warm.

In a large salad bowl, combine the croutons and frisée. Pour in the warm dressing with the bacon pieces and toss to coat. Divide the salad among individual bowls or plates and serve right away.

Bitter Greens with Pecans & Balsamic Vinaigrette

MAKES 4 SERVINGS

3 Tbsp balsamic vinegar

2 Tbsp olive oil

Salt and freshly ground pepper

5 cups (15 oz/470 g) mixed torn sturdy greens and chicories, such as watercress, radicchio, or escarole (Batavian endive)

½ cup (2 oz/60 g) pecans, toasted (page 264)

1 oz (30 g) shaved hard cheese, such as Parmesan

In a small bowl, whisk together the vinegar and olive oil. Whisk in salt and pepper to taste to make a vinaigrette.

Place the greens in a large bowl, drizzle with some of the vinaigrette, and toss to lightly coat. Add the pecans and toss well, adding more vinaigrette if necessary to coat the leaves. Top the salad with the cheese and serve right away.

BUYING ARUGULA

Look for long, slender, young leaves with a vibrant green color and deeply notched or oval-shaped leaves. Whether loose-leaved or still bunched, avoid any with wet or bruised leaves. Wrap the stems of bunched arugula (rocket) in damp paper towels. Store both leaves and bunches in a plastic bag in the refrigerator for up to 2 days.

Arugula

Also known as rocket, this pleasantly peppery green, grown along the Mediterranean since Roman times, has recently grown in popularity around the world. The characteristic sword-shaped, deeply notched leaves are usually no more than 2 to 3 inches (5 to 7.5 cm) long. Some arugula varieties boast leaves that are oval in shape, with fewer notches. Fresh arugula can be found in the market in spring through autumn.

Add arugula to other, milder greens for a salad with a nicely sharp, spicy edge. Arugula is very popular in Italy, where it is also used in pasta sauces and to top pizzas hot from the oven. Arugula can also be stirred into soups, folded in potato salads, made into a flavorful pesto, or wilted to serve as a bed for roasted or grilled meat, fish, and poultry.

WORKING WITH ARUGULA

Handle arugula with care to avoid bruising its delicate leaves. Trim the thick stalk ends, if needed. Arugula bunches can trap soil and grit, so wash them well before serving. Immerse the leaves in cold water and then lift them out, letting the grit settle at the bottom. Repeat as necessary. Dry thoroughly in a salad spinner or gently shake them in a kitchen towel.

Select spinach with crisp and dark leaves free of bruises, tears, and any wetness. For fresh salads, look for smaller tender leaves. For cooking, pick the larger and more flavorful leaves. If you are buying spinach in bunches, look for firm stems with a blush of pink at their ends. Refrigerate the spinach unwashed in a plastic bag for 3 to 5 days.

Spinach

Native to central and southwestern Asia, spinach was first grown by Persians and then carried east to China and west to the Mediterranean during the 7th century. Since then, its dark green leaves and earthy, faintly bitter flavor have become popular on tables around the world. There are two main varieties available at markets. Some fall into the Savoy category, also known as curly leaf spinach for their thick, deeply crinkled leaves. Others have smooth leaves that are tender and trap less grit, making them popular for salads. Small, immature leaves with milder, sweeter flavor and more delicate leaves, often called baby spinach, also make an excellent salad green.

Available year-round, spinach reaches its peak season in spring and autumn. Young spinach is ideal in fresh salads and sandwiches. More mature spinach is excellent sautéed or stir-fried, made into creamy soups, or chopped and cooked with pasta.

WORKING WITH SPINACH

As spinach leaves often trap soil and grit, wash them well before use. Fill a large bowl with cold water, immerse the leaves, and then lift them out, letting the grit settle at the bottom. Repeat with fresh water until completely free of grit. Spin dry in a salad spinner. Trim any roots and, if desired, remove the stems for a more delicate texture.

Arugula, Goat Cheese & Walnut Salad

MAKES 4–6 SERVINGS

2 Tbsp red wine vinegar

3 Tbsp extra-virgin olive oil

1 tsp walnut oil

Salt and freshly ground pepper

½ cup (2 oz/60 g) walnuts, toasted (page 264) and coarsely chopped

6 cups (6 oz/180 g) arugula (rocket)

½ lb (125 g) fresh goat cheese, crumbled

In a small bowl, whisk together the vinegar, olive oil, walnut oil, and salt and pepper to taste to make a dressing. Set aside.

Place the arugula in a serving bowl and add the chopped walnuts. Drizzle with enough of the dressing to lightly coat the leaves and toss well. Sprinkle with the cheese and serve right away.

Spaghetti with Arugula-Mint Pesto

MAKES 4 SERVINGS

5 cups packed (5 oz/155 g) arugula (rocket)

¾ cup packed (½ oz/15 g) fresh mint leaves

½ cup (4 fl oz/125 ml) extra-virgin olive oil

½ cup (2 oz/60 g) shaved aged hard cheese such as Parmesan, plus extra for sprinking

2 cloves garlic

Zest of 1 lemon, plus 2 Tbsp lemon juice

Salt and freshly ground pepper

1 lb (500 g) spaghetti

In a blender, combine the arugula, mint, olive oil, cheese, garlic, lemon zest, and salt and pepper to taste and blend until smooth. Stir in 1 Tbsp of the lemon juice. Taste and adjust the seasoning. Refrigerate until ready to serve.

Bring a large pot of salted water to a boil. Add the spaghetti and cook until al dente, 10–12 minutes or according to the package directions. Reserve ½ cup (4 fl oz/125 ml) of the pasta cooking water. Drain the pasta and return it to the empty pot.

Toss the pesto with the spaghetti. Thin it out with a small amount of pasta water if necessary. Taste, season with salt and pepper, and toss with the additional 1 Tbsp lemon juice. Divide among serving bowls. Sprinkle cheese over each serving and serve right away.

Swordfish with Arugula, Currants & Almonds

MAKES 4 SERVINGS

1½ Tbsp dried currants

4 swordfish steaks, each 5–6 oz (155–185 g) and ½ inch (12 mm) thick

Salt and freshly ground pepper

5 Tbsp (3 fl oz/80 ml) olive oil

2 cloves garlic, finely chopped

Pinch of red pepper flakes

2 lb (1 kg) arugula (rocket)

3 Tbsp almonds, toasted (page 264) and chopped

4 lemon wedges

Put the currants in a small bowl and add hot water to cover. Let stand until plump.

Season the swordfish with salt and pepper. In a large, heavy frying pan over medium-high heat, warm 2 Tbsp of the olive oil. Add the swordfish and cook until opaque throughout, about 3 minutes per side. Remove from the pan and keep warm.

In a frying pan over medium-high heat, warm another 2 Tbsp of the olive oil. Add the garlic and red pepper flakes and sauté until fragrant, about 30 seconds. Add as much arugula as will fit in the pan. As the arugula wilts, add the remaining arugula. Cook until the arugula is wilted, about 4 minutes. If the pan gets too dry, add a splash of water. Remove from the heat. Drain the currants and add to the pan with the almonds and the remaining 1 Tbsp olive oil. Season with salt.

Arrange the swordfish and arugula on plates. Serve right away with the lemon wedges.

SPAGHETTI WITH ARUGULA-MINT PESTO

BAKED EGGS WITH SPINACH & CREAM

Baked Eggs with Spinach & Cream

MAKES 4 SERVINGS

1 Tbsp plus 2 tsp unsalted butter

1½ lb (750 g) baby spinach, large stems removed

4 large eggs

Salt and freshly ground pepper

4 tsp heavy (double) cream

Preheat the oven to 350°F (180°C). Coat four ½-cup (4–fl oz/125-ml) ramekins with the 1 Tbsp butter.

Bring a large saucepan of salted water to a boil. Add the spinach and cook until limp but still bright green, about 4 minutes. Drain well and rinse under cold running water. Drain again and squeeze to remove excess water. Coarsely chop the spinach.

Divide the chopped spinach among the prepared ramekins. Dot each with ½ tsp of the remaining butter. Break an egg into each ramekin and sprinkle each with ½ tsp salt and ¼ tsp pepper. Drizzle each with 1 tsp of the cream. Place the ramekins on a rimmed baking sheet.

Bake until the whites are set and the yolks are firm around the edges but still soft in the center, about 15 minutes. Serve right away.

Baby Spinach with Apples & Pecans

MAKES 4 SERVINGS

⅓ cup (2½ oz/75 g) plus 2 Tbsp plain low-fat yogurt

⅓ cup (2½ oz/75 g) mayonnaise

⅓ cup (3 oz/90 g) sugar

2 Tbsp cider vinegar

1 Tbsp poppy seeds

Salt and freshly ground pepper

4 cups (4 oz/125 g) baby spinach

4 slices thick-cut bacon, cooked and crumbled

1 tart apple, such as Fuji or Gala, cored and cut into cubes

⅓ cup (1½ oz/45 g) chopped candied pecans

1 Tbsp chopped fresh chives

In a small bowl, whisk together the yogurt, mayonnaise, sugar, vinegar, poppy seeds, and season with salt and pepper to make a dressing.

In a large bowl, toss together the spinach, bacon, apple, pecans, and chives. Add enough of the dressing to lightly coat the leaves and toss well. Serve right away.

Sautéed Spinach with Feta & Pine Nuts

MAKES 4–6 SERVINGS

2 Tbsp golden raisins (sultanas)

3 Tbsp extra-virgin olive oil

2 cloves garlic, chopped

Pinch of red pepper flakes

2 lb (1 kg) spinach, stems removed

Salt

¼ cup (1 oz/30 g) pine nuts, toasted (page 264)

½ cup (2½ oz/75 g) crumbled feta cheese

1 lemon wedge

Put the raisins in a small bowl and add hot water to cover. Let stand until plump.

In a frying pan over medium heat, warm 2 Tbsp of the olive oil. Add the garlic and red pepper flakes and sauté until fragrant. Add as much spinach as will fit in the pan. Raise the heat to high and add the remaining spinach as the first batch wilts. Cook until all the spinach has wilted and the water has evaporated, about 5 minutes. If the pan gets too dry before the spinach has fully cooked, add a splash of water. Remove from the heat.

Stir in the remaining 1 Tbsp olive oil and the raisins. Season with salt. Transfer to a platter and top with the pine nuts and cheese. Squeeze the lemon over the top and serve right away.

BUYING CHICORIES

Look for crispness in chicories. Buy firm, fat heads of Belgian endive (witloof) with tight, unblemished leaves. In curly varieties, avoid browning, and pass over heads with thick, tough leaves. Select radicchio heads with white cores that are firm and have no holes, blemishes, or moist leaves. Store in a plastic bag in the refrigerator for up to 5 days.

Chicories

Members of this family of pleasantly bitter greens can also fall into the sturdy lettuces category (page 59). Favorites include Belgian endive (witloof), curly endive, escarole (Batavian endive), frisée, and radicchio. Chicories have a range of uses, from salads to braises to grilled side dishes.

Belgian endive is a torpedo-shaped shoot that sometimes has red tips. Curly endive, also known as chicory or curly chicory, has narrow, spiky, finely curled leaves and a creamy white heart. Frisée, also a sturdy lettuce, is slightly immature curly endive, with a smaller head and more delicate and tender leaves.

Escarole, also known as common chicory, broad chicory, or Batavian endive, has loose, broad, green outer leaves, wide white stalks, and a yellow-green heart. Radicchio, a variety of chicory, is characterized by variegated purplish-red leaves.

WORKING WITH CHICORIES

Cut endives in half lengthwise or separate the leaves. To wash chicories, wash and spin in a salad spinner or immerse in a bowl with cold water. Discard any wilted or yellowed leaves. Lift out the leaves gently and repeat until the water is clear. Dry in a salad spinner or by shaking gently in a clean kitchen towel.

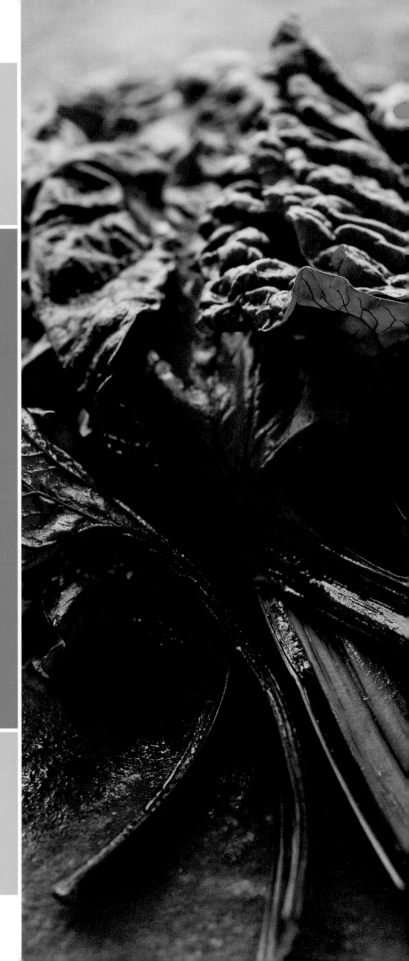

BUYING CHARD & KALE

In both chard and kale bunches, look for dark green color
and crisp, large, spreading leaves. Leaf shape and size will vary
by type. Avoid any bunches that have brown or yellow leaves,
or ribs that are dry or wilted enough to bend. Store in a plastic
bag in the refrigerator for up to 5 days.

Chard & Kale

Kale, a member of the cabbage family, has firm, tightly
crinkled leaves on long stems. The green, sturdy leaves
have an earthy flavor similar to cabbage and keep their
texture well when cooked. Italian varieties have narrower,
more tapered leaves, while dinosaur kale (also called
cavolo nero) can be recognized by its dark green color.
Swiss chard, also known simply as chard, has large,
crinkled leaves on fleshy, ribbed stems. Depending on
the variety, the stems and ribs can be scarlet red, golden
yellow, or pearly white. Red chard, sometimes labeled
ruby chard, has a slightly earthier flavor, while chard
with white stems tends to be sweeter.

Both chard and kale and are available at local farmers'
markets during the autumn and winter. Like other dark,
sturdy greens, they can be highlighted in soups and
sauces, braised or sautéed as side dishes, chopped finely
into fillings, and stirred into starchy accompaniments.

WORKING WITH CHARD & KALE

Wash chard or kale as you would spinach (page 65). If the
stems are fibrous, use a paring knife to cut them away, along
with the tough center vein that runs along the center of each
leaf. Discard the veins. Cut and cook the stems separately from
the leaves, as they will take longer to become tender. Sautéed
or simmered, stem pieces will take 5 to 10 minutes to cook.

Roasted Endive & Pear Salad

MAKES 4 SERVINGS

2 red pears, unpeeled, halved, and cored

4 small heads Belgian endive (chicory/witloof), coarsely chopped

4 Tbsp (2 fl oz/60 ml) walnut oil

⅛ tsp ground cloves

Salt and freshly ground pepper

1 Tbsp Champagne vinegar

2 tsp minced shallot

1 head butter (Boston) lettuce, leaves separated

¼ cup (1 oz/30 g) chopped walnuts, toasted (page 264)

¼ cup (1½ oz/45 g) crumbled blue cheese, such as Roquefort

Preheat the oven to 400°F (200°C). Cut the pear halves lengthwise into slices ½ inch (12 mm) thick. Place the pears and endive on a baking sheet. Brush with 2 Tbsp of the walnut oil and sprinkle with the cloves. Season with salt and pepper. Roast, turning once, until both are softened, 7–9 minutes. Let cool.

In a small bowl, whisk together the remaining 2 Tbsp oil, the vinegar, shallot, and a pinch each of salt and pepper to make a dressing.

Divide the lettuce among individual plates. Arrange the pears and endives on the lettuce and drizzle with the dressing. Sprinkle with the walnuts and cheese and serve right away.

Penne with Radicchio, Bacon & Fontina

MAKES 6 SERVINGS

1 lb (500 g) whole-wheat penne

2 Tbsp extra-virgin olive oil

2 tsp minced garlic

1 cup (8 fl oz/250 ml) dry white wine

2 heads radicchio, cut crosswise into ½-inch (12-mm) strips

½ lb (250 g) bacon, cooked

¼ cup (½ oz/15 g) coarsely chopped fresh flat-leaf (Italian) parsley

⅓ cup (2 oz/60 g) grated soft cow's milk cheese, such as fontina

Bring a large pot of salted water to a boil. Add the penne and cook until al dente, 10–12 minutes or according to the package directions. Reserve 1 cup (8 fl oz/250 ml) of the cooking water and drain the pasta.

Meanwhile, in a large frying pan over medium-low heat, warm the olive oil. Sauté the garlic for 1 minute. Add the wine and bring to a boil, stirring often, until reduced by half, 3–4 minutes. Add the radicchio and cook until slightly wilted, 1–2 minutes more.

Add the pasta and reserved water as needed to the radicchio and stir well. Stir in the bacon, parsley, and half of the cheese. Transfer to a serving bowl and top with the remaining cheese.

Halibut with Braised Escarole & White Beans

MAKES 6 SERVINGS

4 Tbsp (2 fl oz/60 ml) olive oil, plus more for drizzling

3 cloves garlic, thinly sliced

Pinch of red pepper flakes

1 lb (500 g) escarole (Batavian endive), cored and cut into 1½-inch (4-cm) squares

Salt and freshly ground pepper

1 cup (7 oz/220 g) canned white beans such as cannellini, rinsed and drained

6 halibut fillets, each 5–6 oz (155–185 g)

Lemon wedges for serving

In a large frying pan over medium heat, warm 2 Tbsp of the olive oil. Add the garlic and red pepper flakes and sauté for 1 minute. Add as much escarole as will fit in the pan. As the escarole wilts, continue adding the rest. If the pan gets dry, add a splash of water. Cook until the escarole is slightly wilted, 1–2 minutes. Season to taste with salt and pepper.

Stir in the beans and ½ cup (4 fl oz/125 ml) water. Bring to a simmer, cover, and braise until the escarole is very tender and the liquid has thickened, about 10 minutes. Season with salt and pepper. Cover and keep warm.

Season the halibut fillets with salt and pepper. In a large frying pan over medium-high heat, warm the remaining 2 Tbsp olive oil. Add the halibut and cook until opaque throughout, about 2 minutes per side.

Spoon the escarole and beans onto individual plates and top with the halibut. Drizzle with olive oil and serve accompanied by lemon wedges.

TREVISO RADICCHIO

Originating in the Veneto region of Italy but now grown all over the world, Treviso radicchio has elongated red leaves that look similar to those of Belgian endive. (The more common type of radicchio grows as a small, round head.) It has a milder flavor than other types of radicchio and can be served raw in salads, grilled, or baked into a gratin.

GRILLED RADICCHIO WITH ANCHOIADE

In a blender, purée 10 anchovy fillets and 8 cloves garlic. Stir in 3 Tbsp chopped fresh flat-leaf (Italian) parsley. With the machine running, add ⅓ cup (3 fl oz/80 ml) olive oil until a thick paste forms. Halve the radicchio lengthwise, coat lightly with olive oil, and grill (page 264) over medium-high heat until lightly charred, 5–7 minutes. Serve topped with the anchovy-parsley mixture. Makes 6 servings.

HALIBUT WITH BRAISED ESCAROLE & WHITE BEANS

SWISS CHARD, ONION & CHEESE FRITTATA

Wilted Kale with Lemon & Garlic

MAKES 6 SERVINGS

2 Tbsp plus 2 tsp extra-virgin olive oil

2 Tbsp fresh lemon juice

2 cloves garlic, minced

Salt and freshly ground pepper

2 bunches kale, about 2 lb (1 kg) total weight, stems removed

In a small bowl, whisk together the 2 Tbsp olive oil, lemon juice, and garlic. Add salt and pepper to taste to make a vinaigrette. Set aside.

In a large frying pan over medium heat, warm the remaining 2 tsp olive oil. Cut the kale leaves crosswise into 1-inch (2.5-cm) strips and add to the pan. Cover and cook, stirring occasionally, until the kale wilts, 5–7 minutes. Uncover, drizzle the vinaigrette over the top, and toss. Season with salt and pepper.

Transfer to a platter and serve right away.

Orecchiette with Kale, Chickpeas & Sausage

MAKES 6 SERVINGS

1 lb (500 g) orecchiette

1 Tbsp extra-virgin olive oil

1 tsp minced garlic

½ tsp red pepper flakes

½ cup (4 fl oz/125 ml) chicken broth

2 bunches dinosaur kale, stems removed and leaves cut into 1-inch (2.5-cm) pieces

Salt and freshly ground black pepper

¾ lb (375 g) linguiça-style sausage, sliced ½ inch (12 mm) thick

1½ cups (8½ oz/265 g) canned chickpeas (garbanzo beans), rinsed and drained

¼ cup (1 oz/30 g) grated hard cheese, such as Parmesan

Bring a large pot of salted water to a boil over high heat. Add the orecchiette and cook until al dente, 10–12 minutes or according to the package directions. Reserve 1 cup (8 fl oz/250 ml) of the cooking water and drain the pasta.

While the pasta is cooking, in a large frying pan over medium heat, warm the olive oil. Add the garlic and red pepper flakes and sauté until fragrant, about 1 minute. Stir in the broth, kale, and a pinch of salt. Raise the heat to high, cover the pan, and cook until the kale begins to wilt, 1–2 minutes. Remove the cover and add the sausage. Continue cooking until the leaves are tender and the liquid has evaporated, 3–4 minutes more. Stir in the chickpeas and cook until heated through, about 2 minutes.

Add the orecchiette to the kale and stir to combine. Stir in ½ cup (4 fl oz/125 ml) of the pasta water to moisten the mixture, adding more if needed.

Transfer the pasta to a serving dish and sprinkle with the cheese. Serve right away.

Swiss Chard, Onion & Cheese Frittata

MAKES 4–6 SERVINGS

1 bunch swiss chard, about 1¼ lb (625 g)

4 Tbsp (2 fl oz/60 ml) olive oil

1 small yellow onion, thinly sliced

Salt and freshly ground black pepper

6 large eggs

4 cloves garlic, finely chopped

¼ cup (1 oz/30 g) grated hard cheese, such as Parmesan

Pinch of cayenne pepper

Position a rack in the upper third of the oven and preheat to 350°F (180°C). Cut the chard stems crosswise into slices ¼ inch (6 mm) thick. Coarsely chop the leaves.

In a large frying pan over medium heat, warm 2 Tbsp of the olive oil. Add the onion and sauté until tender, about 6 minutes. Add the chard stems, season with salt, and sauté about 4 minutes. Add the chopped leaves and sauté until tender, 2–3 minutes. Transfer to a plate. Set aside.

In a large bowl, lightly beat the eggs with the garlic and cheese. Season with the cayenne, salt, and black pepper.

Gently squeeze the liquid from the chard and stir into the egg mixture. In an 8-inch (20-cm) ovenproof frying pan over medium-high heat, warm the remaining 2 Tbsp olive oil. Add the egg mixture, reduce the heat to medium, and cook until the eggs are set around the edges, about 5 minutes. Transfer to the oven and cook until set, 7–9 minutes longer. Let cool briefly.

If desired, invert the frittata onto a large plate. Cut into wedges and serve right away.

Roots & Tubers

Vegetables that grow below ground, roots and tubers, offer substance to meals that make use of them. Many, such as beets, carrots, and parsnips, are naturally sweet, a characteristic that is intensified during cooking. Others are pleasantly bland or earthy. Still others, such as sharp-flavored radishes, are decidedly bold. Of the many roots and tubers, potatoes may be the oldest, having spread from the Incan civilization of Peru throughout most of the world.

Tubers are distinguished from root vegetables by their ability to reproduce. Unlike roots, potatoes and other tubers are actually round fleshy stems from which a new plant can grow. These new shoots emerge from the eyes of a potato. Roots such as carrots, parsnips, turnips, and rutabagas do not have this potential. But what roots and tubers do share is a dense, hearty texture and a generally long shelf life.

Although roots and tubers are often thought of as winter foods, they also appear in spring: sweet little carrots, tender baby turnips, and tiny multicolored radishes are welcome sights at farmers' markets alongside new artichokes and asparagus.

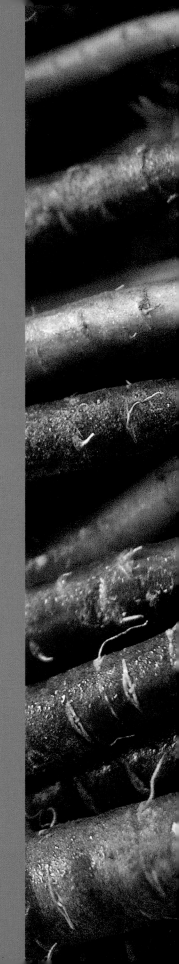

BUYING STARCHY POTATOES

Choose firm potatoes that are not blemished, wrinkled, tinged with green, or cracked. If the potatoes have any buds, commonly called eyes, they should show no sprouting. Potatoes keep well for up to 2 weeks in a cool, dry, dark, and well-ventilated place such as a pantry or drawer. Avoid storing potatoes in the refrigerator to preserve their flavor and texture.

Starchy Potatoes

Native to South America, the starchy potato is an edible member of the nightshade family, along with tomatoes and eggplants. Potatoes are tubers, or enlarged underground stems that store up energy in the form of starch. Starchy potatoes are large and oval, with dry, reddish brown skins. The most common starchy potato variety is the famed Russet Burbank from Idaho. Specialty starchy potatoes include the Lehmi, a large brown potato with white flesh, and the butterfinger, with brown russet skin and golden flesh. All-purpose potatoes, such as the Kennebec of Main work well in a wide range of recipes. The Kennebec is especially prized for making French fries.

Large, fully mature tubers are harvested during late summer. Once cooked, starchy potatoes become light, dry, and fluffy, making them ideal for baking whole, or for mashing.

WORKING WITH STARCHY POTATOES

Starchy potatoes can be used either peeled or unpeeled. In either case, scrub them well with a stiff brush under cold running water to remove any dirt. If peeling, use a vegetable peeler to remove the skin, and cut out the eyes, if any, with a paring knife or the tip of the peeler. Cut away any traces of green spots.

Choose firm potatoes free of blemishes, wrinkles, cracks, or any tinges of green. Look for loose potatoes, as those packaged in plastic bags sprout more readily. Mature waxy potatoes store well for up to 2 weeks in a cool, dry, dark place such as a pantry or drawer. New potatoes should be used as soon after purchasing as possible, as they do not keep well.

Waxy Potatoes

Possessing moister, denser flesh than their starchy cousins, waxy potatoes typically have thin skins and lower amounts of starch. They grow in a wide array of shapes, colors, and varieties. Perhaps the most familiar are the common red or white potatoes. Yellow Finn have yellowish skin and fine-grained, buttery flesh, while Peruvian potatoes have distinctive purple peel and flesh. Specialty varieties include small, oblong fingerling potatoes: Red Gold, with yellow flesh and netted red skin; Red Dale, slightly flat potatoes with white flesh and red skin; All Red, with rosy skin and flesh; and Rose Fir, which have pink skin and yellow flesh.

Available in spring and early summer, freshly dug waxy potatoes have a sweet flavor and creamy texture. Keeping their shape well, waxy potatoes are ideal for roasting, simmering in stews and soups, and boiling or steaming for potato salads.

WORKING WITH WAXY POTATOES

Scrub the potatoes well with a stiff brush under cold running water to remove dirt, taking care not to scrape off thin skins. Green areas on potatoes are known to be mildly toxic, so trim them off before cooking. It is generally not necessary to peel waxy potatoes, but for a decorative look, you can remove a thin strip of peel from the center section of the vegetable.

Crisp Skillet Potato Cake

MAKES 4 SERVINGS

1 lb (500 g) starchy potatoes, peeled and grated

Salt and freshly ground pepper

4 Tbsp (2 oz/60 g) unsalted butter

Place the potatoes in a bowl, season with salt and pepper, and let stand for at least 5 minutes. Squeeze the potatoes to remove as much water as possible. Transfer to a second bowl.

In an 8-inch (20-cm) nonstick frying pan over medium heat, melt 2 Tbsp of the butter. Add the potatoes and press them with a spatula to form an even cake. Cook until the bottom is crisp and deep golden brown, 12–15 minutes.

Remove from the heat and invert the cake onto a large plate. In the same frying pan over medium heat, melt the remaining 2 Tbsp butter. Slide the potato cake back into the pan, browned side up. Cook until the bottom is crisp and deep golden brown, 10–12 minutes. Slide onto a serving plate, season with salt, and cut into wedges. Serve right away.

Perfect French Fries with Ketchup

MAKES 4 SERVINGS

4 russet potatoes, about 2 lb (1 kg) total weight

Canola oil for deep-frying

Coarse salt

Ketchup for dipping

Cut the potatoes lengthwise into slices ½ inch (12 mm) thick. Cut the slices lengthwise into sticks ½ inch (12 mm) thick. Place the potato slices in a bowl of cold water and let stand for 15 minutes. Pat dry before frying.

Pour enough canola oil into a large, heavy pot to reach 2 inches (5 cm) up the sides and heat to 330°F (165°C) on a deep-frying thermometer.

Working in batches, carefully place 3 large handfuls of the potatoes into the pot. Fry until the potatoes are lightly golden, 4–5 minutes.

Using tongs or a long skimmer, transfer the potatoes to a platter lined with paper towels to drain. Between batches, let the oil return to 330°F (165°C) and remove any bits from the oil (the partially fried potatoes will keep at room temperature for up to 2 hours).

Just before serving, reheat the oil to 370°F (188°C). In batches, fry the potatoes in the same manner until golden and crisp, 3–5 minutes. Drain on fresh paper towels. Transfer to a serving bowl, season to taste with salt, and serve with ketchup.

Caution: When deep-frying, do not heat the oil above 375°F (190°C), if it reaches 400°F (200°C), it may start to smoke, then burst into flame.

Spanish Tortilla with Red Peppers

MAKES 6–8 SERVINGS

½ cup (4 fl oz/125 ml) plus 2 Tbsp olive oil

2 lb (1 kg) starchy potatoes, peeled and sliced ¼ inch (6 mm) thick

Salt and freshly ground pepper

2 yellow onions, thinly sliced

6 large eggs

1 large red bell pepper (capsicum), roasted (page 264), peeled, seeded, and cut into thin strips

Position a rack in the upper third of the oven and preheat to 350°F (180°C).

In a large frying pan over low heat, warm the ½ cup (4 fl oz/125 ml) olive oil. Add half of the potato slices to the pan and fry until tender but not browned, 15–20 minutes. Transfer to a plate and season with salt and pepper. Repeat with the remaining potato slices. Leave the oil in the pan.

In another frying pan over medium heat, warm the remaining 2 Tbsp olive oil. Add the onions and sauté until soft and translucent, about 15 minutes. Remove from the heat and let cool.

In a large bowl, whisk the eggs until blended. Stir in the onions and the roasted pepper. Season with salt and pepper. Fold in the cooked potatoes.

Heat the oil remaining in the large frying pan over low heat and pour in the egg mixture. Cook until the eggs are set around the edges, 8–10 minutes. Transfer to the oven and cook until set, 4–5 minutes. Let cool briefly.

Invert the omelet onto a large serving plate. Cut into wedges and serve right away.

PERFECT FRENCH FRIES WITH KETCHUP

ROASTED POTATOES WITH ROSEMARY & BAY

Potato Salad with Mustard Vinaigrette

MAKES 4 SERVINGS

2 lb (1 kg) small, round red-skinned potatoes, each about 1½ inches (4 cm) in diameter

3 Tbsp extra-virgin olive oil

2 Tbsp red wine vinegar

1 Tbsp Dijon mustard

Salt and freshly ground pepper

¼ cup (1 oz/30 g) thinly sliced green (spring) onions, white and light green parts

Place the potatoes in a large saucepan with water to cover. Bring to a boil over high heat, reduce the heat to medium-low, cover, and simmer until the potatoes are tender when pierced with a fork, about 15 minutes. Drain and set aside.

In a large bowl, whisk together the olive oil, vinegar, mustard, ½ tsp salt, and pepper to taste to make a dressing.

As soon as the potatoes are cool, quarter them and add them to the dressing. Add the green onions and toss. Serve right away or at room temperature.

Pan-fried Blue Potatoes with Sage

MAKES 6 SERVINGS

¾ lb (375 g) small blue potatoes

¼ cup (2 fl oz/60 ml) olive oil

10 medium fresh sage leaves

Salt

Place the potatoes in a large saucepan with water to cover. Bring to a boil over high heat and cook until the potatoes are tender when pierced with a fork, about 15 minutes. Drain potatoes and pat dry. When cool enough to handle, slice potatoes ⅜ inch (1 cm) thick, discarding any loose skin.

In a medium frying pan over medium-high heat, heat the olive oil. Arrange the potatoes in a single layer, leaving ¼ inch (6 mm) between slices (you may need to cook in 2 batches). Sauté the potatoes, turning once, until golden and crusty on both sides, 8–9 minutes total. Remove with a slotted spoon and drain on paper towels, blotting dry.

Add sage leaves to the warm pan; they will sizzle and curl slightly. In 10 seconds, turn leaves with tongs and fry for 5 seconds longer. Drain sage on fresh paper towels.

Arrange potatoes on a warmed platter, sprinkle with 1 tsp salt, and top with sage leaves. Serve right away.

Roasted Potatoes with Rosemary & Bay

MAKES 4–6 SERVINGS

2 lb (1 kg) waxy potatoes

1 head garlic, cloves separated

5 sprigs rosemary, each 1 inch (2.5 cm) long

1 bay leaf

3 Tbsp olive oil

Salt

Preheat the oven to 400°F (200°C).

Put the potatoes in a large piece of aluminum foil or a large shallow baking dish just large enough to hold them in a single layer. Add the garlic, rosemary, bay leaf, and olive oil. Season with salt and toss well. Add a splash of water.

Tightly close up the foil or cover the baking dish with foil and bake until the potatoes are tender when pierced with a knife, 40–60 minutes. Serve right away.

NEW POTATOES

New potatoes are small, immature waxy potatoes with a low starch content. They are typically available only in the spring and early summer, although they can be found sporadically at other times. Avoid buying those with cracks, wrinkling, or blemishes. Store them in a cool, dry place, and use within 2 or 3 days of purchase.

ROASTED POTATOES WITH HERBS

In a roasting pan, stir together ¼ cup (2 fl oz/60 ml) olive oil, 2 Tbsp lemon juice, 1 tsp salt, ¼ tsp paprika, and ½ tsp freshly ground pepper. Toss in 2½ lb (1.25 kg) unpeeled new potatoes, rinsed, into the oil mixture. Roast in a preheated 425°F (220°C) oven, turning often, until golden brown, about 45 minutes total. Garnish with 1 Tbsp chopped fresh basil and 1 Tbsp chopped fresh chives. Serve right away. Makes 4–6 servings.

Sweet Potatoes

One of the many contributions of the Americas to the global pantry, the sweet potato typically has either yellow-brown skin and yellow flesh, or dark reddish or purplish skin and dark orange flesh. Specialty varieties of sweet potatoes include white-fleshed, beige-skinned Japanese Sweet; Louisiana's famous copper colored Beauregard; the deep red-orange Jewel; the red-purple Carolina Ruby; and the long, narrow batata originally from the Caribbean.

Sweet potatoes are best in autumn and winter, though they are generally available year-round. Sweet potatoes can be substituted in many recipes for regular potatoes, where roasting, baking, frying, stewing, or steaming highlight their rich flavor and firm texture; they will contribute more moisture to the recipe, so expect a slightly different texture.

BUYING BEETS

Regardless of their size, look for firm, rounded beets (beetroots) with smooth skins and no noticeable bruising. Fresh beets are often sold in bunches with the greens and root ends attached. Do not buy beets with wilted, browning leaves, as the greens are an indicator of freshness. Separate the greens from the beets, and store both in the refrigerator in plastic bags for up to 5 days.

Beets

Once thought of as humble, unglamorous kitchen staples, beets (also called beetroots) are now showing up on fashionable restaurant menus in all their vibrant hues and sizes. Many beets boast a deep, rich red color combined with a sweet, earthy flavor and tender texture, making them a versatile favorite.

Today, markets often stock more than the familiar ruby-red type. It is not unusual to find pink, golden, white, and even striped beets, the best-known variety of which is the visually striking Chioggia, a pink-and-white heirloom from Italy. Although all beets have a characteristic sweetness, the commonly eaten variety is distinct from the larger sugar beet, which is not sold as a vegetable. The greens of beets are edible and should be cooked in the same manner as chard (page 71). Although beets are available year-round, their peak season is late summer and autumn.

WORKING WITH BEETS

Beets are best when cooked whole, peeled, and then sliced, chopped, or mashed. Roasting beets will intensify their flavor and color. Wrap them in aluminum foil for quick cleanup. If boiling, leave about 1 inch (2.5 cm) of the stem and the root end intact to keep the beets from "bleeding" into the water. Remove the stems from beet greens, rinse well, and spin dry.

Mashed Sweet Potatoes with Brown Sugar & Pecans

MAKES 6 SERVINGS

6 sweet potatoes, peeled

4 Tbsp (2 oz/60 g) unsalted butter

2½ Tbsp light brown sugar

Salt

2 Tbsp chopped pecans

Trim the ends from the potatoes. Place the potatoes in a large saucepan with water to cover. Bring to a boil over high heat until the potatoes are tender when pierced with a fork, about 15 minutes. Drain and let cool.

In a small saucepan over low heat, melt the butter. Let cool.

Preheat the oven to 350°F (180°C). Using 1 Tbsp of the melted butter, grease a 6-cup (1.5-l) baking dish.

Place the potatoes in a large mixing bowl and mash with a potato masher or electric mixer until smooth. Stir in 2 Tbsp of the melted butter, 1 Tbsp of the brown sugar, and the ½ tsp salt. Spoon the mashed potato mixture into the baking dish. Dot the remaining 2 Tbsp butter, the remaining 1½ Tbsp brown sugar, and the chopped pecans over the top.

Bake until the sugar melts and the mixture is hot, about 15 minutes. Serve right away.

Baked Sweet Potatoes with Brown Butter & Sage

MAKES 8–10 SERVINGS

½ cup (4 oz/125 g) plus 2 Tbsp unsalted butter, plus extra for greasing

4 lb (2 kg) sweet potatoes, peeled and cut into 1-inch (2.5-cm) cubes

¼ cup (⅓ oz/10 g) chopped fresh sage

Salt and freshly ground pepper

Preheat the oven to 425°F (220°C). Butter a 13-by-9-inch (33-by-23-cm) baking dish and place the sweet potatoes in the dish.

In a heavy frying pan over medium-low heat, melt the butter and cook until golden brown, about 5 minutes. Add the sage and salt and pepper to taste. Continue to cook until the butter is a deep golden brown, about 2 minutes more. Pour the browned butter over the sweet potatoes and season with salt and pepper. Cover the dish with aluminum foil.

Bake the sweet potatoes until tender when pierced with a fork, about 20 minutes. Transfer to a platter and serve right away.

Beef and Sweet Potato Stir-Fry

MAKES 2–4 SERVINGS

½ lb (250 g) flank steak

1½ tsp reduced-sodium soy sauce, plus extra for serving

1½ tsp plus 4 Tbsp (2 fl oz/60 ml) peanut oil

1½ tsp oyster sauce

1 sweet potato, cut into matchsticks

2 small dried red chiles

4 green (spring) onions, cut diagonally into 1½-inch (4-cm) pieces

2 cloves garlic, thinly sliced

1-inch (2.5-cm) piece fresh ginger, peeled and cut into thin slices

Fresh cilantro (fresh coriander) leaves for garnish

Cooked White Rice (page 262) for serving

Cut the steak in half lengthwise. Cut the halves against the grain into slices about ⅛ inch (3 mm) thick. In a small bowl, toss together the beef, the 1½ tsp soy sauce, the 1½ tsp peanut oil, and the oyster sauce. Cover and refrigerate for 2 hours.

In a large, heavy frying pan over high heat, warm 2 Tbsp of the oil. Add the beef and sear for 1 minute without stirring. Stir-fry the beef until the meat is cooked through, about 2 minutes. Remove from the pan.

Return the pan to high heat and heat the remaining 2 Tbsp oil. Add the sweet potato and dried chiles, season with salt, and sear for 1 minute without stirring. Add the green onions and stir-fry until the potatoes are just tender, about 1 minute. Add the garlic and ginger and stir-fry for 1 minute longer. Return the beef to the pan and stir-fry until heated through.

Transfer to a large platter and garnish with cilantro. Serve right away with white rice and soy sauce.

BEEF & SWEET POTATO STIR-FRY

ROASTED BEETS WITH GOAT CHEESE & HERBS

Golden Beet & Blue Cheese Risotto

MAKES 4 SERVINGS

¾ lb (375 g) golden beets

Salt

3 Tbsp unsalted butter

1 small yellow onion, finely diced

5 cups (40 fl oz/1.25 l) chicken broth

1½ cups (10½ oz/330 g) short-grain rice, such as Arborio, Carnaroli, or Vialone Nano

½ cup (4 fl oz/125 ml) dry white wine

⅓ cup (1 oz/30 g) grated hard cheese, such as Parmesan

4 Tbsp crumbled blue cheese

Preheat the oven to 400°F (200°C). Put the beets in a baking dish with water to cover the bottom. Cover tightly with aluminum foil and roast until tender when pierced with a fork, 40–60 minutes. Uncover and let cool. When cool, cut off the beet tops and root ends, peel, and cut into ¼-inch (6-mm) dice. Season with salt.

In a large, heavy pot over medium heat, melt 2 Tbsp of the butter. Add the onion and a pinch of salt and sauté until the onion is soft, about 8 minutes.

Meanwhile, in a saucepan over low heat, bring the broth and 1 tsp salt to a simmer.

Stir the rice into the onion until translucent, about 3 minutes. Add the wine and stir until absorbed. Add ¾ cup (6 fl oz/185 ml) of the broth and simmer vigorously, stirring often, until the liquid is almost absorbed. Add another ladleful of broth. Continue simmering, stirring, and adding more broth until the rice is tender, about 25 minutes. Stir in the beets and heat through, about 1 minute. Stir in the remaining 1 Tbsp butter and the cheese. Let stand for 2 minutes. Season with salt and serve right away.

Roasted Beet Soup with Feta & Dill

MAKES 4 SERVINGS

3 large red beets, trimmed leaving 1 inch (2 cm) of stem

1½ Tbsp olive oil

1 Tbsp unsalted butter

¼ cup yellow onion, chopped

4 cups (32 fl oz/1 l) beef broth

Salt and freshly ground pepper

½ cup (2½ oz/75 g) crumbled feta cheese

1 Tbsp dill, coarsely chopped

Preheat the oven to 350°F (180°C). Put the beets in a baking dish and drizzle evenly with the olive oil, turning them to coat well. Roast until tender when pierced with a fork, about 1 hour, depending on their size. Remove from the oven. When cool, peel the beets and coarsely chop them. Set aside.

In a large saucepan over medium heat, melt the butter. Add the onion and sauté until translucent, about 2 minutes. Add the chopped beets and the broth, bring to a simmer, reduce the heat to low, and cook, uncovered, for about 10 minutes.

Transfer to a blender or food processor and purée until smooth. Return the purée to the saucepan, place over medium heat, and heat through. Season with salt and pepper.

Ladle the soup into individual warmed bowls. Top with the feta cheese and dill and serve right away.

Roasted Beets with Goat Cheese & Herbs

MAKES 4 SERVINGS

6 beets, about 1½ lb (24 oz/750 g) total weight, greens removed

1 tsp chopped fresh thyme

1 tsp chopped fresh chives

3 Tbsp extra-virgin olive oil

Salt and freshly ground pepper

2 oz (60 g) fresh goat cheese, crumbled

Preheat the oven to 400°F (200°C).

Wrap the beets individually in aluminum foil and roast until tender when pierced with a fork, about 1 hour, depending on their size.

When cool, peel and quarter the beets and place in a serving bowl.

In a separate bowl, mix together the thyme, chives, and olive oil. Drizzle the olive oil–herb mixture over the beets, season with salt and pepper, and top with the crumbled goat cheese. Serve right away.

BEET GREENS

Beet greens, the edible leafy green tops attached to beets, are often cut from the beets and discarded but they are actually quite delicious. Similar to chard or spinach, beet greens lend themselves well to stir-frying, sautéing, and braising. Look for them in late summer and autumn when beets are in season.

STIR-FRIED BEET GREENS WITH GINGER

In a large saucepan over medium-high heat, add 1 Tbsp canola oil, 2 tsp peeled and minced fresh ginger, and 1 tsp garlic. Heat until the garlic begins to sizzle, about 10 seconds. Add 1 lb (500 g) beet greens, rinsed and drained and toss to coat. Cover the pan to steam the greens until tender, 9–12 minutes. Season with coarse salt. Transfer to a warmed serving dish and serve at once. Makes 4 servings.

BUYING CARROTS

Look for smooth, firm, brightly colored carrots without cracks or any green near the stem. If the carrots still have their leaves, cut them off before storing. Leave 1 inch (2.5 cm) of the green tops on the carrots to preserve moisture. Keep carrots in a plastic bag in the refrigerator for up to 2 weeks.

Carrots

Relatives of parsley, sweet and crisp carrots are among the most popular of all vegetables. Although the familiar long, tapered, orange Imperator carrot is by far the most widely available, local farmers are increasingly growing special varieties with many different shapes and hues. The Nantes, deep orange and cylindrical in shape, is a delicate carrot only available from smaller growers. The Chantenay, with a short, thick, cone-shaped root, is harvested while still immature for baby carrots. Tiny, finger-shaped Bambina, pointed Horn, and cigar-shaped Bolero are among the other special varieties offered at farmers' markets.

Carrots grow year-round but are at their sweetest from early winter through spring. Use raw carrots in salads and sandwiches. Braised or simmered, they blend into soups, sauces, and stews. Roasted or sautéed, they can star on their own as a colorful side dish.

WORKING WITH CARROTS

If the carrots are small and tender, simply scrub them under cold running water with a soft vegetable brush and use without peeling them. Use a vegetable peeler or paring knife to peel larger vegetables before use. Trim the stems and tough ends before using.

Parsnips

Kin to the carrot, these ivory-colored roots closely resemble their brighter, more familiar cousin. Parsnips have a sweet, slightly earthy flavor and a tough, starchy texture that softens with cooking. It is a popular vegetable across northern Europe, where it thrives in the cool climate, and was carried to North America by the early colonists.

Although they are now available year-round, parsnips are at their peak during the winter, when the frosty weather converts their starches to sugar. Some devotees of the naturally ripened root find that parsnips dug up in the springtime are the sweetest of all. Parsnips lend themselves well to purées and soups. They are also excellent roasted with other root vegetables such as carrots and potatoes.

Carrot Salad with Cumin, Coriander & Cilantro

MAKES 4–6 SERVINGS

1 clove garlic

Salt

1 tsp cumin seeds, toasted
(page 264) and ground

1 tsp coriander seeds, toasted
(page 264) and ground

Pinch of cayenne pepper, or more to taste

¼ cup (2 fl oz/60 ml) fresh lemon juice

1 lb (500 g) carrots, peeled and
shaved into thin strips

¼ cup (2 fl oz/60 ml) extra-virgin
olive oil

⅓ cup (½ oz/15 g) chopped fresh
cilantro (fresh coriander)

Using a mortar and pestle or flat side of
a knife, mash the garlic into a paste with
a pinch of salt. In a small bowl, stir together
the garlic, cumin, coriander, cayenne, and
lemon juice. Put the carrots in a large
serving bowl and season with salt. Add the
garlic mixture, toss well, and let stand for
10 minutes. Add the olive oil and cilantro
and toss. Serve right away.

Carrot Purée with Tarragon

MAKES 4 SERVINGS

4 carrots, peeled and cut into
1-inch (2.5-cm) pieces

2 Tbsp chicken broth

2 Tbsp heavy (double) cream

3 tsp minced fresh tarragon

Salt and freshly ground pepper

Place the carrots in a large saucepan with
water to cover. Bring to a boil over high
heat. Cover and reduce the heat to medium.
Cook until the carrots are tender and can
be pierced with a fork, 15–20 minutes.

Drain the carrots and transfer to a blender
or food processor. Add the chicken broth,
cream, and 1 tsp of the tarragon and process
to a smooth purée. Transfer to a large serving
bowl and season with salt and pepper.
Garnish with the remaining 2 tsp tarragon
and serve right away.

*Serve carrot purée alongside a white fleshed
fish such as halibut.*

Roasted Baby Carrots with Honey Glaze

MAKES 4–6 SERVINGS

1½ lb baby carrots of similar size,
peeled and trimmed, leaving about
½ inch (12 mm) of the carrot top

2 Tbsp unsalted butter

2 Tbsp honey

1 tsp finely grated lemon zest

Salt

If the carrots are larger than ½ inch (12 mm)
in diameter, halve them lengthwise. In a
frying pan large enough to hold the carrots
in a single layer, add the carrots and enough
water to come halfway up the sides of the
carrots. Add the butter, honey, lemon zest,
and 1 tsp salt and bring the water to a boil.
Partially cover the pan, reduce the heat to
medium-high, and continue to boil until the
carrots can easily be pierced with a fork,
about 10 minutes.

Uncover and continue to boil until the
cooking liquid evaporates and the carrots
start to caramelize, about 4 minutes. Season
with salt and serve right away.

MULTICOLORED CARROTS

At farmers' markets in the spring, you can find
carrots in a rainbow of colors such as white,
yellow, red, and purple. The specific colors are
due to a variety of growing conditions such
as temperature, type of soil, water, and number
of daylight hours. While they have only gained
popularity in recent years, multicolored carrots
have been around since ancient times. Use
them in any recipe that calls for carrots.

CRUDITÉS WITH GREEN GODDESS DRESSING

On a large platter, arrange 8 whole multicolored
carrots, 3 cooked red or yellow beets, cut into
chunks, 6–8 cooked new potatoes, cut into
halves, 12 small radishes, and 4 celery stalks,
cut into 3-inch (7.5-cm) lengths. Serve with
Green Goddess Dressing (page 262) on the
side for dipping. Makes 4 servings.

CARROT SALAD WITH CUMIN, CORIANDER & CILANTRO

ROASTED PARSNIPS WITH PEARS & HAZELNUTS

Parsnip & Potato Purée with Chives

MAKES 4–6 SERVINGS

1½ lb (750 g) parsnips, peeled and cut into 2-inch (5-cm) chunks

Salt and freshly ground pepper

1½ lb (750 g) Yukon gold or other waxy potatoes, peeled and cut into 2-inch (5-cm) chunks

½ cup (4 oz/125 g) unsalted butter, cut into pieces

¾ cup (6 fl oz/180 ml) heavy (double) cream or half-and-half (half cream)

¼ cup (½ oz/15 g) finely snipped fresh chives

Put the parsnips and 1 Tbsp salt in a large pot and add water to cover by 1 inch (2.5 cm). In a separate pot, do the same with the potatoes. Bring both to a low boil, reduce the heat, and simmer until the parsnips and potatoes can be pierced with a knife, about 25 minutes. Drain and let cool.

Pass the parsnips and potatoes through a food mill or mash with a potato masher. Return to one of the pots and stir in the butter and cream. Reheat if necessary over low heat, stirring frequently. Season with salt and pepper. Transfer to a bowl and sprinkle with the chives. Serve right away.

Parsnips Glazed with Sherry & Ginger

MAKES 3–4 SERVINGS

1 lb (500 g) parsnips, peeled

½ cup (4 fl oz/125 ml) chicken broth or water

2 Tbsp unsalted butter

2 Tbsp dry sherry

2 tsp minced fresh ginger

1 tsp chopped fresh thyme

Salt and freshly ground pepper

1 tsp fresh lemon juice

Cut the parsnips in half lengthwise, then cut the halves in half again. Cut the pieces in half crosswise. Remove the cores if woody.

Arrange the parsnips in a frying pan large enough to hold them in a single layer. Add the broth, butter, sherry, ginger, and thyme. Season with salt. Partially cover the pan and bring to a simmer over medium heat. Cook until the parsnips are tender when pierced with a knife, 7–9 minutes.

Uncover the pan, raise the heat to high, and continue to cook until the juices are reduced to a glaze, 4–6 minutes. Season with the lemon juice and pepper. Transfer the parsnips to a serving dish and serve right away.

Roasted Parsnips with Pears & Hazelnuts

MAKES 6 SERVINGS

1 lb (500 g) parsnips, peeled and quartered lengthwise

3 pears, such as Bosc or Anjou

3 Tbsp olive oil

Salt

2 Tbsp unsalted butter

3 Tbsp hazelnuts (filberts), toasted (page 264) and finely chopped

Preheat the oven to 400°F (200°C).

Remove the cores from the parsnips. Cut into 3-inch (7.5-cm) lengths, or if the quarters are small, leave as is. Halve the pears lengthwise and remove the cores, leaving the stem attached. Cut the halves into quarters or, if the pears are especially large, into sixths. Put the parsnips and pears on a baking sheet, drizzle with the olive oil, and toss to coat evenly. Spread out in an even layer and season with salt. Roast until tender and browned, 30–40 minutes.

In a small saucepan over medium-high heat, melt the butter. Add a pinch of salt and swirl the pan frequently until the butter browns. Add the hazelnuts and immediately drizzle the butter over the parsnips and pears. Season with salt and serve right away.

Look for firm, medium-sized celery roots (celeriacs), about the size of small grapefruits. They should feel heavy for their size and be free of bruising and soft spots. Tangled root ends are acceptable, as are green stalks growing from the top. Trim any stalks and then store the roots in a plastic bag in the refrigerator for up to 5 days.

Celery Root

Though within the same botanical group, celery root is a distinct variety from the plant that produces the familiar bunches of green stalks that share its name. This plant is cultivated specifically for its large, round, knobby, and deeply gnarled root. Also known as celeriac, celery root is prized for dense, ivory flesh with a pronounced nutty, earthy flavor that evokes celery.

It is at its best from early autumn through early spring. Particularly popular in French kitchens, celery root bakes into smooth, sweet gratins and purées. Shredded or finely julienned, it pairs well with citrus juices, parsley leaves, and bitter greens in fresh salads. It can be substituted for up to half of the potatoes for a new twist on mashed potatoes.

WORKING WITH CELERY ROOT

Scrub the celery root with a stiff brush under cold running water. Trim the root end. With a sharp paring knife or vegetable peeler, peel away the thick skin as deeply as needed to remove any browned furroughs. Immediately sprinkle the root with lemon juice to prevent discoloration. Cut, chop, or shred the hard root using a sharp knife, food processor, mandoline, or grater.

BUYING TURNIPS & RUTABAGAS

Choose turnips and rutabagas (swedes) that are unblemished and firm. Choose large roots that are heavy for their size. Baby turnips should be separated from their greens and stored in plastic bags in the refrigerator for 1 to 2 weeks (the greens can be saved for cooking separately). Rutabagas and turnips will keep for several weeks in a cool, dark, well-ventilated place.

Turnips & Rutabagas

These closely related roots are similar in flavor, uses, and appearance. Turnips usually have creamy fleshed ivory skin, and a purple cap. Some varieties are capped with green, red, white, or even black. Rutabagas (also knows as swedes) are generally bigger and can be brown, yellow, or white, with yellow flesh. The two roots can be substituted for each other in most recipes. Very young turnips are tender and have a mild, sweet flavor. The firm flesh of mature turnips and rutabagas has a strong mustardlike taste that mellows and becomes sweeter when cooked.

Turnips and rutabagas are generally best during the late autumn and early wInter. Roasting these roots brings out their distinctive sweetness. They can also be added to soups and stews, puréed or mashed, or baked into a simple side dish.

WORKING WITH TURNIPS & RUTABAGAS

If you have baby turnips, simply peel and trim for cooking whole. Mature turnips and rutabagas should be peeled and trimmed with a paring knife, and then sliced or cut into chunks. If mature turnips have a strong smell, blanch for 3 to 5 minutes to remove some of the harshness. Prepare turnip greens as you would beet greens (page 85).

Grated Celery Root Salad

MAKES 4 SERVINGS

1 large egg yolk, at room temperature

1 Tbsp Dijon mustard

Salt

¼ tsp cayenne pepper

½ cup (4 fl oz/125 ml) olive oil

2 Tbsp fresh lemon juice

1½ Tbsp heavy (double) cream

1 tsp chopped tarragon

½ tsp caraway seeds

1 celery root (celeriac), about 1 lb (500 g)

In a bowl, whisk the egg yolk, mustard, salt, and cayenne pepper until well blended. Add a little oil and whisk until an emulsion forms then continue to add the oil, a little at a time, beating vigorously after each addition until it is absorbed and the sauce is very thick. Whisk in the lemon juice and 1 Tbsp of the cream. Add more cream if needed to achieve a creamy sauce. Season with the tarragon and caraway seeds. Set aside.

Peel the celery root, removing all of the brown skin. Shred and add about half of the dressing. Mix well. Add more of the dressing as necessary to coat lightly.

Spoon onto plates and serve right away.

Puréed Celery Root with Chives

MAKES 6 SERVINGS

3 Tbsp unsalted butter

3 shallots, chopped

2 cloves garlic, chopped

1–2 celery roots (celeriacs), about 1 lb (500 g), peeled and diced

1 cup (8 fl oz/250 ml) chicken broth

½ cup (4 fl oz/125 ml) heavy (double) cream

Salt and freshly ground pepper

In a large frying pan over medium heat, melt 2 Tbsp of the butter. Add the shallots and garlic and sauté until softened, 1–2 minutes. Add the celery root and sauté until softened and coated with the butter, 5–7 minutes. Pour enough broth to cover the celery root and cook, uncovered, over medium heat, until the celery root is just tender, about 15 minutes. The broth should almost be completely reduced. Remove from the heat and let cool.

When cool enough to handle, transfer to a blender or food processor and purée until smooth, adding cream if needed. Add the remaining cream and blend again. Pour the purée back into a sauté pan over medium-low heat. Season with the salt and pepper. Heat through, then stir in the remaining 1 Tbsp butter.

Remove from the heat, transfer to a serving bowl and serve at once.

Celery Root & Potato Gratin with Thyme

MAKES 6 SERVINGS

2 Tbsp unsalted butter, softened plus extra for greasing

4 large shallots, thinly sliced

Salt and freshly ground pepper

2 celery roots (celeriacs) peeled, halved, and thinly sliced

2 lb (1 kg) russet potatoes, peeled and cut into thin slices

2 Tbsp chopped fresh thyme

2 cups (16 fl oz/500 ml) heavy (double) cream

1 cup (8 fl oz/250 ml) chicken broth

Preheat the oven to 375°F (190°C).

Butter a 14-inch (35-cm) oval gratin dish. Sprinkle half of the shallots on the bottom of the dish and season with salt and pepper. Arrange half of the celery root and potato slices on top of the shallots, sprinkle half of the thyme on top, and season with salt and pepper. Repeat layering with the remaining shallots, celery root, potatoes, and thyme, and season again with salt and pepper.

Bring the cream and broth to a simmer in a saucepan and pour over the vegetables. Dot the remaining 2 Tbsp butter on top and cover tightly with aluminum foil.

Bake until the vegetables are almost tender when pierced with a fork, about 35 minutes. Raise the temperature to 400°F (200°C). Press the vegetables down with a spatula to an even thickness. Continue to bake, uncovered, until the gratin is golden brown, about 30 minutes. Let stand for 5 minutes before serving. Serve right away.

CELERY ROOT & POTATO GRATIN WITH THYME

TURNIP, APPLE & POTATO SOUP

Turnip, Apple & Potato Soup

MAKES 4 SERVINGS

2 Tbsp unsalted butter

1 small yellow onion, finely diced

1 tsp chopped fresh thyme

1 bay leaf

Salt and ground white pepper

1 lb (500 g) turnips, peeled and cut into ½-inch (12-mm) chunks

2 tart apples, such as Braeburn, Granny Smith, Jonagold, or pippin, peeled, cored, and quartered

½ lb (250 g) Yukon gold potatoes, peeled and quartered

2 Tbsp crème fraîche

2 Tbsp chopped fresh flat-leaf (Italian) parsley

In a heavy pot over medium-low heat, melt the butter. Add the onion, thyme, bay leaf, and a pinch of salt and sauté until the onion is tender, about 12 minutes. Add the turnips, apples, potatoes, a pinch of salt, and 1 cup (8 fl oz/250 ml) water. Cover and simmer until the vegetables and apples are tender, 10–15 minutes. Add 4 more cups (32 fl oz/ 1 l) water, raise the heat to high, and bring to a boil. Reduce the heat to low and simmer, uncovered, for 20 minutes. Let cool slightly.

Working in batches, purée the soup in a blender. Return to the pot and reheat. Thin the soup with water if necessary, season with the salt and white pepper. Ladle into bowls, and garnish with the crème fraîche, and chopped parsley. Serve right away.

Baby Turnips & Turnip Greens

MAKES 4 SERVINGS

1 lb (500 g) baby turnips with greens attached, yellow or damaged leaves removed

2 Tbsp olive oil

2 slices bacon, cut crosswise into pieces ¼ inch (6 mm) thick

1 Tbsp unsalted butter

1 large shallot, thinly sliced

Salt and freshly ground pepper

Leaving the greens on the turnips, trim the root ends. If the turnips seem large, cut off the greens, leaving about 1 inch (2.5 cm) attached. Cut the greens into 1½-inch (4-cm) strips, and halve the turnips.

In a large, heavy frying pan over medium heat, warm 1 Tbsp of the olive oil. Add the bacon and cook until the fat has rendered, about 5 minutes. Pour off the fat, leaving the bacon in the pan.

Return the pan to medium-high heat and melt the remaining 1 Tbsp olive oil and the butter. Add the shallot, season with salt, and sauté for 1 minute. Add the turnips and greens, season with salt, and pour in just enough water to cover the bottom of the pan. Cover and cook until both the turnips and the greens are tender, 4–7 minutes, adding water if the pan dries out. If necessary, uncover and continue to cook until the liquid has reduced. Transfer to a serving bowl and season with salt and pepper. Season with salt and pepper and serve right away.

Maple-Glazed Roasted Root Vegetables

MAKES 4–6 SERVINGS

2 carrots, cut into 2-inch (5-cm) pieces

1 large parsnip, cut into 2-inch (5-cm) pieces

1 small turnip, cut into 2-inch (5-cm) pieces

½ rutabaga (swede), cut into 2-inch (5-cm) pieces

1 sweet potato, peeled and cut into 2-inch (5-cm) pieces

1 red onion, cut into 2-inch (5-cm) pieces

2–3 Tbsp olive oil

Salt

¼ cup (2½ fl oz/75 ml) pure maple syrup

2 Tbsp unsalted butter, melted

Preheat the oven to 400°F (200°C).

In a large bowl, toss together the carrots, parsnip, turnip, rutabaga, sweet potato, and onion with olive oil to coat. Season with 2 tsp salt and toss again. Spread the vegetables in a single layer, without touching, on two baking sheets.

Roast, shaking the baking sheets occasionally and turning the vegetables with a spatula to keep them from sticking, until they develop a light crust and are tender, 40–50 minutes.

Meanwhile, in a small bowl, stir together the maple syrup and butter. Brush over the vegetables and continue roasting until they look glazed, about 5 minutes longer.

Transfer the vegetables to a serving dish and serve right away.

BUYING RADISHES

Regardless of shape, size, or color, radishes should be firm, with smooth skins and unwilted green leaves. To ensure freshness, trim away radish greens before storing. Small radishes can be kept in a plastic bag in the refrigerator for up to 1 week; large radishes will keep for up to 2 weeks.

Radishes

Although radishes belong to a single species of mustard, they come to market in a tremendous diversity of sizes, shapes, and colors. In addition to the familiar round red radishes, there are thin white ones, known as icicle radishes; Easter egg radishes of cheerful purple, white, lavender or pink colors; French breakfast radishes with elongated, two-toned red and white roots; and pungently flavored black radishes. Large, watermelon radishes are so called because of their combination of pale green skin and pinkish red flesh.

Small, tender radishes are typically in season in spring and early summer. Larger varieties tend to reach their peak later in summer or autumn. Radishes are best eaten raw in fresh salads, as a palate-cleansing accompaniment to sandwiches, or simply dipped in salt and served with buttered bread.

WORKING WITH RADISHES

Scrub the radishes under cold running water and trim both ends, unless you are serving them as an hors d'oeuvre; in that case, you may want to leave 1 inch (2.5 cm) of the leaves intact as a pretty garnish. If the radishes are not as crisp as you would like, put them into a bowl of ice water and refrigerate for a few hours to refresh them.

Watermelon Radish Salad with Avocado Vinaigrette

MAKES 4 SERVINGS

1 shallot, finely diced

1½ Tbsp fresh lemon juice, plus extra if needed

1½ Tbsp white wine vinegar

Salt

1 avocado, halved lengthwise, pitted, and diced

¼ cup (2 fl oz/60 ml) extra-virgin olive oil

2 heads romaine (cos) lettuce, dark outer leaves cut into ½-inch (12-mm) pieces

1 watermelon radish, thinly sliced

¼ cup (⅓ oz/10 g) chopped fresh cilantro (fresh coriander)

In a small bowl, stir together the shallot, 1½ Tbsp lemon juice, vinegar, and a pinch of salt. Gently stir in the avocado, season with salt, and let stand for 10 minutes, stirring occasionally. Whisk in the olive oil to make a vinaigrette.

In a large bowl, combine the romaine, radish, and cilantro. Stir in the vinaigrette and drizzle over the salad. Toss gently and season with salt and additional lemon juice. Transfer to individual plates. Serve right away.

Radish, Fennel & Parsley Salad

MAKES 6 SERVINGS

2 fennel bulbs

1 small bunch fresh flat-leaf (Italian) parsley, stems removed and leaves minced

12 radishes, thinly sliced

3 Tbsp extra-virgin olive oil

2 Tbsp fresh lemon juice

1 clove garlic, minced

Salt and freshly ground pepper

Cut off the feathery tops and stems from the fennel bulbs and discard. Trim away any yellow or bruised outer leaves and then cut each bulb in half through the stem end. Cut out the tough core portion and place the halves, cut side down, on a work surface. Cut the fennel crosswise into paper-thin slices. Place the slices in a bowl. Mix in the parsley and radishes. Set aside.

In a small bowl, whisk together the olive oil, lemon juice, and garlic. Season with salt and pepper to make a dressing.

Drizzle the dressing over the salad to coat evenly. Transfer to a serving bowl and serve right away.

Tea Sandwiches with Trout, Radishes & Blue Cheese

MAKES 10 SERVINGS

20 thin slices of sandwich bread, crusts trimmed

½ lb (250 g) soft blue cheese

8 oz (250 g) smoked trout

Salt and freshly ground pepper

1 cup (1 oz/30 g) arugula leaves

10–12 radishes, thinly sliced

Spread half of the trimmed bread slices with the blue cheese.

Generously season the smoked trout with salt and pepper. Divide the trout, radishes, and arugula evenly among the cheese-topped slices. Put the remaining bread slices on top and press gently.

Cut each sandwich in half on the diagonal, arrange on a platter and serve right away.

FRENCH BREAKFAST RADISHES

Originally from Southern France, French breakfast radishes (also called flambo or D'Avignon) radishes, have an elongated shape which gives them a more slender appearance than regular radishes. They are red in color but fade to white at the root end. They are available at the market in spring. Use them anytime radishes are called for.

RADISHES WITH BUTTER & SEA SALT

Trim the root end of 30 radishes and then cut in half. Place in a bowl of ice water for 20 minutes. Pack ½ cup (4 oz/125 g) room temperature unsalted butter into a small ramekin. Drain the radishes and pat dry with paper towels, then arrange on a platter. Serve the radishes accompanied by the butter for spreading and coarse sea salt for sprinkling. Makes 6–8 servings.

WATERMELON RADISH SALAD WITH AVOCADO VINAIGRETTE

Squashes

ZUCCHINI

SQUASH
BLOSSOMS

YELLOW SQUASH

PATTYPAN
SQUASH

ACORN SQUASH

BUTTERNUT
SQUASH

DELICATA
SQUASH

PUMPKIN

KABOCHA
SQUASH

Manifesting many colors, sizes, and shapes, the numerous squash varieties are types of gourds, all of which grow on vines. Pattypan squash and zucchini (courgettes) are appreciated for their mild, delicate flesh that lends itself to an array of seasonings. Some, such as acorn squash, kabocha squash, and pumpkin, have dense flesh that becomes sweet and creamy when cooked. Native to the New World, squashes were cultivated thousands of years ago in Mexico and South America.

Squashes are generally divided into two types: summer and winter. Acorn, delicata, kabocha, and other winter squashes are allowed to mature until their flesh is thick and their shells are hard. They tend to have a long shelf life. Zucchini and yellow squash, among other summer varieties, have soft, thin skin and moist flesh. The seeds of many winter varieties and the flowers of summer squash are also edible.

Summer squashes are best when young. Look for small specimens early in the summer. Expect the widest selection of winter squashes in the autumn and winter.

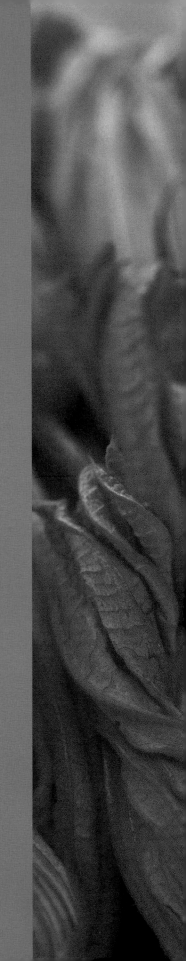

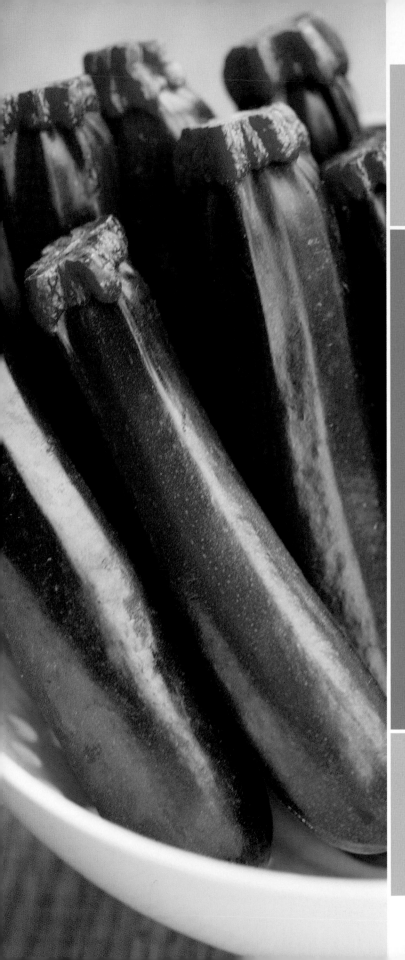

Zucchini

This well-known type of summer squash, zucchini, also called *courgette*, is highly versatile and has a delicious, mild flavor. Served raw or cooked, it appears in many different cuisines, from its native Mexico to Southern Europe, the Middle East to Northern Asia. The vine's large, golden flowers are also edible; they can be filled with cheese and fried or cut into ribbons for soups, pastas, and omelets. In addition to the familiar long, dark green vegetable, new varieties such as golden or round zucchini, known as Ronde de Nice, are becoming increasingly available at farmers' markets.

Zucchini are at their best during the summer. They are ideal sautéed, baked, roasted, or grilled to highlight their delicate texture, but also take well to simmering in soups, quick-steaming, frying, or gentle, slow cooking to bring out their sweetness. Sliced or grated raw, zucchini are excellent in fresh salads and on antipasto plates.

BUYING YELLOW SQUASH

Purchase yellow squashes when small for tender, seedless flesh. As they grow, yellow squash becomes firmer and seedier. Yellow squashes should have bright color and feel heavy and firm for their size. Look for smooth skins with no blemishes. Store the squashes in a plastic bag in the refrigerator for up to 3 days.

Yellow Squash

Tender-fleshed, mild-tasting yellow squashes come in a number of shapes, sizes, and hues. Some are long and cylindrical, resembling zucchini with a bright lemon tint. The bumpy-skinned crookneck type usually has a pale buttery color. Round pattypan squash has a scalloped edge, hence its alternative name: scallop squash.

All yellow squashes reach their peak during the hottest weeks of summer. These versatile vegetables are adaptable to different cooking styles and cuisines, much like their close cousin the zucchini. Sautéed in butter or olive oil, they can top pasta or accompany roasted meat, poultry, or fish. Grilling and roasting brings out their sweetness. They can usually be substituted in recipes that call for zucchini.

WORKING WITH YELLOW SQUASH

Rinse the squashes and trim the ends with a sharp knife. Their thin, flavorful skins do not require peeling. Keep smaller squash whole for roasting. Larger ones can be cut into slices or chunks for grilling or sautéing. If you plan to stuff them, cut yellow squashes in half lengthwise and hollow each one gently with a teaspoon.

Zucchini Carpaccio with Cheese & Pine Nuts

MAKES 4–6 SERVINGS

1 clove garlic

Salt and freshly ground pepper

¼ cup (2 fl oz/60 ml) fresh lemon juice

½ cup (4 fl oz/125 ml) extra-virgin olive oil

1 lb (500 g) zucchini (courgettes), thinly sliced

1 cup (1 oz/30 g) arugula (rocket) leaves

¼ cup (1 oz/30 g) pine nuts, toasted (page 264)

Shaved aged hard cheese, such as Parmesan, for garnish

Mash the garlic into a paste with a pinch of salt. In a bowl, whisk together the garlic paste and lemon juice. Let stand for 10 minutes, then whisk in the olive oil to make a dressing.

Put the zucchini in a bowl, season with salt and pepper, and toss with three-fourths of the dressing. Arrange two-thirds of the zucchini on a large platter. Set aside.

Put the arugula in a small bowl, season with salt, and toss with just enough dressing to coat the greens. Scatter the dressed arugula on top of the zucchini and arrange the remaining zucchini on and around the greens. Sprinkle with the pine nuts and cheese. Serve right away.

Zucchini-Feta Pancakes Topped with Sour Cream

MAKES 6–8 SERVINGS

4 cups (1 lb/500 g) grated zucchini (courgettes)

Salt and freshly ground pepper

⅔ cup (3½ oz/105 g) all-purpose (plain) flour

1 tsp baking powder

1 cup (5 oz/155 g) crumbled feta cheese

4 large eggs, separated

½ cup (1½ oz/45 g) thinly sliced green (spring) onions

2 Tbsp chopped flat-leaf (Italian) parsley

1 Tbsp chopped fresh mint

3 Tbsp olive oil

Sour cream for serving

Put the zucchini in a fine-mesh sieve, sprinkle with 2 tsp salt, and let stand for 15–30 minutes. Squeeze out any excess liquid. In a bowl, stir together the flour, baking powder, ¼ tsp pepper, and 1 tsp salt. In another bowl, stir together the zucchini, feta, egg yolks, green onions, parsley, and mint. Stir in the flour mixture. In a clean bowl, beat the egg whites to soft peaks. Fold into the zucchini mixture.

In a frying pan over medium heat, warm the olive oil. Drop 4 spoonfuls of batter into the pan and fry the pancakes until crisp, about 1½ minutes per side. Transfer to paper towels, season with salt, and keep warm. Add more oil to the frying pan and fry the remaining batter. Serve topped with the sour cream.

Baked Zucchini & Tomato Tian

MAKES 4–6 SERVINGS

2 Tbsp olive oil, plus more for greasing

1 red onion, sliced

Salt and freshly ground pepper

¾ lb (375 g) plum (Roma) tomatoes, sliced

2 small zucchini (courgettes), about ¾ lb (375 g) total weight, sliced

1 Tbsp minced fresh basil

1 Tbsp minced fresh marjoram

¼ cup (2 fl oz/60 ml) chicken broth or water

Preheat the oven to 350°F (180°C). Oil a shallow 2-qt (2-l) baking dish.

In a frying pan over medium heat, warm the 2 Tbsp olive oil. Add the onion and sauté slowly until soft, about 10 minutes. Transfer the onion slices to the baking dish, spreading them evenly over the bottom. Season with salt and pepper.

Arrange the tomato and zucchini slices over the onion in alternate rows. Sprinkle with the basil and marjoram and season with salt and pepper. Pour the broth evenly over the top.

Cover and bake until the vegetables are bubbling and tender, about 40 minutes. Remove from the oven, uncover, and serve right away.

SQUASH BLOSSOMS

Immature zucchini (courgettes) measuring no more than 2–5 inches (5–13 cm) long turn up at the market in the late spring with their brilliant yellow flowers still attached. The flowers, which are edible, can be stuffed, battered, and fried or used as a filling for omelets. Use within 24 hours; place them in a single layer on a baking sheet lined with paper towels and refrigerate until needed.

FRIED SQUASH BLOSSOMS WITH RICOTTA

In a bowl, stir together 1 cup (8 oz/250 g) whole-milk ricotta cheese, ½ Tbsp chopped fresh flat-leaf (Italian) parsley, and 1 Tbsp chopped fresh basil and season with salt and pepper. Add to a pastry (piping) bag fitted with a large plain tip. Remove the stamens from the blossoms. Pipe about 1 Tbsp of the cheese mixture into each blossom. Roll in all-purpose (plain) flour, then in a bowl of 2 beaten eggs, and then in flour again, shaking off the excess. Heat canola oil in a deep-sided frying pan until it reaches 375°F (190°C). Fry a few blossoms at a time, turning once, until golden, 3–4 minutes. Transfer to a paper towel-lined plate, and keep warm in a 200°F (95°C) oven. Allow the oil to return to 375°F (190°C) before adding the next batch. Makes 4–6 servings.

BAKED ZUCCHINI & TOMATO TIAN

GRILLED SQUASH TOSSED IN HERB & GARLIC MARINADE

Yellow Squash & Farro Salad

1½ cups (8 oz/240 g) farro

Salt

2 Tbsp plus ½ cup (4 fl oz/125 ml) extra-virgin olive oil

1 lb (500 g) yellow squash, cut into ½-inch (12-mm) chunks

1 clove garlic

¼ cup (2 fl oz/60 ml) fresh lemon juice

1 small cucumber, about ½ lb (250 g), peeled and cut into ½-inch (12-mm) chunks

5 green (spring) onions, cut on the diagonal into ¼-inch (6-mm) pieces

¼ cup (¼ oz/10 g) chopped fresh basil

¼ cup (¼ oz/10 g) chopped fresh mint

1 cup (5 oz/155 g) crumbled feta cheese

Bring a pot of salted water to a boil. Add the farro and season with salt. Reduce the heat to a low boil and cook until tender, 12–15 minutes. Drain and let cool.

Meanwhile, in a large sauté pan over medium-high heat, warm the 2 Tbsp olive oil. Add the squash, season with salt, and sauté until tender-crisp, 3–4 minutes. Transfer to a plate and let cool.

Mash the garlic into a paste with a pinch of salt. In a small bowl, stir together the garlic and ¼ cup lemon juice and let stand for 10 minutes. Whisk in the remaining ½ cup oil to make a dressing.

Put the farro, squash, cucumber, green onions, basil, mint, and feta in a large bowl. Drizzle with the vinaigrette and toss. Season with salt and serve right away.

Yellow Squash with Tomato Vinaigrette

MAKES 4 SERVINGS

1 clove garlic

Salt and freshly ground pepper

½ lb (250 g) firm but ripe tomatoes, peeled, seeded, and finely diced

2 Tbsp sherry vinegar, or to taste

1½ tsp sweet paprika

½ tsp cumin seeds, toasted (page 264) and ground

¼ cup (2 fl oz/60 ml) extra-virgin olive oil

1 lb (500 g) yellow squash, cut into matchsticks

½ cup (½ oz/15 g) fresh flat-leaf (Italian) parsley leaves

½ cup (½ oz/15 g) fresh cilantro (fresh coriander) leaves

Mash the garlic into a paste with a pinch of salt. In a bowl, stir together the garlic paste, tomatoes, the 2 Tbsp vinegar, paprika, cumin, and a pinch of salt. Let stand for 10 minutes. Stir in the olive oil and season with salt and pepper to make a vinaigrette.

In a bowl, combine the squash, parsley, and cilantro and season with salt. Add enough vinaigrette to lightly coat the squash and herbs, and toss gently. Season with salt and transfer to a platter. Drizzle with any remaining vinaigrette and serve right away.

Grilled Squash Tossed in Herb & Garlic Marinade

MAKES 6–8 SERVINGS

1 cup (8 fl oz/250 ml) extra-virgin olive oil

¼ cup (2 fl oz/60 ml) red wine vinegar

6 cloves garlic, peeled and lightly crushed

6 bay leaves

1 Tbsp *each* fresh minced thyme and rosemary

Salt and freshly ground pepper

2 lb (1 kg) assorted small squash, such as pattypan, Ronde de Nice, or yellow crookneck, cut in half vertically

1 lb (500 g) baby green zucchini (courgettes), cut in half lengthwise

In a nonreactive bowl, mix the olive oil, vinegar, garlic, bay leaves, thyme, rosemary, and ½ tsp each of salt and pepper to make a vinaigrette. Reserve half. Brush the squashes with the other half. Cover and let stand at room temperature for 1–2 hours.

Prepare a gas or charcoal grill for direct cooking over medium-high heat (page 264 or use a grill pan). Oil the grill rack. Remove the squash from the marinade and pat dry to remove any excess. Grill for 3–5 minutes per side. Arrange on a platter; drizzle the additional marinade over the top and serve at room temperature.

PATTYPAN SQUASH

Also known as scallop squash, this pale yellow, green, or white squash is about 4 inches (10 cm) in diameter and has attractive scalloped edges. Pattypans are similar in flavor to yellow squash and zucchini (courgettes) and can be prepared in most of the same ways. They are available at the farmers' market in the summer.

CARAMELIZED SQUASH

Warm 3 Tbsp olive oil in a large frying pan over high heat. Add 1½ lb (750 g) pattypan squashes, cut into wedges ½ inch (12 mm) thick. Season with salt and sauté until tender, 6–8 minutes. Add 2 cloves garlic, chopped, and 1 Tbsp chopped fresh marjoram and sauté for 1 minute. Season with salt and pepper. Squeeze lemon juice to taste over the top. Makes 4 servings.

Acorn Squash & Butternut Squash

Hard-skinned, tough-fleshed winter squashes can appear in an almost infinite variety of colors and shapes, but all have dense flesh and a sweet, slightly nutty flavor. Two of the most common varieties at markets are acorn squash and butternut squash. Acorn squashes are about 6 inches (15 cm) in diameter, with a hard, ribbed, dark green shell and pale orange flesh. Butternut squashes, identifiable by the round bulb at one end, have pale beige skin and rich, meaty, orange-yellow flesh.

True to their name, winter squash are most readily available during the cold winter months. Perhaps the best way to enjoy them is roasting with oil or butter and perhaps a drizzle of honey or maple syrup. Other dishes that highlight their sweet flavor include creamy soups, filled pastas, spicy curries, and long-cooked stews.

WORKING WITH ACORN & BUTTERNUT SQUASHES

Cut long-shaped squash in half lengthwise using a large, sharp chef's knife. Round ones can be more easily cut into thick wedges. With a large metal spoon, scoop out the seeds and strings and discard. If the skin needs to be removed before cooking, use a sharp vegetable peeler or paring knife to peel it away carefully.

Choose pumpkins that feel solid and heavy. As they age, they dry out and become lighter. The skin should be hard, with no cracks or soft spots. The hard shells of pumpkins prevent them from spoiling quickly; whole ones will keep for 1 month when stored in a cool, dry place. Once cut, pumpkins should be wrapped in plastic, refrigerated, and used within 3 or 4 days.

Pumpkin

A popular cold-weather member of the botanical group of gourds, pumpkins are generally available in autumn and winter. They are round to oblong, with a distinctive ridged shell, and range in color from pale ivory to a deep red-tinged orange. For cooking, avoid the large, hollow pumpkins bred for carving into jack-o'lanterns. Instead, look for sweet, thick-fleshed varieties cultivated specifically for the kitchen. Known generally as sugar pumpkins, these include the small, orange sugar pie; the pale beige, deeply ribbed cheese pumpkin; the flat, vibrant red French pumpkin; and the round, heirloom Winter Luxury.

Pumpkins are in season from late autumn to early winter. Many cooks prefer to purée pumpkins for making pies or tarts, muffins or quickbreads. Like other winter squashes, they are also excellent cut into chunks and roasted, braised, or made into soup.

WORKING WITH PUMPKIN

The greatest challenge in working with a pumpkin is cutting it open. Steady the pumpkin on a thick towel, insert a large, heavy knife near the stem, and cut down through the curved side. Always cut away from you. Turn the pumpkin and repeat on the other side. Follow the instructions for Acorn Squash & Butternut Squash (left) for seeding and peeling.

Butternut Squash Soup with Chipotle

MAKES 6 SERVINGS

1 butternut squash, 2½ lb (1.25 kg)

1 Tbsp canola oil, plus extra for greasing

2 slices coarse country bread, cut into ½-inch (12-mm) cubes

1 tsp dried sage

½ yellow onion, chopped

2 small dried chipotle chiles

3½ cups (28 fl oz/875 ml) chicken broth

Salt

Preheat the oven to 350°F (180°C). Lightly oil a baking sheet. Cut the squash in half lengthwise. Scrape out the seeds and any fibers and discard. Place the squash halves, cut sides down, on the baking sheet and bake until easily pierced with a fork, 35–45 minutes. When cool, scoop out the flesh and set aside.

In a large saucepan over medium-high heat, warm the oil. Add the bread cubes and dried sage and sauté until the cubes are browned, about 4 minutes. Transfer to a plate and set aside. Sauté the onion in the pan until softened, about 5 minutes. Stir in the squash, chiles, and broth. Bring to a simmer over medium heat and cook, uncovered, until the squash is soft, about 30 minutes.

Working in batches, purée the soup in a blender. Season with salt. Ladle into bowls. Add the croutons to each and serve hot.

Roasted Squash Purée with Ginger

MAKES 6 SERVINGS

Olive oil for greasing

1 butternut squash, 2½–3 lb (1.25–1.5 kg)

2 Tbsp unsalted butter, at room temperature

½ cup (4 fl oz/125 ml) whole milk

1½ tsp grated fresh ginger

Salt and freshly ground pepper

Preheat the oven to 400°F (200°C). Lightly oil a baking sheet.

Cut the squash in half lengthwise. Scrape out the seeds and any fibers and discard. Place the squash halves, cut sides down, on the baking sheet and bake until easily pierced with a knife, 35–45 minutes. Remove from the oven and set aside to cool. When cool, scoop out the flesh and set aside.

In a small saucepan over medium heat, combine the butter and milk and heat until the butter melts, about 1 minute. Remove from the heat.

Using a ricer or blender, mash the squash until smooth. Stir in the milk mixture and ginger and season with salt and pepper.

Transfer to a heavy saucepan and place over low heat until heated through. Spoon into a serving bowl and serve right away.

Acorn Squash & Chorizo Tart

MAKES 6–8 SERVINGS

Pastry Dough (page 263), rolled into a 13-inch (33-cm) round

½ lb (250 g) acorn squash, peeled, seeded, and cut into ½-inch (12-mm) chunks

2 Tbsp olive oil

Salt

¼ lb (125 g) Spanish-style chorizo, diced

1 yellow onion, finely chopped

1 clove garlic, finely chopped

½ cup (2 oz/60 g) shredded Monterey jack cheese

1 large egg yolk

Position a rack in the bottom third of the oven and preheat to 400°F (200°C). Put the dough round on a baking sheet lined with parchment (baking) paper and refrigerate.

Put the squash on a baking sheet, drizzle with 1 Tbsp of the oil, and toss to coat. Spread in an even layer, season with salt, and roast until almost tender, about 10 minutes. Let cool.

In a frying pan over medium-high heat, warm the remaining 1 Tbsp oil. Add the chorizo and sauté until lightly browned, about 2 minutes. Transfer to paper towels. Pour off all but 1½ Tbsp of the fat and return the pan to medium-high heat. Add the onion and sauté until tender, about 5 minutes. Season with salt, add the garlic, and cook for 1 minute. Let cool.

Remove the dough round from the refrigerator. Spread evenly with the onion mixture, leaving a 1½-inch (4-cm) border. Evenly distribute the squash and chorizo and sprinkle with the cheese. Fold the edge up and over the filling, forming loose pleats. Lightly beat the egg yolk with 1 tsp water and brush the border.

Bake until the crust is browned, about 30 minutes. Cut into wedges, and serve.

DELICATA SQUASH

With green-striped yellow skin and orange-yellow flesh, the delicata squash tastes similar to a sweet potato. It is about 3 inches (7.5 cm) in diameter and 6–8 inches (15–20 cm) long. Unlike other winter squashes, you can eat the skin of delicata squash. Its sweet flesh is excellent cooked and then puréed into a soup or used as a filling for ravioli. It is also delicious cut into slices and roasted.

SQUASH WITH MAPLE BUTTER

Cut a 2 lb (1 kg) delicata squash in half lengthwise. Remove the seeds and fibers. Cut crosswise into slices ½ inch (12 mm) wide, place on a baking sheet, and toss with ⅓ cup (3 fl oz/80 ml) vegetable oil. Season with salt, and roast in a 450°F (230°C) oven until almost tender, about 10 minutes. Drizzle with ¼ cup (2 fl oz/60 ml) maple syrup and roast until tender, about 5 minutes longer. Makes 4 servings.

ACORN SQUASH & CHORIZO TART

BULGUR PILAF WITH PUMPKIN & RAISINS

Roasted Pumpkin Soup with Sage Cream

MAKES 6–8 SERVINGS

1 sugar pie pumpkin, about 2 lb (1 kg)

2 Tbsp unsalted butter

1 yellow onion, chopped

1 carrot, peeled and chopped

1 celery stalk, chopped

6-inch (15-cm) piece fresh ginger, grated

2 cloves garlic, minced

4 cups (32 fl oz/1 l) chicken broth

Salt and freshly ground pepper

Sage Cream (page 262)

Cut the pumpkin into 2-inch (5-cm) chunks. Transfer to a bowl and set aside.

In a large saucepan over medium heat, melt the butter. Add the onion, carrot, and celery and cook, stirring often, until soft, about 5 minutes. Add the ginger and garlic and cook, stirring, about 1 minute.

Add the pumpkin and broth and bring to a boil over high heat. Reduce the heat to medium-low, cover partially, and simmer until tender, about 25 minutes.

Working in batches, purée the soup in a blender. Return to the saucepan and season to taste with salt and pepper. Reheat over medium-low heat.

Ladle into bowls, drizzle the sage cream on top, and serve right away.

Pumpkin Purée with Toasted Pumpkin Seeds

MAKES 4 SERVINGS

½ cup (2½ oz/75 g) pumpkin seeds (pepitas)

1 sugar pie pumpkin, about 2 lb (1 kg)

1 tsp ground cinnamon

½ tsp ground cloves

½ tsp ground nutmeg

Salt

Preheat the oven to 350°F (180°C).

Spread the pumpkin seeds in a dry frying pan over medium heat and cook, stirring continuously, until they just begin to darken. Transfer to a plate to cool; the seeds will continue to darken slightly from residual heat. Set aside.

Place the pumpkin on a baking sheet and bake until the flesh pulls away from the skin, about 1 hour. Cut the pumpkin in half. Scoop out the seeds and discard. Scoop out the flesh and transfer to a blender or food processor. Process to a smooth purée. Stir in the cinnamon, cloves, nutmeg, and salt. Set aside.

To serve, spoon into bowls and top with the toasted pumpkin seeds.

Bulgur Pilaf with Pumpkin & Raisins

MAKES 4 SERVINGS

¼ cup (2 fl oz/60 ml) olive oil

About 1 lb (500 g) peeled and seeded sugar pie pumpkin, cut into ¾-inch (2-cm) cubes

1 yellow onion, finely diced

1 cup (6 oz/185 g) coarse bulgur

Salt

2 Tbsp golden raisins (sultanas)

1 Tbsp sugar

¼ tsp ground cinnamon

1 tsp chopped fresh flat-leaf (Italian) parsley

In a heavy frying pan over medium-high heat, warm the olive oil. Sauté the pumpkin and onion until tender and golden brown, about 8 minutes. Add the bulgur and 1½ cups (12 fl oz/375 ml) water, season with salt, and bring to a boil over high heat. Reduce the heat to a simmer, cover tightly, and cook until the bulgur is tender and the water is absorbed, about 15 minutes.

Stir in the raisins, sugar, and cinnamon and season with salt. Let stand for 5 minutes. Stir in the chopped parsley and serve right away.

KABOCHA SQUASH

This squash, sometimes called Japanese pumpkin, has a dark green skin marked with pale green stripes. The pale orange flesh has a sweet flavor and fluffy texture when cooked. It usually weighs 2–3 pounds (1–1.5 kg) and may be substituted for acorn squash in recipes. Kabocha squash is available year-round but is best in early autumn.

BEEF WITH SQUASH IN CURRY

Put ¼ cup (2 fl oz/60 ml) olive oil and 4 yellow onions, diced, in a large pot. Season with salt and sauté until the onions brown, about 20 minutes. Add 4 cloves garlic, chopped, and 3 Tbsp minced fresh ginger and sauté for 1 minute. Add 1 Tbsp ground toasted (page 264) cumin seeds; 2 Tbsp ground toasted (page 264) coriander seeds; 2½ tsp ground turmeric; and ½ tsp red pepper flakes. Sauté for 15 seconds.

Add 3 lb (1.5 kg) cooked top round beef cut into cubes, 2 cups (12 oz/375 g) chopped canned tomatoes, and 4 cups (32 fl oz/1 l) water. Season with salt and bring to a boil. Reduce the heat to low, cover, and simmer for about 2 hours. Add 1 lb (500 g) kabocha squash, halved crosswise, seeded, and cut into 1-inch (2.5-cm) wedges, and simmer until tender, about 30 minutes. Serve with Cooked White Rice (page 262). Makes 6 servings.

Stalks, Shoots & Bulbs

CELERY

FENNEL

ASPARAGUS

As these three terms suggest, stalk, shoot, and bulb vegetables are those with edible stems. All tend to be mild, though each is characterized by its own distinctive subtle favor. Like many vegetables, celery, fennel, and asparagus were first harvested in the wild. Celery may have been used by the ancient Egyptians, and fennel made an appearance in Roman kitchens before spreading well beyond Italy. Asparagus likewise originated in Europe and is now popular well beyond the continent.

In many ways, however, these three vegetables are quite different. Celery, whose ribbed stalks form in clusters attached to a base, is in the parsley family. Fennel bulbs, which stand out for their faintly aniselike flavor, are also in the parsley family. Though fennel stalks and leaves as well as seeds are used in the kitchen, it is the bulb that is prized. Asparagus, a member of the lily family, grows as individual spears and has a pleasantly grassy flavor.

Of the trio, asparagus spears may be the most beloved not only for their culinary uses but because they mark the beginning of spring at farmers' markets.

BUYING CELERY

Look for tightly bunched celery with firm, crisp stalks, a pronounced light green color, and healthy-looking green leaves. Avoid any bunches that are limp, hollow, or browned. Store whole bunches of celery in a plastic bag in the refrigerator for up to 2 weeks.

Celery

Nearly every refrigerator contains dependable celery, and countless recipes list it as an ingredient. It is indispensable in French *mirepoix*, the aromatic base for numerous stocks and sauces. The pale green, everyday variety with feathery leaves is called Pascal celery. Asian celery has numerous, long, thin stalks that branch into large leaves resembling parsley. It has a slightly more assertive flavor that holds up to stir-frying and pickling. The tender, light-colored ribs at the center, commonly referred to as the heart, are smaller, milder in flavor, and more tender in texture than the outer ribs.

Celery, available all year long, reaches its peak flavor during winter. Enjoy it fresh in salads or with savory dips. Chop and add to salads, stocks, and soups, or braise the stalks gently as an appetizer or side dish. Use the leaves, much like parsley, as garnish on savory dishes.

WORKING WITH CELERY

Separate ribs from the bunch only as needed. Wash them thoroughly and trim off both ends. With few exceptions, new celery varieties are more tender and do not require the removal of tough strings from the ribs. If you find strings, run a vegetable peeler down the length of the stalk to remove them. Refresh limp celery ribs with a 30-minute soak in ice water.

BUYING FENNEL

Choose fennel bulbs that are smooth and tightly layered, with no cracks or bruises. Fat, rounded bulbs that are white and pale green will tend to be more succulent than narrow or yellow ones. Avoid any with dried stalks or wilted fronds. Keep fennel bulbs with the stalks and fronds intact, in a plastic bag in the refrigerator for up to 5 days.

Fennel

Also known as sweet fennel or finocchio (and sometimes mislabeled as "sweet anise"), this aromatic vegetable is the swollen, immature stem of a large, feathery bush. The young stems of the plant overlap at the base to form a bulb with white to pale green ribbed layers. Originating in the Mediterranean, the fennel bulb is popular in Italian and Scandinavian cuisines. Although the stalks are similar to celery both in their appearance and in their crunchy texture, all parts of the plant have a pleasantly sweet, anise-like flavor.

Fennel is abundant during the autumn and winter months. It can be served raw, shaved thinly as a salad or cut into spears for dipping. Grilling or roasting until the layers caramelize highlights its sweetness, and pairing with sausage, salumi, or seafood is a classic way to prepare it in appetizers, soups, and pastas.

WORKING WITH FENNEL

To trim fennel, cut away the green stems and fronds, saving the latter for garnish, if desired. Remove and discard the outer layer of the bulb, trim any discolored areas, cut the bulb in half lengthwise, and remove the base of the core if it is thick and solid. Rinse well to remove any grit between them.

Celery & Rice Soup with Parsley

MAKES 6 SERVINGS

3 Tbsp unsalted butter

1 yellow onion, finely diced

½ cup (3 oz/90 g) finely chopped celery

1 small bay leaf

Salt

6 cups (48 fl oz/1.5 l) chicken broth

⅓ cup (2½ oz/75 g) long-grain white rice

2 Tbsp finely chopped pale green celery leaves

2 Tbsp finely chopped fresh flat-leaf (Italian) parsley

¼ cup (2 fl oz/60 ml) olive oil

In a heavy pot over medium heat, melt the butter. Reduce the heat to medium-low, and sauté the onion, celery, bay leaf, and a pinch of salt until the onion and celery are tender, about 15 minutes. Add the broth and bring to boil. Reduce the heat to low, add the rice, and simmer until tender, about 20 minutes. Season with salt.

In a bowl, stir together the celery leaves, parsley, and olive oil. Season with salt.

Ladle the soup into warmed bowls, garnish with the parsley mixture, and serve right away.

Celery, Parsley & Prosciutto Salad

MAKES 6 SERVINGS

6 stalks celery, thinly sliced on the diagonal

1 fennel bulb, thinly sliced, preferably with a mandoline

4 green (spring) onions, thinly sliced on the diagonal

1 cup (1 oz/30 g) fresh flat-leaf (Italian) parsley leaves

¼ cup (⅓ oz/10 g) small fresh mint leaves

Salt and freshly ground pepper

3 Tbsp olive oil

2 Tbsp fresh lemon juice, or to taste

6 thin slices prosciutto

Shaved hard sheep's milk cheese, such as Pecorino romano

Put the celery, fennel, green onions, parsley, and mint in a bowl and season with salt and pepper. Drizzle with the olive oil and the 2 Tbsp lemon juice and toss gently. Season with salt and more lemon juice, if desired. Place the prosciutto on a serving platter and top with the fennel mixture. Garnish with the shaved cheese and serve at once.

Braised Celery with Lemon

MAKES 4–6 SERVINGS

2 lb (1 kg) celery

1½ cups (12 fl oz/375) chicken broth

¼ cup (2 oz/60 g) finely diced yellow onion

1–2 Tbsp unsalted butter

Salt and freshly ground pepper

¼ cup (2 fl oz/60 ml) dry white wine

1–2 tsp fresh lemon juice

Remove any tough outer strings along the curved edges of the celery stalks. Cut the bottom off the celery and wash the stalks. Cut the stalks into sections about 4 inches (10 cm) long, discarding any of the smaller white stalks in the middle.

In a frying pan over medium-high heat, combine the broth and onion. Bring to a boil, reduce the heat to medium-low, and simmer until reduced to half, about 5 minutes. Add the butter and salt and stir until the butter melts. Add the celery pieces, cover, and simmer until tender, 20–25 minutes. Transfer to a platter, leaving the liquid in the pan.

Add the wine and lemon juice to the liquid in the pan and return to medium-high heat, and boil until thick, 2–3 minutes. Season with salt and pepper. Pour the sauce over the celery and serve right away.

CELERY, PARSLEY & PROSCIUTTO SALAD

ROASTED FISH STUFFED WITH FENNEL & FRESH HERBS

Shaved Fennel Salad with Citrus Dressing

MAKES 4 SERVINGS

2 Tbsp extra-virgin olive oil

2 Tbsp fresh orange juice

Salt and freshly ground pepper

2 fennel bulbs, trimmed and thinly sliced crosswise

Shaved aged hard cheese, such as Parmesan, for garnish

In a small bowl, whisk together the olive oil, orange juice and ½ tsp each salt and pepper to make a dressing.

Place the fennel slices in a bowl and drizzle with the dressing. Toss to combine and place on salad plates. Garnish with cheese shavings. Serve at once.

Olive Oil–Braised Fennel with Lemon

MAKES 6 SERVINGS

4 fennel bulbs, about 2 lb (1 kg)

3 Tbsp extra-virgin olive oil

3 cloves garlic, chopped

1 tsp ground fennel seeds

Salt and freshly ground pepper

1 lemon peel, 2 inches (5 cm) long

2 Tbsp fresh lemon juice

Cut off the stalks and feathery fronds from the fennel bulbs; discard the stalks. Chop the feathery fronds to measure 1 Tbsp and set aside. Remove any damaged outer leaves from the bulb and discard. Cut each bulb into quarters lengthwise and trim away the tough core portions.

In a large saucepan over medium heat, warm the olive oil. Add the garlic and cook, stirring, for 1 minute. Add the fennel quarters and the fennel seeds. Season with salt and pepper. Cook, uncovered, stirring, until the fennel begins to soften, about 5 minutes.

Reduce the heat to medium-low, add 2 cups (16 fl oz/500 ml) water and the lemon peel, cover, and cook until the fennel is tender, 20–25 minutes.

Using a slotted spoon, transfer the fennel to a serving platter and keep warm. Raise the heat to high and cook until only ¾ cup (6 fl oz/180 ml) liquid remains, about 5 minutes. Discard the lemon peel. Add the lemon juice, then season with salt and pepper.

Drizzle the sauce over the fennel and sprinkle with the fennel fronds. Serve right away.

Roasted Fish Stuffed with Fennel & Fresh Herbs

MAKES 6 SERVINGS

2 fennel bulbs, fronds reserved, bulbs thinly sliced crosswise, preferably with a mandoline

2 Tbsp chopped fresh thyme

Salt and freshly ground pepper

Pinch of red pepper flakes

3 sea bass, 1½–2 lb (750 g–1 kg) each, cleaned

Olive oil for drizzling and serving

Lemon wedges for serving

Preheat the oven to 500°F (260°C).

Coarsely chop the fennel fronds and measure about ¼ cup (1 oz/30 g). In a bowl, toss together the sliced fennel, half of the chopped fronds, and thyme. Season with salt, pepper, and red pepper flakes and mix well.

Make 3 diagonal slices about ½ inch (12 mm) deep on each side of fish. Season each side with salt and pepper. Stuff the cavities with the fennel mixture and secure with toothpicks. Scatter the remaining fennel fronds on a sturdy baking sheet, place the fish on top, and drizzle with olive oil. Roast the fish until the flesh flakes easily when lightly pressed, about 15 minutes. Transfer to a platter along with juices from the pan. Discard the fronds on the baking sheet. Remove the toothpicks. Serve right away, passing the olive oil and lemon wedges at the table.

BUYING ASPARAGUS

Choose firm stalks with tight, dry, tips with a slight purple tinge. Avoid those that are soft or broken. The ends of the stems should be fresh and moist. Asparagus is best when very fresh, so use soon after purchasing. If storing is needed, cut 1 inch (2.5 cm) off the stalks at the base and set the bunch upright in a container with a shallow layer of water for up to 4 days.

Asparagus

These crisp-tender spears are the young shoots of a fast-growing, perennial bush. They can be pencil thin or as thick as a thumb; both have their devoted followers. Most asparagus is grassy green in color, with purplish tips, but white asparagus, beloved in Europe, is becoming increasingly popular. It retains a pale, ivory-yellow color and delicate flavor when kept carefully covered to protect the growing stalks from sunlight. There is also a purple variety, which turns green when cooked and tends to be a little sweeter than regular asparagus.

Among the market's favorite harbingers of warming weather, asparagus is most delicious during the early spring. It lends itself to nearly all types of cooking, from steaming to sautéing, roasting to grilling. Raw spears can be eaten fresh out of hand or sliced for salads.

WORKING WITH ASPARAGUS

Gently bend the stem of several spears to find their natural breaking point, or where they leave their tenderness and become tough. The remaining spears can be trimmed to similar lengths. If the spears are thick and have fibrous skin, use a vegetable peeler to pare it away from the stalks to within about 1 inch (2.5 cm) of the tips.

Asparagus Omelet with Chives & Garlic

MAKES 4 SERVINGS

½ lb (250 g) thin asparagus spears, tough ends removed

4 Tbsp (2 fl oz/60 ml) olive oil

2 shallots, finely chopped

8 fresh chives, snipped

2 cloves garlic, minced

5 large eggs

Salt and freshly ground pepper

Position a rack in the upper third of the oven and preheat to 325°F (180°C).

Cut the asparagus into 1-inch (2.5-cm) pieces. Bring a saucepan of salted water to a boil, add the asparagus, and parboil for 3 minutes. Drain, rinse with cold running water, drain again, and pat dry.

In a medium frying pan over low heat, warm 2 Tbsp of the olive oil. Add the shallots and sauté until softened, about 8 minutes. Add the chives, garlic, and asparagus and sauté until the asparagus is tender, about 2 minutes. Remove from the heat.

In a bowl, whisk the eggs until blended. Add the asparagus mixture and season with salt and pepper.

In an 8-inch (20-cm) ovenproof nonstick frying pan, warm the remaining 2 Tbsp olive oil over medium-high heat. Add the egg mixture and reduce the heat to medium. Cook until the eggs are set around the edges, 5–7 minutes. Transfer to the oven and cook until set, 7–9 minutes. Let cool briefly.

Invert the omelet onto a large plate. Cut into wedges and serve right away.

Grilled Asparagus with Rosemary Oil & Parmesan

MAKES 4 SERVINGS

½ tsp chopped rosemary

2 Tbsp extra-virgin olive oil

Salt

2–2½ lb (1–1.25 kg) asparagus, tough ends removed

¼ cup (1 oz/30 g) freshly grated Parmesan cheese

In a small bowl, mix together the chopped rosemary and the olive oil. Cover and let sit for at least 1 hour.

Prepare a gas or charcoal grill for direct grilling over high heat (page 264 or use a stovetop grill pan). Oil the grill rack.

Bring a wide, shallow saucepan of salted water to a boil. Add the asparagus and boil until tender but still crisp, 2–4 minutes. Drain and immerse in a bowl of ice water. When cool, drain and pat dry with a kitchen towel.

Put the spears on a baking sheet and drizzle evenly with the rosemary oil and season with salt.

Grill the asparagus (if using a grill, take care to place them across the bars so they don't fall into the fire) until they blister, 1–2 minutes on each side.

Transfer to a platter and sprinkle with the cheese. Serve right away.

Spaghetti with Roasted Asparagus & Cream

MAKES 6 SERVINGS

½ lb (250 g) asparagus spears, tough ends removed

1 Tbsp extra-virgin olive oil

Salt and freshly ground pepper

1 lb (500 g) dried spaghetti

2 cups (16 fl oz/500 ml) heavy (double) cream

½ cup (2 oz/60 g) grated hard cheese, such as Parmesan

Preheat the oven to 425°F (220°C). Place the asparagus on a large baking sheet, drizzle with the olive oil and a pinch each of salt and pepper. Roast in the oven until tender, 8–10 minutes. When cool enough to handle, cut the asparagus into 1½-inch (12-mm) pieces. Set aside.

Bring a large pot of salted water to a boil. Add the spaghetti and cook until al dente, 10–12 minutes or according to the package directions. Drain and return the pasta to the empty pot.

While the pasta is cooking, in a medium saucepan over medium heat, heat the cream until it reduces by half and thickens slightly, 8–10 minutes. Stir in half of the cheese, and 1 tsp of pepper. Remove from the heat.

Add the cream to the pot with the pasta and stir in the asparagus. Place the pot over medium heat just to warm the pasta.

Transfer to a serving dish. Sprinkle with the remaining cheese and season with salt and pepper. Serve right away.

GRILLED ASPARAGUS WITH ROSEMARY OIL & PARMESAN

Onions & Cousins

ONIONS

SWEET ONIONS

GARLIC

GREEN GARLIC

LEEKS

GREEN ONIONS

Onions and their relatives are all members of the genus *Allium*, and all have an emphatic flavor that provides an essential base for many savory dishes. Pungent when raw, onions and garlic will soften and sweeten during cooking. Vegetables related to today's onion varieties may date back several millennia, before the development of ancient Egyptian, Greek, and Roman civilizations. Garlic, possibly predating onions, can be traced back to the Asian continent.

Onion and garlic fall into loose categories. Globe onions, a name that describes their shape, are mature specimens ranging in color from white to red. Some are sharp in flavor; others are sweet. Green onions, also known as spring onions or scallions, are actually the young shoots of a bulb onion. Garlic also takes two primary forms: the familiar bulb or head and green garlic, a shoot that is harvested before the garlic plant begins to develop cloves. Leeks resemble very plump green onions but are much milder by comparison.

Spring is the time to find green garlic at markets. It is also when leeks are at their best, tender and particularly sweet. Globe onions and garlic are best in the summer.

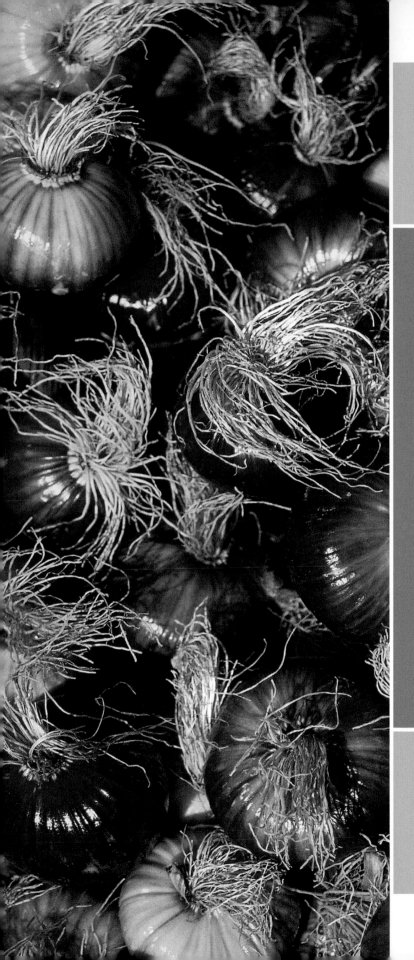

Onions

Since first grown by the ancient Egyptians, this multilayered bulb has become a staple in nearly every cuisine. There are two basic types: green, or spring, onions and dried, or globe, onions. Fresh onions include green onions and such sweet onions as Vidalia, Walla Walla, and Maui. Perhaps the most common all-purpose onion is the familiar yellow globe onion. Other dried types include mild red onions; pink or purple shallots; strongly flavored white onions; small, flat cipolline onions; and tiny pearl onions.

Onions mature from early to late summer, though they may be harvested early for their shoots or for smaller, tender bulbs. Sautéed in oil until soft, onions are the foundation of countless savory dishes around the world. Cooked slowly until caramelized, they can be highlighted in soups, flatbreads, and savory sauces. They are also delicious breaded and fried, grilled, and braised.

Choose plump garlic heads with smooth, firm cloves and creamy white to purple-tinged skin. Pass up those with soft, withered spots or green sprouts. Whole garlic heads keep well when stored in an open container in a cool, dark, well-ventilated place for up to 2 months.

Garlic

Garlic, like the onion, is a pungent member of the *Allium*, or lily, botanical group. Each bulb of garlic consists of 12 to 16 cloves tightly clustered and wrapped with papery white skin. The variety known as Artichoke Garlic is the large, white heads most commonly available. The Purple Stripe, named for the bright, vertical streaks on the bulb's wrapping, has a rich flavor that takes well to roasting. Other varieties include Silverskin, with a strong, spicy flavor; vividly rose-colored and moderately pungent Creole common to the American South; and the highly regarded Rocambole that develops strong, rich flavors in the colder regions where it grows. Elephant garlic, with heads as large as oranges and a flavor that is surprisingly mild, is actually a variety of leek.

Garlic harvested during the middle of the summer will be the freshest and most flavorful that come to market.

WORKING WITH GARLIC

Garlic added to long cooking braises and roasts should be left in large pieces. Minced garlic has a hot, more volatile flavor that will disperse quickly. Crushing garlic will release much more of its aromatic oils. Cooking in oil will bring out its flavor, but avoid scorching, as it will develop unpleasantly bitter flavors.

Fried Onion Rings with Aioli

MAKES 4 SERVINGS

Canola oil for deep-frying

1 large yellow onion, sliced ¼ inch (6 mm) thick

⅔ cup (3½ oz/105 g) all-purpose (plain) flour

1½ cups (3½ oz/105 g) panko bread crumbs

Grated zest of 1 lime

Coarse salt

2 Tbsp chopped fresh cilantro (fresh coriander)

Aioli (page 139)

Pour oil into a deep, heavy saucepan to a depth of 2 inches (5 cm) and heat to 375°F (190°C) on a deep-frying thermometer. Preheat the oven to 250°F (120°C). Line a baking sheet with paper towels.

Separate the onion slices into rings. In a bowl, whisk together ⅔ cup (5 fl oz/160 ml) water and the flour until smooth. Spread the panko on a plate.

When the oil is hot, dip the onion rings, 4–5 at a time, into the batter. Lift out, let the excess batter drip off, and then dip into the panko. Fry the rings, turning them once, until golden, 1–2 minutes. Transfer to the lined baking sheet and place in the heated oven. Repeat until all the rings are cooked.

Transfer the rings to a platter and sprinkle with the lime zest, 1 tsp salt, and cilantro. Serve right away with aioli.

Grilled Marinated Red Onions

MAKES 4 SERVINGS

6 large red onions, cut into slices ¾ inch (2 cm) thick

4 Tbsp (2 fl oz/60 ml) olive oil

1½ Tbsp balsamic vinegar

1 tsp chopped fresh thyme

Salt and freshly ground pepper

Prepare a gas or charcoal grill for direct grilling over high heat (page 264) or use a stovetop grill pan. Oil a grill rack.

Brush each onion slice on both sides with 1 Tbsp olive oil.

In a bowl, whisk together the remaining 3 Tbsp olive oil, vinegar, thyme, and salt and pepper to taste to make a dressing.

Grill the onions until golden on the first side, 5–6 minutes. Turn and continue to grill until tender and golden on the second side, 5–6 minutes more.

Transfer to a platter and drizzle with the vinaigrette. Serve right away.

Serve grilled onions alongside herb-seasoned grilled steak. For 4 servings, use 1¼ lb (20 oz/ 625 g) sirloin, about 1½ inches (4 cm) thick.

Sweet & Sour Onions

MAKES 4 SERVINGS

1 lb (500 g) red and white onions, root and stem ends trimmed

2 Tbsp extra-virgin olive oil

¾ cup (6 fl oz/180 ml) dry red wine

¼ cup (2 fl oz/60 ml) plus 2 Tbsp red wine vinegar

2 bay leaves

1½ Tbsp sugar

Salt

¼ tsp red pepper flakes

Bring a large pot of salted water to a boil, add the onions, and cook for 1 minute. Drain and peel while warm. In a frying pan over medium-high heat, wam the olive oil. Add the onions and sauté until browned, about 4 minutes. Set aside.

In a bowl, combine the red wine, vinegar, bay leaves, sugar, 2 tsp salt, red pepper flakes, and ¾ cup (6 fl oz/180 ml) water. Add the wine mixture to the onions and bring to a boil. Reduce the heat to low and simmer, uncovered, stirring occasionally, until the onions are tender, about 15 minutes. Transfer to a serving bowl and discard the bay leaves. Serve right away.

Serve these onions as a companion to roasted or grilled meats or poultry.

SWEET ONIONS

Sweet onions are cousins to the common onion but have a higher water and sugar content resulting in a sweeter flavor. Their unique taste comes from being harvested in fertile, low-sulfur soils. Most notable varieties are the Walla Walla from Washington, Vidalia from Georgia, and Maui from Hawaii. They are delicious grilled, deep-fried, or baked. Look for them at the market in spring and summer.

ONION MARMALADE

In a large frying pan over medium heat, warm ⅓ cup (3 fl oz/80 ml) olive oil. Add 6 thinly sliced sweet onions, 6 cloves chopped garlic, and ⅔ cup (2½ oz/75 g) chopped pecans. Cook, stirring, until the mixture begins to caramelize, about 30 minutes. Stir in ½ cup (4 fl oz/125 ml) chicken broth, ¼ cup (2 fl oz/ 60 ml) balsamic vinegar, and 1 Tbsp bourbon and cook until the liquid evaporates, about

10 minutes. Let cool, then stir in ¼ cup (3 oz/90 g) honey, ½ cup (2 oz/60 g) grated Parmesan cheese, and 3 Tbsp chopped fresh rosemary. Season with salt and pepper. Serve as an accompaniment to grilled or roasted chicken or steak. Makes 6 servings.

SWEET & SOUR ONIONS

GARLIC AIOLI WITH GARDEN VEGETABLES

Garlic Aioli with Garden Vegetables

MAKES 4 SERVINGS

4 cloves garlic, coarsely chopped

Salt

2 large eggs

2 Tbsp fresh lemon juice

1 tsp Dijon mustard

1½ cups (12 fl oz/375 ml) olive oil

¾ lb (375 g) slender asparagus spears, tough ends removed, blanched (page 264)

½ lb (250 g) green beans, trimmed and blanched (page 264)

8–10 *each* small carrots, blanched (page 264) and small waxy potatoes, halved and blanched (page 264)

1 bunch radishes

6 hard-cooked eggs, peeled and quartered

1 baguette, cut into slices ¼ inch (6 mm) thick

Blend the garlic and ½ tsp salt in a blender. Add the raw eggs, lemon juice, and mustard and blend again. With the motor running, slowly pour in the olive oil and blend until the mixture thickens to the consistency of mayonnaise. Cover and refrigerate until ready to serve.

Serve the aioli on a platter with the blanched vegetables, radishes, hard-cooked eggs, and baguette slices for dipping.

Roasted Garlic–Olive Oil Mashed Potatoes

MAKES 4 SERVINGS

8 cloves garlic, unpeeled

3 Tbsp olive oil

1 Tbsp finely chopped fresh rosemary

3 starchy potatoes, peeled or unpeeled, cut into 2-inch (5-cm) chunks

¼ cup (2 oz/60 g) unsalted butter

½ cup (4 fl oz/125 ml) whole milk

Salt and freshly ground pepper

Preheat the oven to 325°F (165°C). Place the garlic cloves in a baking dish, drizzle with 2 Tbsp olive oil and sprinkle with the rosemary. Cover with aluminum foil and bake until soft, 35–40 minutes. Remove from the oven and, when cool enough to handle, squeeze the garlic from the sheaths into a bowl. Mash with a fork. Stir in the remaining 1 Tbsp of the oil and set aside.

Place the potatoes in a saucepan and add water to cover. Bring to a boil and cook, uncovered, until tender when pierced with a fork, about 10–12 minutes. Just before the potatoes are ready, in a small saucepan over low heat, warm the butter and milk until the butter is melted. Drain the potatoes, transfer to a bowl, and mash with a fork or potato masher. Add the milk mixture and stir until smooth. Mix in the garlic and season with salt and pepper.

Shrimp Sautéed in Garlic-Sherry Oil

MAKES 6 SERVINGS

3 Tbsp extra-virgin olive oil

6 cloves garlic, thinly sliced

Pinch of red pepper flakes

1¼ lb (625 g) shrimp (prawns), peeled and deveined

⅓ cup (3 fl oz/80 ml) dry sherry

Salt and freshly ground pepper

1½ tsp chopped fresh flat-leaf (Italian) parsley

In a large frying pan over medium-high heat, warm the olive oil. Add the garlic and red pepper flakes and cook, stirring, for 15 seconds. Add the shrimp and cook, stirring, about 3 minutes. Add the sherry and continue to cook until reduced by half, about 1 minute. Season with salt and pepper.

Transfer to a serving dish and garnish with the parsley. Serve right away.

GREEN GARLIC

Harvested just before the garlic plant begins to form cloves and available in the spring at farmers' markets, green garlic resembles large green onions with a tinge of pink at the bulb. Green garlic, which has a milder flavor than regular garlic, is delicious in soups, sauces, and with roasted vegetables. It can be stored in a plastic bag in the refrigerator for up to 4 days.

GARLIC SOUP

Melt 1 Tbsp unsalted butter in a heavy pot over medium heat. Add ¾ lb (375 g) green garlic, trimmed of dark green parts and chopped; ½ cup (4 fl oz/125 ml) chicken broth; and a pinch of salt. Reduce the heat to low, cover, and simmer until tender, about 12 minutes. Add 1½ lb (750 g) waxy potatoes, peeled and quartered; 7½ cups (60 fl oz/1.9 l) more broth; and a pinch of salt. Raise the heat to high and bring to a boil. Reduce the heat to low and simmer, covered, until the potatoes are soft, about 20 minutes. Let cool. Working in batches, purée the soup in a blender. Strain into a clean pot. Stir in ¼ cup (2 fl oz/60 ml) heavy (double) cream and 1 Tbsp white wine vinegar and reheat. Season to taste. Ladle into bowls, and garnish with crème fraîche and chopped fresh chervil. Makes 6–8 servings.

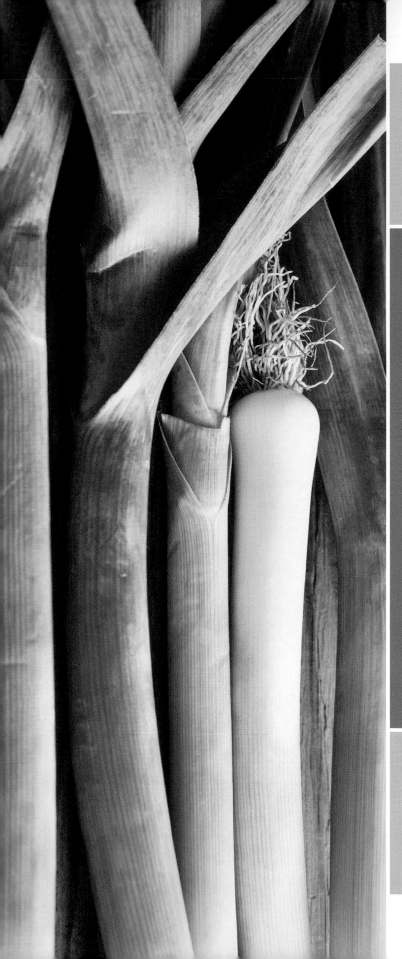

Leeks

Resembling giant green onions, leeks have bright white cylindrical stalks and long, overlapping green leaves. Native to the Mediterranean region and essential to French cuisine, the leek is one of the milder members of the onion family. A particularly prized relative of the leek, gathered in spring, is the wild leek, known as a ramp, which has a strong oniony flavor.

Different varieties of leeks come into season at different times, with some cultivars planted in spring for autumn harvest and others (generally larger and stronger in flavor) grown as an overwintering variety for spring harvest. Gentle cooking preserves their delicate texture and flavor, and they are the star in quiches, soups, salads, and side dishes with potatoes or rice. Very young leeks can also be harvested as shoots and used raw much like chives.

BUYING GREEN ONIONS

The tops of green (spring) onions should be vibrant green in color. They should look fresh and feel firm, not wilted or slimy. The bulb ends should be white. Avoid dried roots or bruised, wet bulbs. Store green onions in a plastic bag in the refrigerator for up to 2 weeks.

Green Onions

Also known as scallions, mild-flavored green (spring) onions are the immature shoots of the bulb onion. They have a narrow white stem that has not yet begun to swell and long, flat green leaves. Although green onions are often equated with spring onions, the latter are actually immature white or red onions and have a slightly swollen white or red base. Similar in flavor, the two are interchangeable.

Green onions can be harvested year round in mild climates. Recipes often specify which part of the onion should be used: the white stem, the green leaves, or both. The milder bite of green onions blends well in dishes where raw onion would be too strong, such as scrambled eggs or omelets, sandwich fillings, or savory salads. In Asia, the bright green leaves commonly garnish soups and dipping sauces.

WORKING WITH GREEN ONIONS

Rinse the green onions thoroughly to remove any sand or grit from the layers. Trim off the root ends and green tops from the onions. Using your fingers, peel off the outer layer of the bulb. Plan to use green onions as soon as they are cut, as they will quickly begin to oxidize and lose their flavor.

Grilled Leeks with Romesco Sauce

MAKES 6 SERVINGS

6 slender leeks, each ¾–1 inch
(2–2.5 cm) in diameter

2 Tbsp olive oil

1 Tbsp chopped fresh thyme

Romesco Sauce (page 262)

Trim the leeks, leaving about 1 inch (2.5 cm) of the tender green tops intact. Halve each leek lengthwise, rinse thoroughly under cold running water, and dry well with paper towels. Brush with the olive oil, then sprinkle with half of the thyme.

Prepare a charcoal or gas grill for direct grilling over high heat (page 264) or use a stovetop grill pan. Oil the grill rack. Place the leeks around the edges of the grill, turning 2–3 times, until softened and golden, 6–9 minutes total. Sprinkle with the remaining thyme and serve with the romesco sauce for dipping.

Green Onion Pancakes

MAKES 6 SERVINGS

2 cups (10 oz/315 g) all-purpose
(plain) flour

1 cup (8 fl oz/250 ml) boiling water

3 Tbsp sesame oil

Coarse salt

1¼ cups (3¾ oz/110 g) chopped green
(spring) onion tops

Canola oil for frying

Sift the flour into a bowl and make a well in the center. Pour the boiling water into the well. Using a wooden spoon, quickly work the water into the flour to make a fairly stiff, but not dry, dough. Knead lightly in the bowl until the dough forms a ball. Remove the dough from the bowl and brush lightly with some of the sesame oil. Invert the bowl over the dough and leave to cool, about 6 minutes.

Knead the dough very lightly until smooth and elastic, brush with more sesame oil, and place in a plastic bag. Set aside for 30–60 minutes.

Using your palms, roll the dough back and forth to form a log about 10 inches (25 cm) long. Cut the log into 6 equal pieces and form each piece into a ball. Roll out each ball into a very thin round about 7 inches (18 cm) in diameter, brush generously with sesame oil, sprinkle with salt, then cover evenly with the chopped green onions. Roll up the round into a cigar shape, twist into a tight coil, and brush the top with sesame oil. On a lightly oiled work surface, flatten the coil with a rolling pin to make a round about 5 inches (13 cm) in diameter. Try to avoid having the onions break through the dough.

Pour canola oil to a depth of 1 inch (2.5 cm) into a large, shallow pan, and place over medium-high heat. When the oil is hot, cook 2 or 3 pancakes, turning once, until golden brown, about 3 minutes per side. Arrange on a platter, sprinkle with salt, cut into quarters, and serve right away.

Savory Leek & Gruyère Soufflé

MAKES 6–8 SERVINGS

2 Tbsp unsalted butter, softened, plus
5 Tbsp (2½ oz/75 g) cold unsalted butter

2 cups (8 oz/250 g) grated Gruyère cheese

2 Tbsp olive oil

4 leeks, about 1½ lb (750 g) total weight,
trimmed and chopped

1 tsp chopped fresh thyme

Salt and freshly ground pepper

5 Tbsp (1¾ oz/50 g) all-purpose (plain) flour

2½ cups (20 fl oz/625 ml) half-and-half
(half cream), warmed

6 large eggs, separated

Position a rack in the upper third of the oven and preheat to 400°F (200°C). Coat a 14-inch (35-cm) oval gratin dish or large soufflé dish with the 2 Tbsp butter and sprinkle the bottom and sides with ½ cup (2 oz/60 g) of the cheese.

In a large frying pan over medium heat, warm the olive oil. Cook the leeks and thyme until the leeks are tender, about 12 minutes. Season with salt and let cool. In a heavy saucepan over medium heat, melt the 5 Tbsp (2½ oz/75 g) butter. Add the flour and whisk for 1 minute until combined. Whisk in the half-and-half and cook, whisking, until the sauce is smooth and thick, about 4 minutes. Transfer to a bowl. Stir in the egg yolks, one at a time. Stir in the remaining 1½ cups (6 oz/185 g) cheese and the leeks. Season with salt and pepper.

In a large bowl, beat the egg whites until they form stiff peaks. With a rubber spatula, fold one-fourth of the whites into the leek mixture. Quickly fold in the remaining egg whites until no white streaks remain. Pour into the prepared dish. Bake until golden brown, about 25 minutes. Serve right away.

SAVORY LEEK & GRUYÈRE SOUFFLÉ

Vegetable Fruits

What initially seems like a contradictory term is a specific category of produce items that are botanically classified as fruits but in the kitchen are used chiefly as vegetables. Nearly all share a key characteristic: the presence of many small seeds, many of them edible. Avocados, an exception, contain a single large, inedible pit. It is easy to think of fresh-picked tomatoes, sweet and juicy, as fruits. In contrast, its hard to imagine chiles as such, their flavor can range from mild and sweet to hot and almost incendiary.

Some vegetable fruits are native to the New World: chiles and sweet peppers to Mexico, avocados to Central America, tomatoes to South America. Eggplants (aubergines) and possibly cucumbers come from India. Over the centuries, these vegetable fruits spread beyond their continents of origin, and now pairings such as eggplants and tomatoes are considered long-standing popular combinations in many international cuisines.

Hundreds of varieties of vegetable fruits have been developed. Many cooks seek out heirloom specimens, particularly tomatoes, for their pure flavor and interesting colors and shapes. Farmers' markets are the ideal places to find these generations-old vegetable fruits, especially from summer to early autumn.

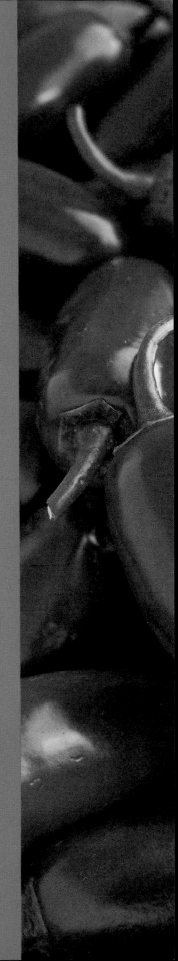

BUYING TOMATOES

Tomatoes are best when eaten at the height of the summer season. For the best flavor, choose those that are ripened on the vine and are bright in color. Tomatoes can be stored at room temperature for up to 3 days. If they are slightly unripe, put them in a sunny place, where they will ripen further.

Tomatoes

Once feared as a poison, tomatoes are botanically a fruit of the nightshade category. Tomatoes, native to South America, have spread during the last few centuries and have adapted to virtually every country on the globe. The tomato comes in a wide range of sizes, from tiny currant tomatoes no bigger than blueberries to fat beefsteaks up to 5 inches (13 cm) in diameter. The colors of heritage varieties span the spectrum, from white to yellow to green zebra stripes, from pink to orange to deep violet black.

The most flavorful tomatoes appear in farmers' markets from mid-summer to early autumn. Purists enjoy them sliced thickly and served with a mere sprinkling of coarse salt. Puréed into soup, layered in sandwiches, tossed into salads, simmered for pasta, or roasted for salsa, tomatoes add color and flavor to our table in a multitude of delicious ways.

WORKING WITH TOMATOES

Rinse, dry, and trim the stem ends just before using. Depending on the recipe, you can leave the tomatoes whole, halve them, slice them crosswise, cut lengthwise into wedges, or chop to the desired sized pieces. To remove seeds for smoother sauces, halve the tomatoes and squeeze each half gently over a bowl.

Cucumbers

This refreshingly juicy, mild-flavored vegetable adds crunch to green salads and crudités platters. First cultivated in India and Western Asia, most varieties of cucumbers now fall into two basic categories: slicing varieties for eating fresh and pickling varieties that keep their crispness after canning. Specialty cucumbers that appear in farmers' markets include delicate, smoothly textured slicers like the familiar English (also called hothouse) cucumbers; narrow, straight Japanese cucumbers; or the unusual, yellow-skinned, egg-shaped lemon cucumbers.

Cucumbers are at their best during the early to mid-summer months. They star in refreshing salads when tossed with simple vinaigrettes, creamy dressings, or cumin-spiked yogurt. Diced and cooked briefly in sauces, cucumbers become a delicate foil for fish and seafood. They are also delicious additions to chilled soups.

Chunky Tomato Conserve

MAKES 4 SERVINGS

3 Tbsp olive oil, plus extra for brushing and storage

5 lb (2.5 kg) tomatoes, cored and cut into small chunks

Salt

In a large frying pan over high heat, warm the olive oil. Add the tomatoes and 1 tsp salt, bring to a boil and cook until soft, about 2 minutes. Pass the tomatoes through a food mill.

Rinse the frying pan, dry, and return to high heat. Add the tomatoes and bring to a boil, reduce the heat to low, and cook stirring often, until reduced by two-thirds, about 2 hours.

Preheat the oven to 250°F (120°C). Lightly brush a baking sheet with olive oil and spread out the tomatoes in an even layer. Bake, turning the tomatoes as their surface darkens, until the liquid evaporates and the tomatoes have reduced to a thick, shiny, brick-colored paste, about 1 hour.

Transfer the conserve to a glass jar, top with about ½ inch (12 mm) of olive oil, and store in the refrigerator for up to 3 days. Top with olive oil after each use.

Serve this chunky conserve on top of crackers or toasted bread slices.

Spaghettini with Fresh Plum Tomato Sauce

MAKES 4 SERVINGS

⅓ cup (3 oz/90 g) unsalted butter

1 small white onion, thinly sliced crosswise

1 lb (500 g) plum (Roma) tomatoes, peeled, sliced lengthwise, and seeded

Salt

8 fresh basil leaves, torn into small pieces

1 lb (500 g) spaghettini

Grated hard cheese such as Parmesan

In a large frying pan over medium heat, melt the butter. Add the onion and ¼ cup (2 fl oz/60 ml) water, cover, and cook gently, stirring occasionally, until tender and translucent, about 10 minutes.

Add the tomatoes, cover partially, and cook over low heat until creamy, about 20 minutes. If the sauce begins to dry out, add more water to the pan.

Stir in salt to taste and the basil. Remove from the heat and let stand, covered, for 2 minutes. Set aside.

Bring a large pot of salted water to a boil. Add the spaghettini and cook until al dente, 7–9 minutes or according to the package directions. Drain and place in a large, shallow bowl. Add the sauce and toss. Top with the cheese and serve right away.

Rustic Tomato & Mozzarella Tart

MAKES 6–8 SERVINGS

2–3 ripe red and yellow tomatoes, about 8 oz (250 g) total weight, cored and cut into slices ⅛ inch (3 mm) thick

Salt

1 clove garlic, finely chopped

1 Tbsp unsalted butter, melted

8-by-10-inch (20-by-25-cm) rectangle of frozen puff pastry, cut in half and thawed in the refrigerator

¾ cup (3 oz/90 g) shredded whole-milk mozzarella cheese

4 Tbsp (1 oz/30 g) grated hard cheese, such as Parmesan

2 Tbsp chopped fresh basil

Olive oil for drizzling

Position a rack in the upper third of the oven and preheat to 400°F (200°C). Place the tomato slices on paper towels, season with salt, and let drain, 30–60 minutes.

In a small bowl, combine the garlic and butter. Place the puff pastry rectangles on a baking sheet lined with parchment (baking) paper. Brush with the garlic butter and season with salt. Leaving a ¼-inch (6-mm) border, sprinkle the pastry evenly with the mozzarella and 2 Tbsp of the Parmesan. Arrange the tomato slices on top. Sprinkle with the remaining 2 Tbsp Parmesan. Bake until puffed and golden, 25–30 minutes. Sprinkle with the basil and drizzle with the olive oil and serve right away.

HEIRLOOM TOMATOES

Heirloom tomatoes are old-fashioned varieties that have been reintroduced by farmers and gardeners. These tomatoes are full of flavor, but they may not keep as long as more commonly available varieties, and they may have thinner skins, qualities that make them less desirable for commercial processing. Many new tomato varieties often also classified as heirloom have also been introduced.

HEIRLOOM TOMATOES WITH SHALLOT VINAIGRETTE

In a small bowl, whisk together 3 Tbsp extra-virgin olive oil, 1 Tbsp balsamic vinegar, and 1 large shallot, minced. Season with salt and pepper. Let stand for 30 minutes. Core 1–1¼ lb (500–625 g) heirloom tomatoes. Halve the tomatoes, then cut into thin wedges. Arrange on a platter, drizzle the vinaigrette, and serve. Makes 4 servings.

RUSTIC TOMATO & MOZZARELLA TART

GRILLED BLACK COD WITH CUCUMBERS & GINGER

Cucumber Salad with Yogurt-Dill Sauce

MAKES 4 SERVINGS

4 English (hothouse) cucumbers, peeled and thinly sliced

Salt and ground white pepper

3 cloves garlic

⅔ cup (5 oz/150 g) plain yogurt

1 Tbsp fresh lemon juice

2 Tbsp minced fresh dill

3 Tbsp extra-virgin olive oil

Place the cucumber slices in a single layer on a plate. Salt lightly and let stand for about 1 hour. Drain off excess liquid.

Mince the garlic cloves and put into a small bowl. Add the yogurt, lemon juice, and dill. Season with salt and white pepper to taste. Add the olive oil and stir until blended to make a dressing.

Place the drained cucumber slices in a salad bowl, pour the dressing over the top, and toss. Refrigerate for 1 hour, then serve.

Chilled Spicy Cucumber Gazpacho

MAKES 4 SERVINGS

4¼ cups (1½ lb/690 g) peeled, seeded, and coarsely chopped English (hothouse) cucumbers

¾ cup (6 fl oz/180 ml) plus 1 Tbsp extra-virgin olive oil, plus extra for drizzling

½ cup (4 fl oz/125 ml) ice water

1 small clove garlic

¼ cup (2 fl oz/60 ml) plus 2 tsp white wine vinegar

1 Tbsp fresh lemon juice

Salt

1 small shallot, finely diced

1 small jalapeño chile, seeded and finely chopped

1 Tbsp finely chopped basil

Combine 4 cups (1¼ lb/625 g) of the cucumbers, ¾ cup (6 fl oz/180 ml) olive oil, ice water, garlic, the ¼ cup (2 fl oz/60 ml) vinegar, and lemon juice in a blender and purée. Pour into a serving bowl and season with salt. Cover and refrigerate for at least 1 hour before serving or up to overnight.

In a small bowl, stir together the shallot, the 2 tsp vinegar, and a pinch of salt. Let stand for 10 minutes. Stir in the remaining ¼ cup (1 oz/30 g) cucumber, jalapeño, basil, and the 1 Tbsp oil. Season with salt.

Ladle the soup into chilled bowls, garnish with the jalapeño mixture, and drizzle with oil. Serve right away.

Grilled Black Cod with Cucumbers & Ginger

MAKES 6 SERVINGS

2 English (hothouse) or Japanese cucumbers, thinly sliced

1 cup (3½ oz/105 g) thinly sliced red onion

Salt and freshly ground pepper

3 Tbsp chopped pickled ginger

1 Tbsp rice vinegar

3 Tbsp canola oil, plus extra for greasing

4 black cod fillets, about 1½ lb (750 g) total weight

Prepare a charcoal or gas grill for direct grilling over high heat (page 264) or use a stovetop grill pan. Oil the grill rack.

In a bowl, combine the cucumbers and onion and 1½ tsp salt. Let stand for 15 minutes. Stir in the ginger, vinegar, and 2 Tbsp of the canola oil. Set aside.

Brush the fillets on both sides with the remaining 1 Tbsp oil. Sprinkle on both sides with ½ tsp each salt and pepper.

Place the fish, skin side down, over the fire and grill, turning once, until just opaque throughout, about 8 minutes total.

Transfer the fillets to a serving platter and top with the cucumber salad. Serve right away.

PICKLING CUCUMBERS

Small, finger-length pickling cucumbers (also called gherkins or cornichons) show up in market bins for a few weeks during the summer. Their sweet taste and crunchy texture make them ideal for brining and turning into pickles, but they are also delicious raw in recipes or for eating out of hand.

SWEET-AND-SOUR CUCUMBER SALAD

Peel 2 lb (1 kg) pickling cucumbers and cut in half lengthwise. Scrape out the seeds, then cut again crosswise into thin slices ¼ inch (6 mm) thick. Place in a colander, sprinkle with 1 tsp salt, and toss to mix. Set aside and let drain for 1 hour. In a small saucepan, combine ½ cup (4 fl oz/125 ml) rice vinegar, 2 Tbsp sugar, and 1 tsp salt. Bring to a simmer over medium heat and cook, stirring to dissolve the sugar. Set aside to cool. Pat the cucumbers dry with paper towels. In a large bowl, combine the cucumbers; 4 shallots, thinly sliced; 1 chile, cut into thin rings and seeded; and 2 Tbsp chopped fresh cilantro (fresh coriander). Pour the vinegar mixture over the cucumber mixture and toss to coat. Cover and refrigerate for 2 hours or up to overnight. Serve chilled. Makes 4–6 servings.

Sweet Peppers

Sweet peppers, like their cousins the spicy chiles, are native to South America. Also called bell peppers or capsicums, sweet peppers are crisp and juicy. Green peppers usually have a sharper flavor and a characteristic vegetal note. Red peppers, allowed to ripen to maturity, come from the same plant as green ones. Other colors of peppers, such as yellow, orange, brown, and purple, are different varieties that have the same sweet flavor of red peppers, but can add colorful variety to dishes.

Sweet peppers are most abundant and flavorful from mid- to late summer. They can be sliced and enjoyed raw in salads, diced and sautéed until silken in texture and even sweeter in flavor, roasted or grilled for antipasti platters and sandwiches, or baked whole and filled with savory stuffings.

Chiles

Over centuries of domestication, hundreds of varieties of chiles have been developed from the earliest plants grown in Latin America. Requiring hot summers, they grow well in tropical areas. Among the most popular mild varieties for serving whole are long, grass-green Anaheims; dark green, triangular poblanos; and narrow, yellow banana chiles. Hotter varieties used for salsas and sauces include long, hot Fresno chiles; bell-shaped habaneros; the thin, bullet-shaped serranos; and the ubiquitous, tapered jalapeños.

Chiles are at their peak season from late summer to early autumn. In addition to contributing heat and depth of flavor to sauces and salsas, chiles can be stuffed with cheese, meat, or vegetables and then fried or baked. Roasted and sliced into ribbons, milder chiles can be stirred into soups or tossed with shredded meat for tacos, sandwich fillings, or egg dishes.

Pepper Salad with Sherry Vinegar & Ricotta Salata

MAKES 4 SERVINGS

3 red bell peppers (capsicums), seeded

2 Tbsp extra-virgin olive oil

2 Tbsp sherry vinegar

Salt and freshly ground pepper

¼ lb (125 g) ricotta salata

Cut the bell peppers into matchsticks, about ⅛ inch (3 mm) thick and 2–3 inches (5–7.5 cm) long.

In a large serving bowl, whisk together the olive oil and vinegar to make a vinaigrette. Add the bell peppers, season with salt and pepper, and toss. Marinate for at least 10 minutes or up to 1 hour.

Arrange on individual salad plates and shave the ricotta salata over the top. Serve right away.

Piperade with Mixed Bell Peppers

MAKES 4 SERVINGS

⅓ cup (3 fl oz/80 ml) plus 2 Tbsp extra-virgin olive oil

6 garlic cloves, thinly sliced

2 large yellow onions, cut into ¼-inch (6-mm) slices

1 yellow bell pepper (capsicum), seeded and chopped

2 red bell peppers (capsicums), seeded and chopped

1½ Tbsp chile powder

2 large tomatoes, seeded and chopped

Salt and freshly ground pepper

In a small saucepan, combine the ⅓ cup of the olive oil and half of the garlic over low heat. Cook until the garlic is soft, about 5 minutes. Remove from the heat and set aside. Once cooled, mash the garlic against the side of the pan with a fork.

In a large frying pan over medium heat, warm the remaining 2 Tbsp oil. Add the onions, bell peppers, and the remaining garlic; sauté until the vegetables begin to soften, about 6 minutes. Add the chile powder and cook for 1 minute longer. Add the tomatoes and sauté until soft, about 3 minutes. Season with salt and pepper. Remove from the heat and set aside. Serve right away.

Make this recipe into a main dish by serving it with seared ahi tuna fillets cut into thin strips.

Roasted Red Peppers with Fresh Mozzarella

MAKES 8 SERVINGS

6 red bell peppers (capsicums), about 3 lb (1.5 kg) total weight

2 cloves garlic

Salt

2 Tbsp small capers, preferably salt-packed, rinsed well

2 Tbsp chopped fresh marjoram or basil

2–3 Tbsp extra-virgin olive oil

Pinch of cayenne pepper

1½ tsp red wine vinegar, or more to taste

1 lb (500 g) small fresh mozzarella cheese balls (bocconcini)

Halve the peppers lengthwise and remove the stems and seeds. Cut into strips ½ inch (12 mm) wide and put in a bowl.

Mash the garlic into a paste with a pinch of salt. Add the garlic paste, capers, marjoram or basil, and olive oil to the peppers and toss. Season with salt, cayenne, and the red wine vinegar and toss again. Let stand at room temperature for at least 10–20 minutes or up to several hours. Just before serving, season with salt and more vinegar if desired. Transfer the peppers to a platter. Scatter the mozzarella balls on top and serve right away.

Serve this dish as a first course for an Italian-themed meal.

PADRÓN PEPPERS

Named after the Spanish town where their seeds originated, Padrón peppers are a recent find at the farmers' market. Small and green, their flavor is usually sweet and mild but can be hot and spicy making every bite suspenseful. Padrón peppers are best fried or grilled and served with coarse salt sprinkled on top. They're available in the summer when other chiles appear.

GRILLED PADRÓN PEPPERS WITH COARSE SALT

Prepare a gas or charoal grill for direct-heat cooking over high heat (page 264) or use a stovetop grill pan. In a bowl, toss 1 lb (500 g) Padrón peppers with 1 Tbsp extra-virgin olive oil. Grill the peppers, turning with tongs, until the skin has blistered on all sides, 3–4 minutes. Season with coarse salt and serve right away. Makes 4 servings.

PIPERADE WITH MIXED BELL PEPPERS

JALAPEÑOS STUFFED WITH SAUSAGE & CHEESE

Quesadilla with Queso Fresco & Chiles

MAKES 6 SERVINGS

4 poblano chiles, roasted (page 264)

5 Tbsp (3 fl oz/80 ml) canola oil

1 large yellow onion, halved and thinly sliced

1 large clove garlic, minced

Salt and freshly ground pepper

6 flour tortillas, each 10 inches (25 cm) in diameter

3 cups (12 oz/375 g) shredded *queso fresco* or feta cheese

6 Tbsp (⅓ oz/10 g) chopped fresh cilantro (fresh coriander)

Halve the chiles lengthwise and discard the core and seeds, then cut into strips ¼ inch (6 mm) wide.

In a large frying pan over medium-low heat, warm 1 Tbsp of the canola oil. Add the onion until soft, about 15 minutes. Sauté the garlic for 1 minute. Stir in the chiles and season with salt and pepper. Cook, stirring, for 5 minutes. Remove from the heat. If the mixture has released any juices, drain in a colander and set aside.

In a large frying pan over medium-high heat, warm 2 tsp of the oil. Add 1 tortilla and reduce the heat to medium. Sprinkle half the surface with ½ cup (2 oz/60 g) of the shredded cheese, keeping the cheese away from the edges. Top the cheese evenly with one-sixth of the chile-onion mixture and 1 Tbsp of the cilantro. Fold the untopped half over the filling, pressing gently. Move the quesadilla into the center of the frying pan and cook until the bottom is nicely browned, about 1 minute. Turn and cook until the other side is nicely browned, about 1 minute longer. Repeat with the remaining ingredients, using 2 tsp of the oil for each tortilla. Serve right away.

Fried Eggs with Charred Chiles & Crème Fraîche

MAKES 2–4 SERVINGS

½ lb (250 g) poblano chiles, roasted (page 264)

3 Tbsp olive oil

1 small white onion, cut into slices ¼ inch (6 mm) thick

2 cloves garlic, finely chopped

½ tsp dried oregano

Salt and freshly ground pepper

½ cup (4 oz/125 g) crème fraîche

3 Tbsp chopped fresh cilantro (fresh coriander)

4 large eggs, fried

Halve the chiles lengthwise and discard the core and seeds, then cut into strips ¼ inch (6 mm) wide.

In a large frying pan over medium-high heat, warm 1 Tbsp of the oil . Sauté the onion, until not quite tender, about 5 minutes. Add the garlic and oregano and sauté for 30 seconds. Add the chiles, season with salt, and cook until heated, about 1 minute. Transfer to a blender. Add half of the crème fraîche and cook over medium heat for 1 minute, scraping the pan bottom to remove any caramelized bits. Add the warm crème fraîche, remaining crème fraîche, and cilantro to the blender and purée. Arrange the fried eggs on plates, top with the sauce, and season with salt and pepper.

Jalapeños Stuffed with Sausage & Cheese

MAKES 6–8 SERVINGS

½ lb (250 g) mild Italian sausage, casings removed

1 cup (5 oz/155 g) grated teleme cheese

½ tsp fennel seeds, coarsely ground

2 Tbsp chopped fresh flat-leaf (Italian) parsley

Salt

12 large jalapeño chiles, halved lengthwise and seeded

Preheat the oven to 400°F (200°C).

Crumble the sausage in a bowl. Add the cheese, fennel seeds, and parsley and season with salt. Stir to combine. Set aside.

Season the jalapeños with salt and spoon about 1 Tbsp of the sausage mixture into each half.

Arrange the jalapeños in a single layer on a baking sheet, stuffed side up, and bake until golden, about 20 minutes. Serve right away.

DRIED CHILES

Dried chiles first appear in the markets in late autumn, after the fresh chiles have disappeared. Look for flexible pods rather than brittle ones. They will be wrinkled and perhaps a little twisted, but they should have a good uniform color. Store dried chiles in an airtight container away from light and moisture. They will keep for up to 6 months.

SPICY HOT COCOA

Release the seeds of 1 ancho chile into a saucepan. Add 6 Tbsp (1 oz/30 g) unsweetened cocoa powder, 3 Tbsp sugar, and ⅓ cup (3 fl oz/80 ml) water. Place over low heat and stir until a paste forms. Pour in 2½ cups (20 fl oz/625 ml) whole milk, and stir until the paste dissolves. Cook until hot, about 2 minutes. Strain into mugs and garnish with cinnamon sticks. Makes 4 servings.

Avocados

Beneath its thick, dark rind, the egg-shaped avocado reveals green-golden flesh with a silken texture and buttery flavor. Most that come to market fall into two broad categories. The green-black, pebbly-skinned Guatamalan varieties like Hass (also spelled Haas), Zutano, and Bacon are widely popular for their long growing seasons and their high oil content. Trees from the Mexican varieties, such as Fuerte and Gwen, bear larger fruit with smoother, lighter colored skins and generally lower fat content.

Avocados have a long season and come to market, depending on the variety, from early spring through late autumn in temperate regions. The fruit is at its best when served raw or only slightly heated, as its flavor does not hold up to cooking. Ripe avocados are especially popular mashed into guacamole, spread onto sandwiches, diced for salsas, and sliced to garnish salads.

BUYING EGGPLANTS

Choose smooth, firm, glossy-skinned eggplants (aubergines) with green caps and stems. Whether purple, white, green, or another color, avoid any that are wrinkled, torn, bruised, or scarred or that have brown, dried caps. Store eggplants in a plastic bag in the refrigerator for up to 5 days.

Eggplants

Native to Africa and Asia, eggplants, also known as aubergines, are named for the appearance of the oldest varieties, which were small, white, and egg shaped. Now, eggplants from around the world appear at farmers' markets. Among the most familiar remains the large, purple-black globe eggplant common in Mediterranean cuisines. Chinese and Japanese eggplants are long, thin vegetables with denser flesh and thinner skins that range in color from pink to lavender to dark purple. Specialty varieties may be ivory, rose colored, striped or striated, or even green, as with the tiny, round Thai eggplant.

Eggplants are at their best and most abundant in late summer. Large globe eggplant are ideal for roasting, broiling, and grilling, after which they excel in puréed spreads, pasta sauces, and chilled antipasti. Asian eggplants lend themselves well to stir-frying, braising in curry sauces, and pickling.

WORKING WITH EGGPLANTS

Rinse the eggplants. Using a large knife, trim the green top. If an eggplant is large with numerous seeds, or if the flesh looks dark and watery, extract the bitter juices by sprinkling salt on it after slicing and place in a colander set in the sink for 30 minutes. Salting also prepares eggplant for deep-frying. Young eggplants or Asian varieties can be cooked without salting or peeling.

Classic Guacamole with Tortilla Chips

MAKES 4 SERVINGS

1 ripe avocado

2 Tbsp fresh lime or lemon juice

¼ cup (⅓ oz/10 g) fresh chopped fresh cilantro (fresh coriander)

1 green (spring) onion, chopped

1 serrano chile, seeded and minced

1 clove garlic, minced

Salt

Tortilla chips for serving

Halve the avocado lengthwise, cutting around the pit. Rotate the halves to separate and remove the pit. Remove the flesh and put in a small bowl.

Mash the avocado flesh with a fork. Add the lime or lemon juice, cilantro, green onion, serrano chile, and garlic. Mix the ingredients until well incorporated. Season to taste with salt.

Serve the guacamole right away alongside tortilla chips.

Avocado & Shrimp Summer Rolls

MAKES 6 SERVINGS

6 rice-paper rounds, each 8 inches (20 cm) in diameter

6 red-leaf or butter (Boston) lettuce leaves

1 avocado, pitted, peeled, and cut into slices ¼ inch (6 mm) thick

½ small cucumber, seeded and shredded

2 oz (60 g) cellophane noodles, soaked in boiling water for 15 minutes and drained

9 medium peeled, deveined, and cooked shrimp (prawns), cut in half lengthwise

18 *each* fresh mint leaves and fresh cilantro (fresh coriander) leaves

Asian Dipping Sauce (page 262)

Fill a wide, shallow bowl with warm water. Working with 1 rice-paper round at a time, soak in the warm water until softened, about 10 seconds. Shake off the excess water and place on a work surface. Set a lettuce leaf horizontally on the bottom half of the rice paper. In a line across the base of the lettuce, place 1½ slices of avocado, 1 tsp of the cucumber, and several strands of the noodles; do not overstuff the rolls. Lift the bottom edge of the rice paper and roll up halfway into a tight cylinder. Place 3 shrimp halves and 3 each of the mint and cilantro leaves along the inside seam of the roll. Fold in the sides of the rice paper and continue to roll into a cylinder. Moisten the edge of the roll to seal.

Cut the rolls in half and place seam side down on a platter. Serve right away with the dipping sauce.

Avocado, Bacon & Tomato Tartines

MAKES 4 SERVINGS

4 slices course country bread, each ½ inch (12 mm) thick

½ cup (4 oz/125 g) Aioli (page 139)

2 tomatoes, cut into slices ¼ inch (6 mm) thick

Salt

8 thin slices bacon, cooked

1 avocado, cut into thin slices

Preheat the broiler (grill).

Arrange the bread in a single layer on a baking sheet and put under the broiler until lightly toasted, 2–3 minutes.

Spread the aioli on the bread and top with a few tomato slices, pressing the tomato into the bread. Season with salt and top the tomato with the bacon slices, then with the avocado and a light sprinkle of salt. Serve right away.

AVOCADO, BACON & TOMATO TARTINES

ROLLED EGGPLANT WITH SAUSAGE & MOZZARELLA

Smoky Roasted Ratatouille

MAKES 6–8 SERVINGS

1 lb (500 g) plum (Roma) tomatoes, halved lengthwise

4 large cloves garlic, sliced

1 large yellow onion, cut crosswise into slices ¼ inch (6 mm) thick

1 small eggplant (aubergine), trimmed and cut into 1-inch (2.5-cm) chunks

1 small zucchini (courgette), trimmed and cut crosswise into slices ½ inch (12 mm) thick

1 small yellow crookneck squash, trimmed and cut crosswise into slices ½ inch (12 mm) thick

1 green bell pepper (capsicum), seeded and cut into 1½-inch (4-cm) squares

5 Tbsp (3 fl oz/80 ml) olive oil

Salt and freshly ground pepper

¼ cup (⅓ oz/10 g) finely shredded fresh basil

2 Tbsp chopped fresh thyme

Preheat the oven to 425°F (220°C). Place the tomatoes, garlic, onion, eggplant, zucchini, squash, and bell pepper in a bowl, coat with the olive oil and season with salt. Place the vegetables in single layer on a large rimmed baking sheet.

Roast the vegetables, stirring 1–2 times, for 20 minutes. Remove from the oven and sprinkle with the basil and thyme. Continue to roast, stirring 1–2 times, until tender when pierced with a fork, 5–10 minutes longer. Remove the pan from the oven and season with salt and pepper.

Transfer to a serving bowl. Serve hot, warm, or at room temperature.

Rolled Eggplant with Sausage & Mozzarella

MAKES 4 SERVINGS

1½ lb (750 g) Italian or Asian eggplant (slender aubergine) trimmed and cut lengthwise into slices ¼ inch (6 mm) thick

¼ cup (2 fl oz/60 ml) plus 2 Tbsp olive oil

Salt and freshly ground pepper

5 oz (155 g) Italian sausage, casings removed

2 cups (16 fl oz/500 ml) tomato sauce

1 cup (8 oz/250 g) whole-milk ricotta

4 oz (125 g) fresh mozzarella cheese, cut into small pieces

4 Tbsp (2 oz/60 g) grated hard cheese, such as Parmesan

1 Tbsp chopped flat-leaf (Italian) parsley

Preheat the oven to 450°F (230°C). Brush the eggplant on both sides with the ¼ cup (2 fl oz/60 ml) of the olive oil and season with salt. Place in an even layer on a baking sheet and bake until lightly browned on the bottom, about 10 minutes. Turn the slices and bake until tender, 5–7 minutes. Remove from the oven and reduce the oven temperature to 350°F (180°C).

In a frying pan over medium-high heat, warm the remaining 2 Tbsp olive oil. Sauté the sausage until cooked through, about 3 minutes. Stir in the tomato sauce and bring to a boil. Reduce the heat to low and simmer for 5 minutes.

In a bowl, stir together the ricotta, the mozzarella, 2 Tbsp of the Parmesan, and the parsley. Season with salt and pepper. Spread half of the sauce on the bottom of a 9-inch (23-cm) baking dish. Place a spoonful of the cheese mixture near the wide end of each eggplant slice, roll up, and place upright or upside down in the sauce. Spoon the remaining sauce between the rolls. Sprinkle with the remaining 2 Tbsp Parmesan. Bake until the sauce is bubbling, about 20 minutes. Serve right away.

Soy-Glazed Broiled Eggplant

MAKES 4 SERVINGS

2 Tbsp olive oil plus extra for greasing

¼ cup (2 fl oz/60 ml) white miso

2 Tbsp rice wine vinegar

1 Tbsp soy sauce

1 Tbsp sugar

1 tsp grated fresh ginger

4 Asian eggplants (slender aubergines)

2 Tbsp chopped fresh basil

Preheat the broiler (grill). Brush a large baking sheet with olive oil.

In a small bowl, whisk together the miso, vinegar, soy sauce, 1 Tbsp water, the sugar, and ginger to make a glaze.

Cut the eggplants (aubergines) in half lengthwise and place cut side up on the baking sheet. Brush with the 2 Tbsp of oil. Broil until they begin to soften and turn golden, about 5 minutes. Remove from the oven, brush with the glaze, and broil again for 2 minutes longer. Remove from the oven and turn the baking sheet 180 degrees. Continue to broil until the eggplant is tender and the glaze is golden brown, 4–5 minutes.

To serve, arrange the eggplant slices on a platter and sprinkle evenly with the chopped basil. Serve right away.

Other Vegetables

MUSHROOMS

SWEET CORN

ARTICHOKES

BABY
ARTICHOKES

Several vegetables found at farmers' markets bear little relation to other groups of produce and claim distinct characteristics of their own. Mushrooms are edible types of fungi. Corn, an important crop worldwide, is a type of grass that produces grains, or kernels, borne on sizable ears. Artichokes are the flower buds of a type of thistle. Mushrooms have an unmistakable earthiness. Fresh corn is so sweet and juicy that the kernels can be eaten raw. Artichokes are prized for their mild buttery flavor.

Each of these vegetables has a different lineage. The exact geographic origin of mushrooms is unclear, but food historians theorize that the earliest edible fungi date to prehistoric times. The ancient Greeks and Romans may have been the first to cultivate mushrooms. Now, thousands of mushroom varieties exist worldwide, though a limited number come to market. Corn is a New World crop. Artichokes, native to the Mediterranean, were enjoyed by the Romans.

Mushroom varieties, wild and cultivated, are harvested throughout the year. Be sure not to miss summer's crop of sweet corn, best when eaten the day ears are picked from the stalks. Watch for the primary harvest of artichokes in early spring.

BUYING MUSHROOMS

Fresh mushrooms should be firm and have smooth, unblemished caps. Avoid any that are broken, limp, wrinkled, soggy, or moldy. Stems with gray, dried ends indicate that the mushrooms are old. As mushrooms age, they dry out, so the heaviest ones are the freshest. Store all mushroom varieties in a paper bag in the refrigerator for up to 4 days.

Mushrooms

Almost 40,000 varieties of mushrooms grow in the wild, but only a fraction of these make it to the table, where they are enjoyed for their rich, earthy flavor. For culinary purposes, mushrooms are divided into two categories. Many are cultivated, like the familiar button or white mushroom and the large, dark, wide portobello. Wild mushrooms include the popular, all-purpose shiitake; the deeply aromatic Italian porcini (also called cèpes); the highly prized morel with its elongated caps and furrowed ridges; the pale and delicate oyster mushroom; the pine-scented matsutake; and the flared, apricot-scented chaterelle that grows in striking golden-orange or black color.

The most flavorful mushrooms are still gathered by experienced foragers during cool, moist days in spring and autumn. Sautéing, grilling, roasting, and drying concentrate the rich, woodsy flavors of mushrooms.

WORKING WITH MUSHROOMS

Mushrooms absorb water easily, becoming soggy and flavorless if left to soak. If possible, wipe the mushrooms clean with a damp cloth or soft brush. If needed, rinse mushrooms quickly and dry thoroughly with paper towels just before cooking. Trim the dried end of tender stems. Tough stems, such as those of shiitakes, should be removed entirely.

Creamy Mushroom Soup with Sherry

MAKES 6 SERVINGS

1 oz (30 g) dried porcini mushrooms

6 Tbsp (3 oz/90 g) unsalted butter

2 yellow onions, chopped

2 lb (1 kg) fresh mushrooms, brushed clean and thinly sliced

5 cups (40 fl oz/1.25 l) chicken broth

¼ cup (2 fl oz/60 ml) dry sherry

1 cup (8 fl oz/250 ml) heavy (double) cream

Salt and freshly ground pepper

Rinse the porcini and place in a bowl. Add 1 cup (8 fl oz/250 ml) hot water and let stand for 1 hour. Lift out the porcini, squeezing over the bowl to remove moisture, and chop finely. Strain the liquid through a sieve lined with damp cheesecloth (muslin).

In a heavy saucepan over low heat, melt 2 Tbsp of the butter. Add the onions and cook, stirring occasionally, until translucent, about 10 minutes. Remove from the heat.

In a large frying pan over medium heat, melt the remaining 4 Tbsp (2 oz/60 g) butter. Add the mushrooms and sauté slowly, stirring, until soft, 10–15 minutes.

Add the cooked mushrooms, the chopped porcini, and the strained liquid to the sautéed onions and return to medium-high heat. Pour in the broth and bring to a boil. Reduce the heat to low and simmer, uncovered, about 20 minutes.

Working in batches and using a slotted spoon, transfer the mushrooms and onions to a blender or food processor. Add a little of the cooking liquid and purée until smooth. Transfer to a clean saucepan. Thin the purée with as much of the remaining liquid as needed. Add the sherry and cream and season with salt and pepper. Reheat over low heat. Serve right away.

Wild Rice & Mushroom Pilaf

MAKES 6 SERVINGS

1 Tbsp unsalted butter

1 small leek, white part only, chopped

1 lb (500 g) mixed fresh mushrooms such as white button, shiitake, morel, and wood ear, brushed clean

1 cup (6 oz/185 g) wild rice, rinsed and drained

¼ cup (⅓ oz/10 g) chopped fresh flat-leaf (Italian) parsley

Salt and freshly ground pepper

In a large saucepan over medium heat, melt the butter. Add the leek and the mushrooms and sauté until the leeks are soft and translucent and the mushrooms begin to brown, about 8 minutes.

Add the wild rice, parsley, salt, pepper, and water to cover by 1 inch (2.5 cm). Bring to a boil, reduce the heat to low, cover, and cook until the rice is tender, about 45 minutes. Drain off any excess water. The cooking time will vary with different batches of rice. The wild rice is ready when the grains puff up and the inner, lighter part is visible.

Transfer to a warmed serving dish and serve right away.

Seared Halibut with Wild Mushroom Ragout

MAKES 4 SERVINGS

1 cup (8 fl oz/250 ml) chicken broth

2 tsp unsalted butter

1 Tbsp plus 2 tsp olive oil

1 lb (500 g) fresh button mushrooms, brushed clean and halved

1 lb (500 g) mixed morel, oyster, and shiitake mushrooms, brushed clean and cut into pieces the same size as the button mushroom halves

½ cup (2 fl oz/60 ml) heavy (double) cream

2 cloves garlic, minced

2 Tbsp chopped fresh flat-leaf (Italian) parsley

Salt and freshly ground pepper

4 skinless halibut fillets, each about 6 oz (185 g)

In a small saucepan, bring the chicken broth to a boil until reduced by half, 3–5 minutes. Remove from the heat and set aside.

In a large frying pan over medium-high heat, melt the butter with the 2 tsp olive oil. Add all the mushrooms and sauté until golden, 5–6 minutes. Add the chicken broth, the cream, garlic, parsley and simmer over medium heat until reduced by half, 3–4 minutes. Season with salt and pepper. Cover the pan and turn the heat to low.

Heat a large nonstick frying pan over medium-high heat for 2–3 minutes. Add the remaining 1 Tbsp oil. Add the halibut and sauté, turning once, until browned on both sides and opaque throughout when pierced with a knife, about 8 minutes total. Transfer to a cutting board and cut the fillets into equal pieces. Spoon the mushrooms over the halibut, and serve right away.

WILD RICE & MUSHROOM PILAF

Sweet Corn

Actually a grain whose large, fleshy seeds are cooked and eaten as a vegetable, corn was first cultivated nearly 7,000 years ago in Central America. It is also known as maize and has long been celebrated as one of the most important foods in the world. Most ears found at farmers' markets are tender, high-sugar varieties with small yellow kernels. Look for specialty types with white kernels; a combination of white, yellow, and red; or even deep purplish blue, a special hybrid primarily grown in the Southwest United States and Mexico.

Corn lovers eagerly anticipate its arrival at markets during the summer. Purists insist on cooking corn on the cob only until warmed through, either boiled or steamed, to preserve its sweetness and crunch. Cut from the cob, the fresh kernels can be added raw to salads and salsas, cooked until creamy for soups and chowders, deep-fried in fritters, or folded into savory quickbreads and fillings.

CHILE-RUBBED CORN ON THE COB

Chile-Rubbed
Corn on the Cob

MAKES 6 SERVINGS

6 ears of corn, husks intact

Salt and freshly ground black pepper

1 tsp chile powder

½ tsp ground cumin

⅛ tsp cayenne pepper

2 Tbsp unsalted butter, melted

Pull back the husks from each ear of corn but leave them attached to the base. Pull off and discard the silks. Rinse under cold running water and then place in a bowl with cold water to cover. Let soak for 20 minutes.

Prepare a gas or charcoal grill for direct grilling over medium-high heat (or use a stovetop grill pan). Oil the grill rack.

In a small bowl, stir together ½ tsp salt, ¼ tsp black pepper, the chile powder, cumin, cayenne, and butter. Spread the butter mixture on the corn and rewrap the husks around them. Wrap each ear of corn in aluminum foil.

Place the corn on a grill rack about 4 inches (10 cm) from the fire. Grill, turning occasionally, until tender, about 15 minutes.

Remove the foil and arrange on a platter. Serve right away.

Corn Pudding
with Chives

MAKES 4 SERVINGS

8 ears of corn, husks and silk removed

Salt and freshly ground pepper

2 Tbsp chopped fresh chives

1 Tbsp unsalted butter

Holding each ear of corn by its pointed end, and steadying its stalk end on a cutting board, cut down along the ear with a sharp knife to strip off the kernels, turning the ear with each cut. Then stand the ear upright on a plate or in a shallow bowl and scrape a spoon down each row to remove all of the pulp and juices, leaving behind the kernel skins. You should have about 3 cups (18 oz/560 g).

Put the corn in a nonstick saucepan and place over medium heat. Add ¼ tsp salt and bring to a simmer. Cook, stirring often with a wooden spoon, until one-third of the liquid has evaporated and the consistency is thick, 8–10 minutes. The corn will bubble and sputter, but it should not boil vigorously. If you are not using a nonstick pan, a brown crust will form on the bottom and sides of the pan. Do not try to scrape this off to mix it with the corn. Instead, simply stir the corn without breaking up the crust.

Stir in the chives and butter. Season with salt and pepper.

Spoon into a bowls and serve right away.

Risotto with Fresh
Corn & Basil Oil

MAKES 4 SERVINGS

2–3 ears of corn, husks and silk removed

2 Tbsp unsalted butter

1 cup (3 oz/90 g) thinly sliced leeks, white and pale green parts only

2 cups (16 fl oz/500 ml) chicken broth

1½ cups (10 oz/330 g) short-grain rice such as Arborio, Carnaroli, or Vialone Nano

Salt and freshly ground pepper

2 Tbsp snipped fresh chives

4 Tbsp (2 fl oz/60 ml) Basil Oil (page 262)

Holding each ear of corn by its pointed end, and steadying its stalk end on a cutting board, cut down along the ear with a sharp knife to strip off the kernels, turning the ear with each cut. Set aside.

In a saucepan over medium heat, melt the butter. Add the leeks and stir to coat. Cover, reduce the heat to medium-low, and cook until translucent, about 5 minutes.

Pour the broth and 3 cups (24 fl oz/750 ml) water into a saucepan and place over medium heat. Adjust the heat to keep the mixture hot but not simmering.

Raise the heat under the leeks to medium, add the rice, and cook, stirring, until the rice is translucent, about 3 minutes. Begin adding the hot liquid ½ cup (4 fl oz/125 ml) at a time, stirring constantly and adding more liquid only when the previous addition has been absorbed. After 10 minutes, stir in the corn. It should take about 20 minutes for the rice to absorb all the liquid and become al dente and creamy. If you need more liquid, use boiling water. Season with salt and pepper.

Remove from the heat and stir in the chives and 2 Tbsp of the basil oil. Divide among bowls and top with the remaining 2 Tbsp basil oil. Serve right away.

Artichokes should feel heavy for their size. Look for tightly closed, olive green leaves and moist, healthy stems. Some may have black streaks, which indicate slight frost damage, but this will not affect their flavor. Sprinkle artichokes with a few drops of water and store in a plastic bag in the coldest part of the refrigerator for up to 1 week.

Artichokes

Few vegetables look as forbidding as the artichoke, or have as high a proportion of inedible matter. Beneath its armor of fibrous, thorny leaves, this ungainly thistle bud offers a culinary treasure: a tender, delicious heart with a mild flavor. Native to the Mediterranean, artichokes are popular across Italy, France, and Spain.

The primary artichoke season is in early spring, followed by a second, shorter season in late autumn or early winter. Artichokes come to market in wide range of sizes, from tiny baby artichokes tender enough to eat whole to immense globes that weigh nearly a pound each. The easiest way to enjoy them is simply by steaming or boiling until tender and serving with a fresh herb vinaigrette or garlicky aioli for dipping. Trimmed to the heart, they can be sliced and tossed into salads or pastas, puréed into soups or spreads, or used whole as a bed for poached eggs or seafood salads.

WORKING WITH ARTICHOKES

To trim an artichoke, start at the base, pulling off and discarding the tough outer leaves. Trim away the prickly tips of the remaining leaves with kitchen shears. Use a serrated knife to slice off the top 1 to 2 inches (2.5 to 5 cm) to reveal the frilly choke, which should be scooped out with a spoon. Prevent discoloration after cutting the artichoke by it rubbing with fresh lemon juice.

Shaved Artichoke & Blue Cheese Salad

MAKES 4 SERVINGS

2 lemons, halved

8 small to medium artichokes

4 Tbsp (2 fl oz/60 ml) extra-virgin olive oil

¼ cup (½ oz/15 g) frisée

Salt and freshly ground pepper

2 Tbsp crumbled blue cheese

⅓ cup (2 oz/60 g) almonds, toasted (page 264) and chopped

Squeeze the juice of 2 lemon halves into a large bowl of cold water. Add the peels. Pull off the tough outer leaves of each artichoke until you reach the pale green inner leaves. Using a small knife, trim the dark green portions from the stem and base, and trim the stem. Cut 1 inch (2.5 cm) off from the tops. Halve the artichoke lengthwise and using a small spoon, remove the fuzzy choke. As the artichokes are trimmed, immerse them in the lemon water.

Slice the artichokes thinly lengthwise. Put in a bowl, drizzle with 2 Tbsp of the olive oil, and toss well. Add the frisée, season with salt and pepper, drizzle with the remaining 2 Tbsp olive oil, and squeeze the juice from 1 lemon half. Toss gently and season with salt and with more lemon juice, if needed. Transfer to a platter, scatter the blue cheese and almonds on top, and serve right away.

Steamed Artichokes with Dill Mayonnaise

MAKES 4 SERVINGS

4 medium to large artichokes

1 large egg yolk

1 cup (8 fl oz/250 ml) olive oil

2 Tbsp finely chopped fresh dill

1–2 tsp fresh lemon juice

Salt

Pull off the tough outer leaves of each artichoke at the base of the stem. Trim the stem even with the base. Arrange the artichokes, stem end up, in a single layer on a steaming basket. Transfer to a pot, pour in 1 inch (2.5 cm) of water, cover tightly, and bring to a boil. Steam, checking the water level periodically, until the bottoms can be easily pierced with a knife, 30–40 minutes.

Meanwhile, whisk together the egg yolk and ½ tsp water in a small bowl. When the mixture thickens and turns opaque, add the olive oil in a steady drizzle, whisking constantly. Stir in the dill and lemon juice and season with salt. If the mayonnaise is too thick, add water.

Place the artichokes on a platter and serve right away with the mayonnaise for dipping.

Artichokes Stewed with Lemon & Garlic

MAKES 6 SERVINGS

2 lemons

18 small artichokes

10 cloves garlic, halved

5 fresh thyme sprigs

2 bay leaves

½ tsp salt

¼ cup (2 fl oz/60 ml) olive oil

1 tsp chopped fresh flat-leaf (Italian) parsley

Using a vegetable peeler, remove the zest from the lemons and set aside.

Fill a large bowl halfway with cold water. Halve 1 lemon and squeeze the juice into the water. Working with 1 artichoke at a time, break off the tough outer leaves to reach the pale green, tender inner leaves. Using a small knife, trim the dark green portions from the stem and base, and trim the stem. Cut 1 inch from the tops. Cut the artichoke in half lengthwise and slip the halves into the lemon water. Trim the remaining artichokes in the same way.

Drain the artichokes and place in a saucepan. Halve the remaining lemon and squeeze the juice into the saucepan. Add the reserved lemon zest, the garlic, thyme sprigs, bay leaves, salt, and olive oil. Add water to cover and place a piece of parchment (baking) paper the diameter of the pan on top of the artichokes. Weight the parchment with a heatproof plate that rests directly on the artichokes. Bring to a boil over medium-high heat, reduce the heat to medium, and simmer for 5 minutes. Remove from the heat and let cool in the pan, about 1 hour or until tender when pierced with a knife. Sprinkle the parsley on the top and serve right away.

BABY ARTICHOKES

These small artichokes are grown lower down on the plant than their globe counterparts. They should be olive green in color and have tightly closed leaves. They can be as tiny as a nut and may not have developed chokes, but you will still need to trim the stems, pull off the dark outer leaves, and cut away the spiny tops before cooking.

FRIED BABY ARTICHOKES WITH AIOLI

Break off the outer leaves of 12–16 baby artichokes. Cut off the top one-fourth of the leaves, and trim the stems. Cut lengthwise into slices ¼ inch (6 mm) thick, and drop into water with the juice of 1 lemon. Warm ¼ cup (2 fl oz/60 ml) olive oil in a frying pan over medium-high heat. Fry the artichokes until crisp, 3–4 minutes. Transfer to paper towels and sprinkle with 1 tsp salt. Serve with Aioli (page 139).

ARTICHOKES STEWED WITH LEMON & GARLIC

Berries

In contrast to fruits that have a single large pit or concentrations of seeds at their center, berries are generally distinguished by tiny edible seeds dispersed throughout their flesh. Many varieties grow on vines or canes, a term referring to slender, often thorny stems. Some berries, such as blueberries and huckleberries, are grown on bushes. Among the group of berries here, shiny red cranberries are unusual, as they grow on bushes in bogs or special beds, which are flooded in fall so the buoyant berries can be harvested. The intense sweetness and succulence of many of these small fruits overshadow their small size. For example, when strawberries, raspberries, and blackberries are at their peak of ripeness, they can be extraordinarily fragrant.

Several berries, including raspberries, strawberries, and blackberries, are native to both the Old World and the New World and are also found in Asia. In ancient times, people gathered berries in the wild, and though the custom is still followed today, the berries found at farmers' markets are mostly cultivated. Two varieties, huckleberries and cranberries, originated in North America.

Because most berries are delicate, they are carefully harvested by hand when they mature in spring and summer.

Strawberries

Bursting with sweet flavor and blessed with a heady fragrance, vibrant red strawberries are members of a large botanical family that includes apples and pears, raspberries and blackberries. It derives its name from an Anglo-Saxon word meaning "spreading berry," for the abundant, sprawling shoots that grow out from each mother plant.

Strawberries are among the first fruit to come to market in spring and early summer. Other strawberry types include the small, juicy alpine strawberry, also known as *fraises des bois* in French, and the musk strawberry. Shopping for strawberries at farmers' markets will lead you to similarly flavorful berries, as local growers can cultivate these more delicate varieties. Strawberries are among the most popular fruits for eating fresh out of hand. They are also made into jams, piled onto tarts, layered into cakes, and heaped on pancakes and waffles.

Blackberries & Raspberries

The first sighting of plump, elongated, midnight-hued blackberries and the delicate, cupped fruit of raspberries heralds summer's sweetest flavors. Raspberries tend to carry tart flavor qualities and are typically scarlet in color, though some varieties produce golden fruit. Blackberries and raspberries grow on thorny, rambling bushes called brambles and thrive in sunny fields and meadows across North America and Europe. Both appear at farmers' markets from late spring to early autumn and taste their best during the height of summer.

Raspberries and blackberries can be substituted for one another or combined in recipes. They are delicious when eaten simply fresh, but can also be sprinkled over ice cream or fruit salads, baked into flaky pies, or transformed into luscious, jewel-toned jams.

Fresh Strawberry & Spinach Salad

MAKES 6 SERVINGS

¼ cup (2 fl oz/60 ml) rice vinegar

2 Tbsp sugar

2 tsp poppy seeds

½ tsp dry mustard

Salt and freshly ground pepper

¾ cup (6 fl oz/180 ml) canola oil

6 cups (6 oz/185 g) baby spinach leaves

2 cups (8 oz/250 g) strawberries, hulled and sliced

¼ cup (1 oz/30 g) thinly sliced red onion

¼ cup (1 oz/30 g) pecans, toasted (page 264) and coarsely chopped

In a small bowl, whisk together the vinegar, sugar, poppy seeds, dry mustard, and a pinch each of salt and pepper. Whisking constantly, slowly add the oil, and continue to whisk until the vinaigrette is well combined.

In a large bowl, toss together the spinach, strawberries, onion slices, and pecans. Add half of the vinaigrette and toss gently. Add more vinaigrette as needed to lightly coat the ingredients. Serve right away.

Strawberry–Crème Fraîche Ice Cream

MAKES 6 SERVINGS

1 vanilla bean, split lengthwise

1 cup *each* (8 fl oz/250 ml) heavy (double) cream and whole milk

¾ cup (6 oz/185 g) sugar

Pinch of salt

4 large egg yolks

2 cups (8 oz/250 g) strawberries, hulled and cut into ½-inch (12-mm) pieces

1 tsp fresh lemon juice

1 cup (8 oz/250 g) crème fraîche

Combine the vanilla seeds and pod, the cream, milk, ½ cup (4 oz/125 g) of the sugar, and the salt in a saucepan and bring to a boil, stirring until the sugar is dissolved. Turn off the heat. In a large bowl, whisk the yolks. Whisk in 1 cup (8 fl oz/250 ml) of the warm cream mixture to the egg yolks. Add the yolk mixture back to the cream mixture and cook over low heat, stirring, until it coats the back of a spoon. Strain into a heatproof bowl and set into a bowl of ice water. Stir often until cool, about 30 minutes.

Purée half of the strawberries, the remaining ¼ cup (2 oz/60 g) sugar, and the lemon juice in a food processor. Stir the purée and crème fraîche into the cream mixture. Freeze in an ice cream maker. Just before the ice cream is done, add the remaining strawberries and finish freezing.

Strawberry Cornmeal Shortcake

MAKES 6 SERVINGS

3 cups (12 oz/375 g) strawberries, hulled and halved

4 Tbsp (2 oz/60 g) sugar, or to taste

Fresh lemon juice

1 cup (8 fl oz/250 ml) heavy (double) cream

¼ tsp pure vanilla extract

Cornmeal Shortcake (page 263), baked into one 9-inch (23-cm) round or six 2-inch (5-cm) rectangles

In a large bowl, stir together the strawberries and 3 Tbsp of the sugar, or more to taste. Let stand for 15 minutes to let the berries macerate. Add lemon juice to taste.

In another bowl, using a blender or whisk, beat the cream, remaining 1 Tbsp sugar, and the vanilla until soft peaks form.

Spoon the berries and their juice over the shortcake(s). Top with the whipped cream and serve right away.

FRAISES DES BOIS

Also called wild, wood, or alpine strawberries, these tiny foraged strawberries originating from France have an intense aroma that begins to fade as soon as they are picked. *Fraises des bois* are especially sweet and make an attractive presentation when used in tarts, parfaits, or as a simple garnish. Look for them in the spring, and use them as you would strawberries.

FRAISES DES BOIS PARFAIT

In a large bowl, whisk together ½ cup (4 fl oz/125 ml) cold heavy (double) cream, ¼ cup (1 oz/30 g) confectioners' (icing) sugar, 2 cups (16 oz/500 g) whole milk ricotta cheese and 1 tsp pure vanilla extract until smooth. Set aside. Using 1½ cups (6 oz/150 g) *fraises des bois*, place half in the bottom of 4 parfait glasses. Divide half of the ricotta mixture among each of the glasses. Divide 1 cup (5 oz/155 g)

chopped toasted almonds (page 264) evenly into each glass, then add another layer of the fraises des bois to each. Finish each parfait with another layer of the ricotta mixture and sprinkle any leftover fraises des bois or almonds on top. Makes 4 servings.

STRAWBERRY CORNMEAL SHORTCAKE

BABY ARUGULA SALAD WITH BERRIES & GORGONZOLA

Breakfast Polenta
with Blackberries

MAKES 4 SERVINGS

½ cup (5½ fl oz/170 ml) maple syrup

1½ tsp salt

1 cup (5 oz/155 g) coarse-ground polenta

1 cup (8 fl oz/250 ml) whole milk

½ cup (4 oz/125 g) mascarpone

1 cup (4 oz/120 g) blackberries

In a small saucepan over low heat, warm the maple syrup. Keep warm.

In a large, heavy saucepan, bring 3 cups (24 fl oz/750 ml) water and the salt to a boil. In a small bowl, stir together the polenta and milk. Gradually stir into the boiling water. Stirring constantly, bring the mixture back to a boil, about 2 minutes. Reduce the heat to medium-low and cook, stirring often, until the polenta is thick and creamy, about 25 minutes. Add up to ½ cup (4 fl oz/125 ml) water, 1 Tbsp at a time, if the polenta begins to stick. (Be careful, as the hot polenta can bubble and spatter.)

Divide the polenta among 4 shallow bowls. Drizzle each serving with 2 Tbsp of the warm maple syrup and top with about 2 Tbsp of the mascarpone. Top with the blackberries and serve right away.

Baby Arugula Salad with
Berries & Gorgonzola

MAKES 4–6 SERVINGS

3 Tbsp extra-virgin olive oil

2 Tbsp balsamic vinegar

Salt and freshly ground pepper

6 cups (6 oz/185 g) baby arugula (rocket)

½ lb (250 g) firm blue cheese, crumbled

1 cup (4 oz/125 g) fresh blackberries or blueberries

In a small bowl, whisk together the oil, vinegar, and salt and pepper to taste.

Place the arugula in a bowl. Add the cheese and toss to combine. Drizzle with the dressing and toss to coat evenly. Divide among serving plates, top with the berries, and serve right away.

Make this salad into a main course by adding Grilled Marinated Red Onions (page 136) and thinly sliced grilled steak.

Mixed Berry Cobbler
with Cinnamon

MAKES 4–6 SERVINGS

6 cups (1½ lb/750 g) mixed blackberries and raspberries

½ cup (4 oz/125 g) plus 2 Tbsp sugar

2 Tbsp all-purpose (plain) flour

1 Tbsp fresh lemon juice

¼ tsp ground cinnamon

Cobbler Crust (page 263)

Preheat the oven to 425°F (220°C). Lightly butter a shallow 2-qt (2-l) baking dish.

In a large saucepan over medium-high heat, warm the berries, the ½ cup sugar (4 oz/125 g), flour, lemon juice, and cinnamon until the juice begins to boil. Let cool.

Pour the berry mixture into the prepared dish, spreading evenly. Arrange the cobbler topping evenly on top, then sprinkle with the 2 Tbsp sugar.

Bake until the filling is bubbling and the topping is golden brown, about 25 minutes. Let cool to room temperature and serve right away.

GOLDEN RASPBERRIES

Harder to find than their red-colored counterparts, golden raspberries look similar to red raspberries except that their color ranges from pale yellow to deep gold and they have a slightly sweeter, honey-like flavor. Golden raspberries are in season only for a few weeks during the summer. Snap them up if you see them at the market, as their season is very short.

GOLDEN RASPBERRY TART

Process 8 graham crackers in a food processor until fine crumbs form. Add ½ cup (4 oz/125 g) unsalted butter, melted, and 2 Tbsp light brown sugar and process until combined. Transfer to a 9-inch (23-cm) tart pan with a removable bottom. Press into the bottom and up the sides of the pan. Bake in a preheated 350°F (180°C) oven until set, about 10 minutes. Let cool completely on a rack. In a bowl, beat 1 cup

(8 oz/250 g) room-temperature mascarpone, 1 tsp pure vanilla extract, and ⅓ cup (1½ oz/45 g) confectioners' (icing) sugar and beat until fluffy. Spread the mixture evenly over the cooled crust. Place 4 cups (1 lb/500 g) golden raspberries on top of the mascarpone. Heat ¼ cup (2½ oz/75 g) apricot jelly with 1 tsp water. Brush over the fruit. Makes 6–8 servings.

BUYING BLUEBERRIES

For the freshest fruit, look for firm, dry, and smooth blueberries that retain a powdery white bloom on their surfaces. They can be refrigerated in an airtight container for up to 1 week or frozen to enjoy during the off-season. Freeze blueberries in a single layer on a baking sheet and then transfer them to an airtight container.

Blueberries

The smooth, dark blue spheres of blueberries range in size from the diameter of a small pea up to a marble. The smallest yet most intensely flavored varieties grow wild on low-growing bushes in colder climates. Wild blueberries from Maine and Nova Scotia are legendary among cooks, who prize them for their complexity and richness in pies, cobblers, and jams. Some farmers have succeeded in cultivating close cousins of these wild varieties. Look for these smaller, darker blueberries in markets during the mid-summer months to enjoy their balance of tartness and sweetness.

Blueberries are especially popular at the breakfast table. They can be folded easily into batters for pancakes, coffee cakes, or muffins, and spooned over waffles, yogurt, or cereal. Like many of their cousins in the berry family, blueberries shine beautifully in tarts, pies, ice cream, and other colorful desserts.

WORKING WITH BLUEBERRIES

Ripe blueberries are fragile and should be handled with care. If any stems remain, pinch them off and discard. Rinse the berries with cool water just before using and let drain on paper towels. To encourage even distribution in muffin or cake batters, gently toss the berries while still moist with a small amount of flour reserved from the recipe before folding them in.

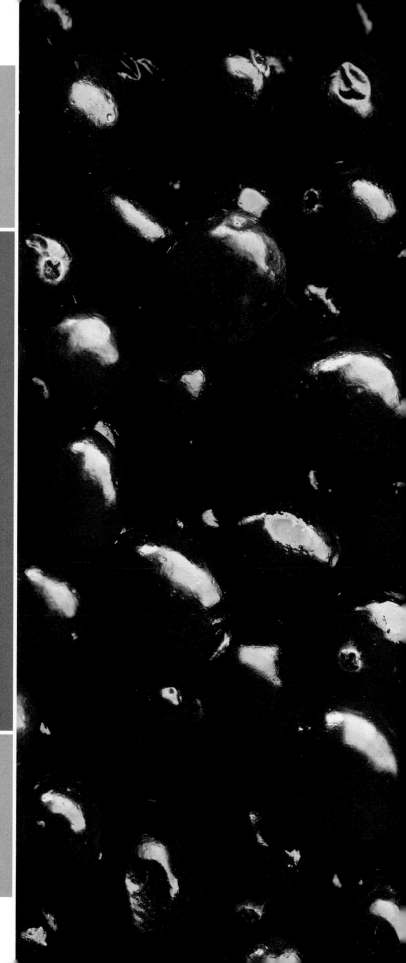

BUYING CRANBERRIES

Ranging from light red to deep scarlet, cranberries should be plump, firm, shiny, and dry. Avoid berries that are shriveled or have a dull skin. Cranberries can be stored in a tightly covered container in the refrigerator for at least 1 month. They can also be frozen for up to 10 months.

Cranberries

One of the few fruits native to North America, the bright red, round cranberry is an integral part of American cooking. Cranberry relishes, jellies and sauces provide essential counterpoints of refreshing tartness in the holiday feasts of the autumn and winter months. Native to wetland areas, cranberries are now harvested from specially flooded fields across the northern regions of the continent.

Look for fresh, whole cranberries throughout the late autumn and early winter months. For sweet and savory preparations, they marry well with nuts, grains, and other autumn fruits such as apples and pears. Too sour and astringent to eat raw on their own, the berries typically appear with sweet ingredients to balance their assertive flavors. Some farmers dry their cranberries and offer them as colorful alternatives to raisins for pilafs, fillings, breads, and desserts.

WORKING WITH CRANBERRIES

Rinse cranberries in cold water just before using. Discard any that show brown spots or feel soft to the touch. Chop them while fresh to cook in pilafs and fillings. For a smoother texture, simmer cranberries in stock, wine, liqueur, orange juice, or water until they burst. There is no need to thaw frozen cranberries before cooking them.

Buttermilk Blueberry Pancakes

MAKES 6–8 SERVINGS

2 cups (10 oz/315 g) all-purpose (plain) flour

2 tsp baking powder

1 tsp *each* baking soda (bicarbonate of soda) and salt

2 large eggs

2 cups (16 fl oz/500 ml) buttermilk

4 Tbsp (2 oz/60 g) unsalted butter, melted and cooled, plus extra for greasing

2 cups (8 oz/250 g) blueberries

In a bowl, sift together the flour, baking powder, baking soda, and salt. In another bowl, beat together the eggs and buttermilk. Mix the liquids into the dry ingredients with a large wooden spoon until a smooth batter forms. Fold in the 4 Tbsp (2 oz/60 g) melted butter and the blueberries.

Preheat a large frying pan over medium-high heat. Brush with melted butter. For each pancake, ladle 2 Tbsp of the batter, forming circles 4–5 inches (10–13 cm) in diameter. Cook until browned on the bottom and bubbles appear on the surface, about 3 minutes. Turn and cook until lightly browned on the second side, about 3 minutes longer. Transfer to a plate and keep warm in a low oven. Brush the pan with more butter as needed between batches. Serve right away.

Blueberry-Vanilla Panna Cotta

MAKES 4 SERVINGS

2½ tsp (1 package) unflavored gelatin

¼ cup (2 fl oz/60 ml) whole milk

2 cups (16 fl oz/500 ml) heavy (double) cream

¼ cup (2 oz/60 g) sugar

1 vanilla bean

1 tsp pure vanilla extract

2 cups (8 oz/250 g) blueberries, plus extra for garnish

In a bowl, sprinkle the gelatin over the milk. Let stand for about 2 minutes. In a saucepan over medium heat, stir together the cream and sugar. Using a small knife, split the vanilla bean in half lengthwise. Scrape the seeds into the cream and add the pod. Heat, stirring, until small bubbles appear around the edges of the pan. Let cool briefly.

Remove the vanilla bean. Slowly add the warm cream to the gelatin mixture, stirring constantly until dissolved. Stir in the vanilla extract and 2 cups blueberries and then pour into four ¾-cup (6–fl oz/180-ml) ramekins, dividing evenly. Cover and refrigerate for 4 hours or up to overnight.

Run a thin knife around the inside of each ramekin, and invert onto a dessert plate. Garnish with blueberries and serve right away.

Blueberry Summer Pudding

MAKES 6–8 SERVINGS

6 cups (1½ lb/750 g) blueberries

½ cup (4 oz/125 g) granulated sugar

1 Tbsp fresh lemon juice

2 tsp finely grated lemon zest

Pinch of salt

1 tsp pure vanilla extract

12 slices challah, about ½ inch (12 mm) thick

1 cup (8 fl oz/250 ml) heavy (double) cream

2 Tbsp confectioners' (icing) sugar

½ tsp ground cinnamon

In a large saucepan, combine 2 cups (8 oz/250 g) of the blueberries, the granulated sugar, lemon juice and zest, and the salt and bring to a boil over high heat. Reduce the heat to medium, and cook, stirring occasionally and gently crushing some of the berries as they soften, until the berries are juicy and thickened, 6–8 minutes. Remove from the heat and stir in the remaining 4 cups (1 lb/500 g) berries and the vanilla.

Line a 6-cup (48–fl oz/1.5-l) bowl with plastic wrap, leaving a 3-inch (7.5-cm) overhang. Line the prepared bowl with the bread, covering it completely and cutting the bread so that it fits in a single layer. Pour in the berry mixture and top with the remaining bread slices to cover completely. Cover with the overhanging plastic wrap and then with a plate just slightly smaller than the diameter of the bowl. Weight with a can. Refrigerate overnight or for up to 24 hours.

To serve, in a bowl, whip the cream, confectioners' sugar, and cinnamon until soft peaks form. Remove the can, plate, and plastic wrap from the pudding. Unmold onto a plate. Cut the wedges and serve right away with the whipped cream.

HUCKLEBERRIES

A close relative of the blueberry, huckleberries are also called whortleberries. They tend to be seedier and a little tarter. One variety grows on the East Coast and another on the West Coast of the United States. Use them in recipes that call for blueberries or for sauces for wild game. Look for them in the summer when other berries are in season at the market.

HUCKLEBERRY CRISP

Stir together ⅔ cup (5 oz/155 g) sugar, ¼ cup (1½ oz/45 g) flour, ⅛ tsp salt, 1 Tbsp grated orange zest, and 1 tsp pure vanilla extract. Scatter the sugar mixture over 6 cups (1½ lb/750 g) huckleberries and mix well. Pour into a 10-inch (25-cm) buttered baking dish. Pat Crisp Topping (page 263) evenly over the top. Bake in a 350°F (180°C) oven until the topping is golden brown, 25–30 minutes. Makes 4 servings.

BLUEBERRY-VANILLA PANNA COTTA

TART CRANBERRY SORBET

Fresh Cranberry Scones

MAKES 10–12 SCONES

1½ cups (7½ oz/235 g) all-purpose (plain) flour

1½ Tbsp sugar

½ tsp baking powder

¼ tsp salt

7 Tbsp (3½ oz/105 g) chilled unsalted butter, cut into small pieces

1 cup (4 oz/125 g) cranberries

1 egg, lightly beaten

2 Tbsp fresh orange juice

Preheat the oven to 400°F (200°C).

In a bowl, whisk together the flour, sugar, baking powder, and salt. Cut in the butter with a pastry blender or 2 knives until the mixture resembles rolled oats. Stir in the cranberries. Using a fork, mix in the egg and orange juice until a soft dough forms.

On a floured work surface, roll out the dough into a round ½ inch (12 mm) thick. Using a 2-inch (5-cm) round cookie cutter, cut out as many rounds as possible. Gather the dough scraps, roll out again, and cut more rounds. Place on an ungreased baking sheet.

Bake until lightly golden, about 15 minutes. Watch carefully so that the bottoms do not burn. Transfer to a rack and let cool, 2–3 minutes. Serve warm.

Cranberry-Orange Relish

MAKES 4 SERVINGS

1 thin-skinned orange with peel intact, cut into 8 wedges

3 cups (¾ lb/375 g) cranberries

¾ cup (6 oz/185 g) sugar, or to taste

Remove any seeds from the orange wedges, then cut each wedge in half crosswise. In a food processor, finely combine half of the orange pieces, the cranberries, and ¾ cup sugar. Transfer to a bowl. Repeat with the remaining orange pieces, cranberries, and sugar. Add to the bowl. Taste and add more sugar, if the relish is too tart. Cover and refrigerate until well chilled.

This relish is a delicious accompaniment to simple pan-seared turkey cutlets or chicken breasts, or as a condiment for traditional roast turkey.

Tart Cranberry Sorbet

MAKES 4 SERVINGS

2 cups (8 oz/250 g) cranberries

½ cup (4 fl oz/125 ml) cranberry juice

1½ cups (10½ oz/330 g) superfine (caster) sugar

In a small saucepan over medium-low heat, heat the cranberries and cranberry juice, stirring occasionally, until the cranberries pop, 5–7 minutes. Stir in the sugar until it has dissolved. Let cool, cover, and refrigerate until well chilled, about 2 hours.

Pour the cranberry mixture into an ice-cream maker and freeze according to the manufacturer's instructions. Serve right away.

For a firmer texture, pack into freezerproof containers and freeze until firm, about 3 hours.

Citrus

The family of flowering plants classified as citrus are marked by pulpy flesh and slightly bumpy skin with yellow, orange, and red tones. They grow on trees or large shrubs with evergreen leaves that also produce intensely scented white flowers. Nearly all parts of a citrus fruit—the flesh, the juice, and the zest—are consumed or used in cooking. The flesh can be tart, like that of most lemons and grapefruits, or sweet, like that of oranges and tangerines. Even individual varieties of a fruit, such as pomelos, can range from sweet to pleasingly acidic.

Analysis of fossil records suggests that citrus fruits are among the oldest known fruits. Most citrus fruits familiar today originated in Asia and gradually spread to Europe and the Americas. The trees thrive in tropical and temperate climates, such as areas of China, the Mediterranean, South America, and the United States including Florida, Texas, Arizona, and parts of California. Many citrus hybrids have been discovered or intentionally propagated. The popular sweet-tart Meyer lemon, for instance, is believed to be a cross between a lemon and a mandarin orange.

In those regions where citrus fruits can be grown, a type of citrus is being harvested in every season.

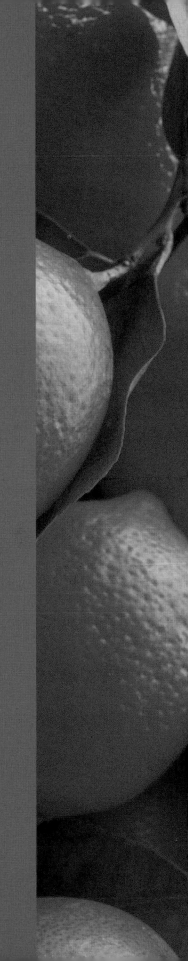

Lemons

Lemons have long been important in kitchens around the world and play a fundamental role in the cuisines of the Mediterranean region. The fruit's tart juice and aromatic, oil-rich zest contribute flavor to countless dishes. Small and oval in shape, the lemon was first cultivated in tropical regions of Asia. Lisbon and Eureka are the most popular varieties among growers for their large fruit, distinct sourness, and thick, protective piths. The smaller, rounder, more fragile Meyer lemon has a floral fragrance and sweeter flavor.

Though widely available throughout the year, lemons come to peak season in the winter and early spring in the mild climates where they are grown. They brighten soups, finish sauces, marinate meats, garnish vegetables, and flavor refreshing drinks and classic cocktails. Lemon's fruity tartness makes it one of the most popular flavors for sweets and desserts.

Limes

Smaller than lemons, the fruits of the evergreen lime tree have a distinctive sweetness that tempers their tartness. Their green zest offers a fragrant, almost floral aroma. Limes are an essential souring ingredient in the cuisines of Latin America, Africa, India, Southeast Asia, and the Pacific Islands. The most common variety sold in North America and Europe is the round, dark green Persian lime (also known as Tahitian lime) that grows in tropical zones. Key limes, the star of Florida's famous pies, and Mexican limes, are much smaller and more delicate than the Persian lime. Tiny calamansi limes have orange flesh and fragrant, sour juice that smells and tastes of tangerines.

Limes are at their peak flavor from late summer to late autumn. Their sour, slightly bitter juice holds up well in savory dishes such as ceviche, desserts such as lime curd bars, and in countless drinks and cocktails.

Fusilli with Lemon Zest & Ricotta

MAKES 6 SERVINGS

1 Tbsp olive oil

1 Tbsp minced garlic

1 cup (8 oz/250 g) ricotta cheese

1 cup (8 fl oz/250 ml) heavy (double) cream

1 Tbsp grated Meyer lemon zest plus extra for garnish

2 tsp fresh lemon juice

Salt and freshly ground pepper

1 lb (500 g) dried fusilli pasta

Bring a large pot of generously salted water to a boil over high heat.

In a small frying pan over medium heat, warm the olive oil. Add the garlic and sauté until golden brown, 2–3 minutes. Transfer to a bowl and set aside.

Add the ricotta, cream, 1 Tbsp lemon zest, lemon juice, a pinch of salt, and 1 tsp pepper to the bowl.

Add the fusilli to the boiling water and cook until al dente, 8–10 minutes or according to the package directions. Drain and return to the pot. Add the ricotta mixture and stir well. Heat over medium heat for 1–2 minutes. Spoon into individual bowls, garnish with lemon zest and serve right away.

Sautéed Snapper Fillets with Caramelized Lemons

MAKES 4 SERVINGS

4 snapper fillets, about 6 oz (180 g) each, skin removed

Salt and freshly ground pepper

2 Tbsp unsalted butter

3 Tbsp olive oil

1 fennel bulb, trimmed, cored and thinly sliced

1 lemon, cut into slices ⅛ inch (3 mm) thick

½ tsp sugar

2 tsp minced fresh dill

Sprinkle the fillets generously with salt and pepper. In a large nonstick frying pan over medium-high heat, melt 1 Tbsp of the butter with 1 Tbsp of the oil. Add the fennel and a pinch each of salt and pepper. Cook, stirring, until the fennel is just tender, about 5 minutes. Transfer to a platter and cover with aluminum foil. Add the remaining 1 Tbsp butter and another 1 Tbsp of oil to the pan. Add the fillets, skin side down, and cook, turning once, until opaque, 2–3 minutes on each side. Place on top of the fennel.

Add the remaining 1 Tbsp olive oil and the lemon slices to the pan. Sprinkle with the sugar and cook, stirring, until the lemons are golden, 2–3 minutes. Scatter the caramelized lemons over the fish and fennel, and add any juices from the pan. Sprinkle with the dill and serve right away.

Lemon Sorbet with Fresh Basil

MAKES 6 SERVINGS

1½ cups (12 oz/375 g) sugar

½ cup (½ oz/15 g) fresh basil leaves

1 cup (8 fl oz/250 ml) fresh lemon juice

Pinch of salt

In a saucepan over medium-high heat, cook 2½ cups (20 fl oz/625 ml) water, the sugar, and half of the basil leaves, stirring until the sugar is dissolved, 3–4 minutes. Let cool completely. Strain the resulting sugar syrup into a bowl and discard the basil. Stir in the lemon juice and the salt.

Transfer the mixture to an ice cream maker and freeze according to the manufacturer's instructions. About 10 minutes before the sorbet is done, cut the remaining basil into thin ribbons. Add the basil to the ice cream maker and finish freezing the sorbet. Serve right away.

For a firmer texture, pack into freezerproof containers and freeze until firm, about 3 hours.

MEYER LEMONS

The Meyer lemon, a hybrid imported from China, was discovered in 1908. It now proliferates in California and other Mediterranean climates and is believed to be a cross between a Eureka lemon and a mandarin orange, as hinted at by its rounder shape, yellow orange color, sweeter flavor, and flowery fragrance. It's peak seasons are winter through spring. Use in savory dishes and desserts.

MEYER LEMON CURD

In the top of a double boiler, whisk together 3 large eggs; 3 large egg yolks; ¾ cup (6 fl oz/ 180 ml) Meyer lemon juice, strained; and 1 cup (8 oz/250 g) sugar until the sugar dissolves. Place over (not touching) barely simmering water and add 6 Tbsp (3 oz/90 g) unsalted butter, cut into ¾-inch (2-cm) cubes. Using a large wooden spoon, stir constantly until the butter melts and the mixture is thick enough to coat the back of a spoon, about 12 minutes. Remove from over the water and strain through a fine-mesh sieve placed over a bowl. Let cool, cover, and place in the refrigerator for 3–5 hours to thicken. The curd will keep in the refrigerator for up to 3 days. Use as a spread for scones and muffins or stir into whipped cream and serve with fresh strawberries. Makes 1 cup (9 oz/280 g).

FUSILLI WITH LEMON ZEST & RICOTTA

LIME CURD BARS WITH COCONUT CRUST

Ceviche with Lime & Herbs

MAKES 6 SERVINGS

1 lb (500 g) boneless firm white-fleshed fish, such as snapper or halibut, cut into ½-inch (12-mm) pieces

1⅓ cups (11 fl oz/330 ml) fresh lime juice

¼ cup (1½ oz/45 g) minced white onion

1 red jalapeño chile, minced

1 avocado, peeled, pitted, and diced

¼ cup (⅓ oz/10 g) minced fresh cilantro (fresh coriander)

2 Tbsp finely chopped fresh mint

Salt and freshly ground pepper

Tortilla chips for serving

In a bowl, stir together the fish pieces, lime juice, onion, and jalapeño. Cover and refrigerate until the fish is opaque throughout, 30–60 minutes.

Using a slotted spoon, transfer the fish, onions, and jalapeño to another bowl, leaving the liquid behind. Stir in the avocado, cilantro, mint, and a pinch each of salt and pepper. Taste, and add some of the marinade if desired for more acidity. Serve right away with the tortilla chips.

Lime & White Chocolate Mousse

MAKES 6 SERVINGS

8 oz (250 g) good-quality white chocolate, finely chopped

½ cup (4 oz/125 g) sugar

2 Tbsp fresh lime juice

1½ Tbsp finely grated lime zest

Pinch of coarse salt

1½ cups (12 fl oz/375 ml) heavy (double) cream

Put the white chocolate in a heatproof bowl. In a small saucepan over medium-high heat, cook the sugar, 3 Tbsp water, the lime juice, half of the lime zest, and the salt, stirring occasionally, until the sugar dissolves, 2–3 minutes. Pour over the chocolate, let stand for 1 minute, and then stir until smooth. Let stand at room temperature, about 15 minutes.

In a bowl, whip the cream until it holds stiff peaks. Gently fold the cream into the white chocolate mixture. Transfer to 6 serving dishes. Garnish with the remaining lime zest. Serve right away (for a thicker, denser mousse, cover and refrigerate 4–6 hours before garnishing and serving.)

Lime Curd Bars with Coconut Crust

MAKES 2 DOZEN BARS

1 cup (8 oz/250 g) unsalted butter, softened

⅓ cup (2½ oz/75 g) light brown sugar

2 cups (10 oz/315 g) all-purpose (plain) flour

Grated zest of 1 lime, plus extra for garnish

½ cup (2 oz/60 g) shredded dried coconut

¼ tsp salt

1¾ cups (14 oz/440 g) granulated sugar

1 Tbsp cornstarch (cornflour)

1 tsp baking powder

4 large eggs

¾ cup (6 fl oz/180 ml) fresh lime juice

Confectioners' (icing) sugar for dusting

Preheat the oven to 350°F (180°C). Line a 9-by-13-inch (23-by-33-cm) baking dish with aluminum foil, overhanging the edges by 1 inch (2.5 cm). In a mixer fitted with the paddle attachment, beat the butter and brown sugar until fluffy, 3–4 minutes. Add the flour, half of the lime zest, coconut, and half of the salt and mix until the dough just holds together. Press into the pan and prick with a fork. Bake until golden, 20–25 minutes.

In the mixer, combine the granulated sugar, cornstarch, baking powder, and remaining lime zest and salt. Slowly beat in the eggs and lime juice. Pour into the crust. Bake for 20–25 minutes. Cool and then refrigerate until set, 1–2 hours. Cut into 24 bars and dust with confectioners' sugar and lime zest.

KEY LIMES

Grown in southern Florida and Mexico, Key limes, are small, round fruits that have a thin, leathery skin, a yellowish rind, and green flesh with an abundance of seeds. Extremely tart, Key limes lend their flavor and name to the famous pie and can also be used in other desserts, such as lime curd bars. Look for them in the summer.

KEY LIME PIE

Process 8 gingersnaps in a food processor until fine crumbs form. Add ½ cup (4 oz/125 g) unsalted butter, melted, and 2 Tbsp light brown sugar and process until combined. Transfer to a 9-inch (23-cm) pie pan. Press into the bottom and up the sides of the pan. Bake in a preheated 350°F (180°C) oven until the crust is set, about 10 minutes. Let cool completely on a rack. Keep the oven on. In a bowl, whisk together

7 large egg yolks and 4 tsp key lime zest. Add 2 cans (14 fl oz/430 ml) sweetened condensed milk and 1 cup (8 fl oz/250 ml) fresh Key lime juice, strained (from about 24 limes) and whisk again until well blended. Pour the filling into the graham cracker crust. Bake until the filling is firm in the center 20–24 minutes. Transfer to a wire rack and let cool. Refrigerate until firm, 2–3 hours. Serve with whipped cream. Makes 8 servings.

BUYING ORANGES

The juiciest oranges are heavy for their size and have firm, smooth skins free of bruising, mold, deep wrinkles, or soft spots. Valencia oranges may sport green-tinged areas, which will not affect their flavor. Better quality navel oranges have smaller, tighter navels. Oranges can be stored at room temperature for several days or refrigerated in a plastic bag for up to 3 weeks.

Oranges

First cultivated in China over 2,000 years ago, orange trees now grow in mild climates around the world. Many varieties of the fruit fall into two broad categories: sweet and bitter. Among the most popular sweet orange is the Valencia, considered best for juicing because of its thin skin and juicy pulp. Navel oranges are sweet, easy to peel, and ideal for eating out of hand. Blood oranges have distinctive deep red colored flesh and sweet flavor. The two most common bitter oranges are Seville and Bergamot.

Oranges are in peak season during late winter and early spring. In Latin America, orange juice is the base of marinades for meat and seafood. In Europe, its candied peel appears in desserts and holiday breads, while throughout Asia, oranges are given as auspicious gifts. Bitter oranges have a pungent sourness that holds up to sugar. Their peels are used to make marmalades, liqueurs and confections.

WORKING WITH ORANGES

Before peeling an orange, squeeze it between your palms or roll it on a countertop, pressing down firmly. This will make the orange a little juicier and easier to peel. To juice an orange, cut the orange in half and use a juicer or reamer to extract the liquid. To remove the zest from an orange or to segment oranges, see page 264.

BUYING TANGERINES & MANDARINS

Choose fruits that are deep in color, heavy for their size, and free of dull or soft spots. Although some will have loose skins, avoid those that appear overly bumpy, which indicates that they are overripe. The fruits will keep at room temperature for up to 1 week or in a plastic bag in the refrigerator for up to 1 month.

Tangerines & Mandarins

Named after officials in Chinese imperial courts who once wore orange robes and headpieces topped with large, round buttons, mandarins tend to be smaller and slightly flatter in shape than oranges. Tangerines, most notably the red-orange Darcy from Florida, are the most recognizable class within the mandarin family. Other popular members include the Satsuma, originally from Japan; the smooth, seedless Clementine widely grown in Algeria and Spain; and tangelos such as the honey-flavored Minneola tangelo.

Like other citrus fruit, they come to market from early winter to early spring. They are ideal for flavoring and garnishing desserts such as ice cream, sorbets, custards, and cream-filled cakes and pastries. They also shine in delicate sauces for fish, pork, chicken, and duck.

WORKING WITH TANGERINES & MANDARINS

Juice mandarins as you would other citrus: bring them to room temperature, cut them in half, use a reamer or juicer attachment, and strain seeds and membranes before adding to recipes. Their segments should be added at the end of cooking and just heated through to preserve their delicate texture. To segment the fruits, see page 264.

Orange & Red Onion Salad

MAKES 6 SERVINGS

6 navel oranges, segmented (page 264), with juice reserved

½ tsp grainy mustard

Salt and freshly ground pepper

3 Tbsp extra-virgin olive oil

2 hearts romaine (cos) lettuce, cut crosswise into ½-inch (12-mm) pieces

1 small red onion, thinly sliced

Small wedge of aged hard cheese, such as Pecorino

2 Tbsp minced fresh chives

Place 2 Tbsp of the orange juice in a small bowl. Add the mustard and a generous pinch each of salt and pepper. Whisking constantly, slowly add the oil until well combined.

Place the orange segments in a large bowl. Add the romaine and onion. Add half of the dressing and toss to coat. Add more dressing if needed to coat the lettuce leaves. Using a vegetable peeler, shave the cheese evenly over the top. Sprinkle with the chives and serve right away.

Pan-Seared Scallops with Sautéed Oranges

MAKES 4 SERVINGS

1 *each* navel orange and blood orange, with juice reserved

Salt and freshly ground pepper

½ tsp ground cumin

1 lb (500 g) large sea scallops

1 Tbsp olive oil

2 tsp sherry vinegar

1 Tbsp unsalted butter

2 tsp chopped fresh cilantro (fresh coriander)

Cut the oranges into thin rounds. In a small dish, combine a pinch each of salt and pepper with the cumin. Sprinkle the scallops with the seasoning mixture. In a frying pan over medium-high heat, warm the olive oil. Cook until browned on the bottom side, 1–2 minutes. Turn and cook on the other side until just firm to the touch and still a bit translucent in the center, 1–2 minutes longer. Transfer to a plate and keep warm.

Add the vinegar and reserved orange juice to the pan and cook until reduced by half, 1–2 minutes. Add the orange slices and cook for 1 minute. Remove from the heat and stir in the butter. Return the scallops along with and any juices to the pan and stir to coat with the sauce. Transfer to plates, top with the sauce and oranges, sprinkle with cilantro, and serve right away.

Orange Custard with Caramelized Oranges

MAKES 6 SERVINGS

¾ cup (6 oz/185 g) sugar

¼ cup (1 oz/30 g) cornstarch (cornflour)

1 vanilla bean, split lengthwise

2 cups (16 fl oz/500 ml) whole milk

½ cup (4 fl oz/125 ml) heavy (double) cream

3 large egg yolks

½ cup (4 fl oz/125 ml) fresh orange juice

2 Tbsp unsalted butter

Pinch of salt

1 navel orange

½ tsp ground cinnamon

In a saucepan, whisk together ½ cup (4 oz/125 g) of the sugar and the cornstarch. Scrape the seeds from the vanilla bean and add to the pan with the pod. Whisk in the milk and cream. Bring to a boil over medium-high heat, then reduce the heat to medium-low.

In a small bowl, whisk together the egg yolks. Whisk ½ cup (4 fl oz/125 ml) of the warm milk mixture into the yolks. Return to the saucepan with the cream mixture and stir gently until thickened, 2–3 minutes. Remove from the heat and stir in the orange juice, 1 Tbsp of the butter, and the salt.

Divide the mixture among 6 custard cups and let cool. Cover with plastic wrap and refrigerate for 4 hours or for up to overnight. Remove from the refrigerator 30 minutes before serving.

Before serving, cut away the skin and white pith from the orange (page 264), then cut crosswise into 6 slices. Heat the remaining 1 Tbsp of butter in a nonstick frying pan over medium heat. Add the remaining ¼ cup (2 oz/60 g) sugar and the cinnamon and cook, stirring, until the sugar begins to caramelize. Add the orange slices and cook, turning once, until caramelized, 2–3 minutes. Place an orange slice on top of each custard and serve right away.

BLOOD ORANGES

Originally from Sicily, blood oranges have a distinctive red flesh and juice and a flavor reminiscent of berries. Varieties include Moro, Cara Cara, and Sanguinello. As versatile as they are dramatic, blood oranges can be eaten out of hand or used in salads, sauces, desserts, and drinks.

BLOOD ORANGE MIMOSA

Squeeze the juice from 2–4 blood oranges. Measure ½ cup (4 fl oz/125 ml) juice; reserve the rest for another use. In a small pitcher, combine the orange juice, and ¼ cup (2 fl oz/60 ml) orange liqueur. Divide the mixture among 4 Champagne flutes. Top with Champagne or Prosecco and stir to combine. Garnish each glass with a blood orange slice and serve right away. Makes 4 servings.

PAN-SEARED SCALLOPS WITH SAUTÉED ORANGES

TOASTED POUND CAKE WITH SPICED CLEMENTINES

Tangerine, Fennel & Olive Salad

MAKES 6 SERVINGS

2 Tbsp extra-virgin olive oil

4 seedless tangerines, segmented (page 264) with juice reserved

Salt and freshly ground pepper

2 fennel bulbs, fronds reserved

½ cup (½ oz/15 g) fresh flat-leaf (Italian) parsley leaves

⅔ cup (3 oz/90 g) kalamata olives, pitted and halved

In a small bowl, stir the olive oil into the reserved tangerine juice with a pinch each of salt and pepper to make a dressing.

Using a sharp knife, shave the fennel bulb into thin slices. Place in a bowl and drizzle with a spoonful of the dressing. Arrange on a platter. Toss the tangerine slices in some of the dressing and arrange on top of the fennel. Top with the parsley and olives, and drizzle with more dressing. Coarsely chop 2 Tbsp of the fennel fronds and sprinkle over the top. Serve right away.

Tangerine Relish with Shallots & Mint

MAKES 4 SERVINGS

2 seedless tangerines, segmented (page 264) with juice reserved

2 tsp minced shallot

2 tsp chopped fresh mint

1 tsp balsamic vinegar

1 tsp chopped fresh flat-leaf (Italian) parsley

Salt and freshly ground pepper

1 Tbsp extra-virgin olive oil

Cut the tangerine segments into ¼-inch (6-mm) pieces and put in a bowl. Add the shallot, mint, vinegar, parsley, and 1 Tbsp of the reserved tangerine juice and stir to combine. Stir in a pinch each of salt and pepper and the olive oil. Serve right away.

Serve tangerine relish alongside seared duck breast halves or roast pork tenderloin.

Toasted Pound Cake with Spiced Clementines

MAKES 6 SERVINGS

½ cup (4 oz/125 g) sugar

4 allspice berries, lightly crushed

2 *each* cinnamon sticks and peppercorns, lightly crushed

1 star anise, lightly crushed

1 vanilla bean, split lengthwise

6 clementines

6 slices purchased pound cake, each about ½ inch (12 mm) thick

¼ cup (⅓ oz/10 g) fresh mint leaves, cut into thin ribbons

In a saucepan, combine the sugar, allspice, cinnamon sticks, peppercorns, and star anise with ½ cup (4 fl oz/125 ml) water. Scrape the seeds from the vanilla bean and add to the pan with the pod. Bring to a boil, stirring to dissolve the sugar. Remove from the heat and let steep for 30 minutes. Strain into a bowl, discarding the spices.

Cut away the skin and pith from the clementines (page 264). Cut crosswise into thin slices. Add to the syrup, cover, and refrigerate overnight. Bring to room temperature before using.

Preheat the oven to 400°F (200°C). Place the cake slices on a baking sheet. Bake until lightly browned on both sides, 5–6 minutes. Place the clementines and syrup in a serving bowl and sprinkle with mint. Serve right away alongside the toasted pound cake slices.

SATSUMA MANDARINS

Originally from Japan, the Satsuma is a sweet, seedless type of mandarin orange that is distinguishable by its thin, loose, and leathery skin, which allows it to be peeled very easily. Select Satsumas that are slightly soft, yet heavy for their size. Avoid fruits that are overly soft or are starting to show even small spots of brown. Use in salads, desserts, or simply eat out of hand.

MANDARIN & DATE COMPOTE

In a saucepan over medium heat, warm 1 cup (8 fl oz/250 ml) water and 1 cup (8 oz/250 g) sugar, stirring often until the sugar dissolves and a thin syrup forms, 6–7 minutes. Add 1 Tbsp grated orange zest, reduce the heat to low, and simmer, uncovered, to blend the flavors, about 30 minutes. Cut away the skin and pith (page 264) from 6 Satsuma mandarins, removing as much of the white membrane as possible.

Cut crosswise into slices ¼ inch (6 mm) thick. Place in a heatproof bowl, pour in the hot syrup, and let stand at room temperature for 1 hour. Spoon the Satsuma slices and some of the syrup into bowls and add 8 dates, pitted and halved. Makes 4 servings.

BUYING GRAPEFRUITS

Choose smooth-skinned grapefruits that are firm and heavy for their size. Avoid those that have bruises or soft spots. Small and shallow blemishes do not generally indicate poor quality, nor does the color of the peel reveal the sweetness or ripeness of the fruit within. Store at room temperature for 1 week or in a plastic bag in the refrigerator for up to 3 weeks.

Grapefruits

The grapefruit first appeared in the eighteenth century as a hybrid of the orange and the pomelo. Its name refers to how the fruit grows in large clusters on the tree much like grapes on the vine. The large fruit has a wealth of juice and a tart, refreshing flavor that varies by type. Some can be quite sweet, while others carry pleasantly bitter undertones. All grapefruit have yellow peels, and some display varying intensities of pink or red blush covering the fruit. Their pulp ranges in color from white to pale pink to ruby red. Popular varieties include Ruby Red, Rio Red, Ruby Sweet, and Oroblanco.

Grown in warm climates, grapefruit reaches peak flavor during the winter months. Ubiquitous on breakfast tables, simply sliced in half or pressed into juice, grapefruit also appears in savory dishes such as butter sauces for fish or refreshing salads, especially when paired with buttery avocado or earthy spinach.

WORKING WITH GRAPEFRUITS

To halve grapefruits, cut them along their equators between the stem and blossom ends. For easier eating, use a paring knife to cut along each membrane wall and just inside the white pith. To obtain whole segments free of peel and pith, see page 264.

Broiled Grapefruit with Brown Sugar

MAKES 6 SERVINGS

3 grapefruits

6 Tbsp (2½ oz/75 g) light brown sugar

Preheat a broiler (grill). Line a baking sheet with aluminum foil.

Halve the grapefruits crosswise. Arrange the grapefruit halves, cut sides up, on the prepared sheet. Sprinkle each half evenly with 1 Tbsp of the brown sugar. Place under the broiler about 4 inches (10 cm) from the heat source. Broil (grill) until the sugar has melted and is bubbling, 2–3 minutes. Transfer to a platter and serve right away.

Any grapefruit variety can be used for this dish. If desired, use a serrated knife to separate the segments before broiling the fruit.

Grapefruit, Avocado & Crab Salad

MAKES 6 SERVINGS

2 pink grapefruits, segmented (page 264) and juice reserved

2 tsp white wine vinegar

1 Tbsp minced shallot

1 Tbsp minced fresh chives

Salt and freshly ground pepper

3 Tbsp extra-virgin olive oil

1 head butter (Boston) lettuce, leaves separated and torn into small pieces

2 firm but ripe avocados, cut into ½-inch (12-mm) slices

½ lb (250 g) fresh lump crabmeat

In a small bowl, whisk together 2 tsp of the grapefruit juice with the vinegar, shallot, chives, and a pinch each of salt and pepper. Whisking constantly, slowly add the oil until well combined to make a vinaigrette.

In a bowl, toss the lettuce with 1 Tbsp of the vinaigrette. Divide the lettuce leaves among 6 salad plates. Gently toss the avocado slices in 1 Tbsp of the vinaigrette and place a few slices on each plate. Place the grapefruit slices, lettuce, avocado, and crabmeat on a platter or in a serving bowl. Drizzle some of the vinaigrette over the top and toss until lightly coated. Season with salt and pepper, and serve right away.

Mint-Infused Grapefruit Sorbet

MAKES 6 SERVINGS

1 cup (8 oz/250 g) sugar

½ cup (½ oz/15 g) fresh mint leaves

1½ cups (12 fl oz/375 ml) fresh grapefruit juice

Pinch of salt

In a saucepan, heat 2 cups (16 fl oz/500 ml) water, the sugar, and half of the mint leaves over medium-high heat, stirring until the sugar is completely dissolved, 3–4 minutes. Let cool completely. Strain the resulting sugar syrup into a bowl and discard the mint. Stir in the grapefruit juice and the salt. Transfer to an ice cream maker and freeze according to the manufacturer's instructions. About 10 minutes before the sorbet is done, cut the remaining mint into thin ribbons. Add to the ice cream maker and finish freezing the sorbet.

For a firmer texture, pack into freezerproof containers and freeze until firm, about 3 hours.

POMELOS

An ancestor of the grapefruit, the pomelo is thought to have originated in Malaysia. Ranging in color from yellow to light pink, they are larger than a grapefruit and have a sweet-tart flavor. Available primarily in the winter, choose pomelos that are heavy for their size, free of blemishes, and fragrant. Use them as you would grapefruits.

POMELO, CILANTRO & CASHEW SALAD

Separate 2 pomelos into segments (page 264). Place in a bowl, add 1 minced red jalapeño chile and ¼ cup chopped fresh cilantro (fresh coriander), and toss. In a small bowl, stir together 1 Tbsp Asian fish sauce, 1 tsp light brown sugar, and the zest and juice of 1 lime. Pour over the pomelo and toss gently. Stir in ½ cup (2 oz/60 g) toasted and coarsely chopped cashews. Makes 6 servings.

GRAPEFRUIT, AVOCADO & CRAB SALAD

Melons

CANTALOUPE

HONEYDEW

GALIA MELON

WATERMELON

The term melon describes a large round or oval fruit with skin that ranges from thin to very thick and encloses juicy flesh surrounding a central core of small seeds. Before they are even cut into, most melons have an alluring aroma that hints of the sweet, smooth flesh inside.

The earliest forms of melons, probably gathered from the wild, were appreciated in ancient Egypt. The fruits were later grown in the Middle East before being embraced in Europe and the Americas. Watermelons, however, originated in Africa.

The many melon varieties fall into two groups: muskmelons and watermelons. The former includes a wide array of melons, from the cantaloupe with its textured skin to the smooth-skinned honeydew, to recent hybrids such as the Galia melon, which resembles a cantaloupe but has a pale green flesh. Watermelons, which occupy a category of their own, can be rounds the size of large honeydews or ovals so large and weighty that they need to be hefted with both hands. Their seeds may be scattered throughout the flesh.

Some melons are harvested throughout the year, but most reach farmers' markets during the summer months.

Cantaloupe & Honeydew

Both orange-fleshed cantaloupe and juicy, pale green honeydew melons fall under the banner of muskmelons, the large and fragrant fruit of trailing vines native to Asia. Depending on the variety, their protective rinds range from creamy white to pale yellow, celadon to dark green, or a striped or speckled combination of all these hues. The flesh of muskmelons can be ivory, yellow, orange, or green. Heritage varieties much sought for their intensely flowery fragrance and complex flavors include the pale, oval Crenshaw; the green-striped Charentais from France; and the round, wrinkled, bright yellow casaba.

Muskmelons are at their peak from mid- to late summer. They are popular in fruit salads, on antipasti platters with prosciutto, puréed to make drinks, or sliced into wedges as a refreshing treat during summer's hottest months.

Watermelon

Originating in Southern Africa, watermelons are the quintessential summertime fruit. Their crisp, sweet flesh is loved for its refreshing juiciness. The most familiar variety sports stripes of light and dark green on its rind and has bright red flesh within. Some retain their shiny black seeds, though seedless varieties have become more popular. Capable of exceeding 100 pounds, most watermelons come to market between 10 to 15 pounds. New watermelon varieties have become more widely available. They may have flesh that ranges from yellow or orange to deep pink. Some are oblong, while others are small and round like a cantaloupe.

Watermelons are at their best during the summer. Cut into wedges, they help define summer picnics and barbecues. More formally, watermelons lend themselves to sorbets, fruit salads, or appetizers when paired with salty feta cheese or drizzled with balsamic vinegar.

Cantaloupe Cubes in Spiced Syrup

MAKES 4 SERVINGS

½ cup (4 oz/125 g) sugar

2 Tbsp grated fresh ginger

1 star anise

2 Tbsp fresh lemon juice

1 tsp grated lemon zest

1 cantaloupe, peeled, seeded, and cubed

Heat the sugar and ½ cup (4 fl oz/125 ml) water in a saucepan over medium heat, stirring until the sugar dissolves. Add the ginger, star anise, and lemon juice and zest and simmer gently for 10 minutes to make a syrup. Let cool and then strain.

Spoon the cantaloupe into a bowl and drizzle with the spiced syrup. Serve at once.

Grilled Salmon with Spicy Melon Salsa

MAKES 4 SERVINGS

½ cup (3 oz/90 g) *each* finely chopped honeydew, cantaloupe, and watermelon

1 serrano chile, minced

2 Tbsp coarsely chopped fresh cilantro (fresh coriander)

1 Tbsp honey

2 tsp grated lime zest

1 tsp fresh lime juice, or more to taste

Salt and freshly ground pepper

4 salmon fillets, 6 oz (185 g) each, skin removed

1 Tbsp canola oil, plus extra for the grill

In a bowl, stir together the melons, chile, cilantro, honey, lime zest and juice, and a generous pinch each of salt and pepper. Stir well and let stand at room temperature for 15–30 minutes. Taste and adjust the seasonings with lime juice, salt, or pepper.

Prepare a grill for direct-heat over medium-high heat (page 264) or use a stovetop grill pan. Sprinkle the salmon pieces all over with salt and pepper, then drizzle with the canola oil. Lightly oil the grill rack and place the fish on the grill. Cook until browned on one side, 3–4 minutes. Turn and cook until browned on the other side and just opaque in the center, 3–4 minutes more.

Transfer the salmon to a serving platter and serve right away with the salsa.

Honeydew-Lime Ice Pops

MAKES 6 SERVINGS

½ cup (4 oz/125 g) sugar

1 lime

1 honeydew melon, peeled, seeded, and diced (about 4 cups/24 oz/750 g)

Pinch of salt

Combine ½ cup (4 fl oz/125 ml) water and the sugar in a small saucepan. Using a vegetable peeler, remove 2 large strips of zest from the lime and add to the saucepan. Bring to a boil. Cook, stirring, until the sugar has dissolved, 3–4 minutes. Let the resulting syrup cool and then strain.

Purée the sugar syrup, melon, and the salt in a food processor until very smooth. If desired, pour the mixture through a fine-mesh strainer to remove any remaining chunks of melon. Taste and add lime juice, if needed, to cut the sweetness.

Pour the mixture into eight ½-cup (4-fl oz/125-ml) ice pop molds, add sticks, and freeze until solid, 6–8 hours. (The mixture can also be poured into small paper cups and frozen just until barely firm; add the sticks and freeze until solid. Peel away the cups and serve.)

GALIA MELON

A type of muskmelon, the Galia is a hybrid developed in Israel and now grown where other melons thrive. With its netted skin, it resembles a cantaloupe but is somewhat larger, and the flesh, rather than orange, is yellowish green and very sweet and juicy. The best way to choose a Galia is by its aroma, detected at the stem end. Galia melons are available in the summer, use as you would a cantaloupe.

FROZEN MELON MARGARITA

Working in batches, purée 3 cups (15 oz/420 g) melon cubes in a blender and transfer to a bowl. Stir in ½ cup (4 oz/125 g) sugar and the juice of 2 limes. For each of 3 batches, fill a blender with 2½ cups (20 oz/625 g) ice. Add 1 cup (8 fl oz/250 ml) of the melon purée, ½ cup (4 fl oz/125 ml) tequila, and ¼ cup (2 fl oz/60 ml) triple sec. Purée until blended and pour into salt-rimmed glasses. Makes 8 servings.

HONEYDEW-LIME ICE POPS

WATERMELON, FETA & MINT SALAD

Watermelon, Feta & Mint Salad

MAKES 6 SERVINGS

¾ cup (¾ oz/20 g) fresh
mint leaves

1 Tbsp sugar

1 serrano chile, seeded and chopped

2 Tbsp rice vinegar

1 Tbsp fresh lime juice

3 Tbsp extra-virgin olive oil

Salt and freshly ground pepper

1 small seedless watermelon, about
3 lb (1.5 kg), peeled, seeded, and cut
into 1-inch (2.5-cm) cubes

6 oz (185 g) feta cheese, crumbled
into ¼-inch (6-mm) pieces

Process ½ cup (½ oz/15 g) of the mint
leaves and the sugar in a food processor
until well blended. Add the chile, vinegar,
and lime juice and process again. With the
motor running, drizzle in the olive oil. Transfer
the vinaigrette to a bowl and season with
a pinch each of salt and pepper.

Place the watermelon and cheese into
individual bowls and drizzle the vinaigrette
on each. Garnish with the remaining mint
leaves and serve right away.

Summer Watermelon Granita

MAKES 4 SERVINGS

½ cup (4 oz/125 g) sugar

½ cup (4 fl oz/125 ml) white grape juice

1 small seedless watermelon about
3 lb (1.5 kg), peeled, seeded, and cut
into 1-inch (2.5-cm) chunks

1 Tbsp fresh lemon juice

Add the sugar and juice in a small
saucepan and bring to a boil, stirring often,
3–4 minutes. Cook, stirring, until the sugar
has dissolved, 1–2 minutes. Pour the resulting
syrup into a heatproof bowl and let cool.
Cover and refrigerate for about 1 hour.

Process the watermelon in a food processor
until a thin, watery, and somewhat grainy
purée forms, about 30 seconds.

In a bowl, stir together the sugar syrup,
lemon juice, and watermelon purée. Pour
into a shallow 9-by-13-inch (23-by-33-cm)
baking pan. Cover with aluminum foil, then
place in the freezer. Freeze until a thin layer
of ice forms on the surface and the edges
begin to harden about ½ inch (12 mm)
in from the sides, about 1 hour.

Remove the pan from the freezer and use
a sturdy fork to break up the surface of the
mixture, breaking up any frozen areas into
small shards. Cover the pan and freeze for
30 minutes, then repeat the scraping and
mixing 3 or 4 times, for a total of about
2½ hours freezing time. The mixture will
be icy and grainy. To serve, spoon into
individual bowls and serve right away.

Watermelon Wedges with Hot Pepper Salt

MAKES 6 SERVINGS

2 tsp red pepper flakes

2 tsp grated lime zest

3 Tbsp coarse salt

6 watermelon wedges

To make the hot pepper salt, in a small bowl,
gently stir together the red pepper flakes,
lime zest, and salt. (The salt can be stored
for up to 5 days in an airtight container.)

Sprinkle the hot pepper salt on the
watermelon wedges. Serve right away.

*Watermelon wedges sprinkled with hot
pepper salt are the perfect treat for a picnic
or summer outing.*

Stone Fruits

Stone fruits are so named because they contain a pit, or stone, in the middle of the flesh. Regardless of size, stone fruits from the smallest cherries to the largest peaches grow on trees. When at their peak, each member of this group has its own sweet flavor and juicy flesh that seems to melt in the mouth.

Most stone fruits originated in Asia. Peaches, for example, were mentioned in ancient Chinese literature. According to food historians, traders probably brought some of these fruits to Europe, and from there they were transported to the New World. In modern times, growers have developed numerous varieties of these popular fruits, as well as hybrids such as the pluots and apriums—both crosses of plums and apricots—that fill the market crates in the summer. Dozens of peach and nectarine varieties have been created to bring out desirable colors, flavors, and other characteristics.

Depending on the region, stone fruits are first harvested in spring, beginning with cherries. Plums and the last of the peaches can appear in markets through September.

Look for fresh apricots with a deep golden color and sweet fragrance. They should be soft enough to give slightly when gently pressed. Avoid any hard fruit, as it will never ripen fully on the counter. Lightly green-tinged fruit may become sweeter if enclosed in a paper bag at room temperature for 1 or 2 days. Once ripe, apricots should be eaten as soon as possible.

Apricots

Like its close cousin, the peach, the apricot was first cultivated in China thousands of years ago, where they still grow wild. Since the delicate fruit does not travel well, the best apricots are found in markets where local growers can offer longer ripening on the tree and extra care in handling. Some varieties are golden, while others display a soft blush of pink on the fruit's skin. The Blenheim variety is legendary among bakers and jam-makers for its honeysuckle aroma and sweet-tart flavor.

They have a short season peaking in early to midsummer. Apricots have small pits that are easy to remove, and their delicate skins can be left on in most recipes. Apricots are much loved for their bright color and delicate texture atop tarts, between cake layers, or puréed into sauces. Made into relishes, compotes or shimmering glazes, apricots make excellent foils for poultry and roasted meats such as pork and lamb.

WORKING WITH APRICOTS

Apricots should be handled very gently, as they bruise easily. To peel the fruit: trim away the stem, cut a shallow X in the blossom end, and plunge the apricots into a large pot of boiling water until the skin peels away, 20 to 60 seconds, depending on ripeness. With a slotted spoon, transfer the fruit to ice water to cool. Drain and then peel with your fingers or a small paring knife.

BUYING CHERRIES

Make sure that cherries are large, plump, smooth, and still have stems and leaves that are firm and green. Avoid any that are wet, sticky, bruised, excessively soft, or have shriveled stems. Cherries should be used as soon as possible after purchasing. If needed, refrigerate them in a shallow container covered with a clean cloth or paper towels for up to 5 days.

Cherries

Perfectly ripe cherries are an unrivaled treat. Two primary types exist: sweet cherries and sour cherries. Sweet cherry varieties, best for eating fresh, include the deep red, plump Bing and the bright red, late-blooming Lambert. The more delicately flavored Royal Ann, Rainier, and other golden cherries may be only softly tinged with pink or red. Sour cherry varieties, also known as tart cherries, include the light red Montmorency and the deeply red Morello. They tend to be smaller and softer and are prized for their flavor and texture when cooked in pies, jams, and dessert sauces.

Cherries have a short season, late spring to early summer depending on the variety. They are perfect for summer pies, pastries, and ice cream. They also pair well in savory dishes with poultry and meats, especially duck, pheasant, pork, and venison.

WORKING WITH CHERRIES

Try to keep the stem on the cherries until ready to use, since once they are removed, the fruit spoils quickly. To prevent them from molding, wash cherries under cold running water just before using. To use cherries in recipes, pit the fruit with a cherry pitter or a small, sharp knife.

Sautéed Apricots with Mascarpone & Almonds

MAKES 6 SERVINGS

3 Tbsp unsalted butter

1 vanilla bean, split lengthwise

¼ cup (2 oz/60 g) light brown sugar

Pinch of salt

¼ tsp pure almond extract

12 firm but ripe apricots, pitted and cut into ½-inch (12-mm) wedges

1 cup (8 oz/250 g) mascarpone cheese, at room temperature

2 Tbsp confectioners' (icing) sugar

1 Tbsp whole milk

½ cup (2 oz/60 g) sliced (flaked) almonds, toasted

Heat a frying pan over medium heat. Add the butter and cook until it melts, foams, and turns a light, nutty brown color. Scrape the seeds from the vanilla bean into the brown butter. Add the brown sugar and the salt. Cook, stirring, until the brown sugar is melted, 1–2 minutes. Stir in the almond extract and apricots, reduce the heat to medium-low, and cook, stirring, until the fruit is warmed through, 1–2 minutes.

Using an electric mixer on low speed, beat together the mascarpone, confectioners' sugar, and milk until smooth, 1–2 minutes.

Spoon the apricots into serving dishes. Top with the mascarpone mixture, sprinkle with the almonds, and serve right away.

Crisp Apricot Turnovers

MAKES 8 SERVINGS

¾ lb (375 g) firm but ripe apricots, pitted and cut into slices ½ inch (12 mm) thick

¼ cup (2 oz/60 g) plus 2 tsp sugar

1 Tbsp cornstarch (cornflour)

1 Tbsp unsalted butter

1 tsp *each* fresh lemon juice and grated lemon zest

¼ tsp ground cinnamon

Pinch of salt

Pastry Dough (page 263), chilled and rolled out until ⅛ inch (3 mm) thick

1 large egg beaten with 1 Tbsp whole milk

Combine the apricots, ¼ cup sugar, the cornstarch, butter, lemon juice and zest, cinnamon, and salt in a saucepan. Cook over medium heat, stirring often, until the apricots break down slightly, 25–30 minutes. Let cool.

Preheat the oven to 375°F (190°C). Line a baking sheet with parchment (baking) paper. Cut the dough into eight 5-inch (13-cm) rounds. Fill each round with a spoonful of the apricot mixture. Fold the dough and press the edges with a fork to seal. Brush with the egg-milk mixture, sprinkle with the 2 tsp sugar, and prick the tops with a fork. Place on the prepared baking sheet. Bake until lightly browned, 25–30 minutes. Let cool and serve right away.

Chicken Thighs with Roasted Apricots

MAKES 4 SERVINGS

8 bone-in chicken thighs

Salt and freshly ground pepper

2 tsp olive oil

1 small yellow onion, diced

1 tsp *each* minced garlic and fresh ginger

¼ cup (2 fl oz/60 ml) fresh orange juice

1 cup (8 fl oz/250 ml) dry vermouth

8 firm but ripe apricots, halved and pitted

2 Tbsp honey

Preheat the oven to 400°F (200°C). Season the chicken with salt and pepper. In an ovenproof sauté pan over medium-high heat, brown the chicken in the olive oil and set aside on a plate. Pour out all but 2 Tbsp fat from the pan. Add the onion, garlic, ginger, and a pinch of salt. Cook, stirring, until the onions are translucent, 4–5 minutes. Add the orange juice and vermouth and bring to a boil, scraping up the brown bits on the pan bottom. Cook until the liquid is reduced by half, 4–5 minutes. Return the chicken, skin side up, to the pan, cover, and cook in the oven until the chicken is tender, about 25 minutes.

Meanwhile, place the halved apricots, cut side up, in a small baking dish. Drizzle the apricots with honey and sprinkle with a generous amount of pepper.

When the chicken is tender, remove the cover and raise the oven temperature to 450°F (230°C). Place the dish of apricots in the oven and cook both for 10 minutes longer. The chicken should be nicely browned and the apricots should have just a bit of color.

When the chicken is done, transfer it to a serving platter with the juices from the pan. Nestle the apricots around the chicken and serve right away.

PLUOTS

A pluot (pronounced "plue-ott") is a hybrid of a plum and an apricot. Pluots range in size from small like an apricot to slightly larger like a plum. Their skin is more similar to a plum but can range from red to slightly orange to green. They are slightly fragrant, sweet, and several varieties exist. Among the most popular are Dapple Dandy, Candy Stripe, and Flavor King. Use pluots as you would apricots or plums.

PLUOT GALETTE

Roll Pastry Dough (page 263) into a 15-inch (38-cm) round and put on a baking sheet. Cut 1½ lbs (750 g) pluots into thin slices and arrange on the dough, leaving a 2 inch (5 cm) border. Sprinkle with 2 Tbsp sugar. Fold the dough over the fruit, leaving the center open and brush with 1 egg yolk whisked with 1 tsp water, sprinkle with another 1 Tbsp sugar. Bake in a 425°F (220°C) oven for 50 minutes. Makes 8 servings.

CRISP APRICOT TURNOVERS

SWEET DARK CHERRY CLAFOUTI

Crostini with Smoked Duck & Cherry Relish

MAKES 6 SERVINGS

1 cup (6 oz/185 g) pitted cherries

1 baguette, cut into slices ¼ inch (6 mm) thick

2 Tbsp extra-virgin olive oil, plus extra for brushing

¼ cup (1 oz/30 g) thinly sliced green (spring) onions, white and light green parts

1 Tbsp minced shallot

2 tsp balsamic vinegar

Salt and freshly ground pepper

2 cups (12 oz/390 g) shredded smoked duck meat

Cut ½ cup (3 oz/90 g) of the cherries in half and finely chop the rest. Preheat the oven to 450°F (230°C).

Brush the baguette slices with olive oil and place on a baking sheet. Toast until lightly browned, 5–6 minutes.

In a bowl, combine the halved and chopped cherries, green onions, shallot, balsamic vinegar, and the 2 Tbsp olive oil. Add a generous pinch each of salt and pepper.

Top each toasted bread slice with a spoonful of the shredded duck and then top with a spoonful of the cherry mixture. Place on a serving platter and serve right away.

Fresh Ricotta & Cherry Parfaits

MAKES 4 SERVINGS

1½ lb (750 g) cherries, pitted and halved

1 Tbsp granulated sugar

1 tsp kirsch

2 cups (16 oz/500 g) fresh whole-milk ricotta cheese

2 Tbsp confectioners' (icing) sugar

1 tsp pure vanilla extract

⅛ tsp pure almond extract

¼ cup (2 oz/60 g) almonds, toasted and coarsely chopped

In a bowl, gently toss together the cherries, granulated sugar, and kirsch. Let stand at room temperature for at least 10 minutes or up to 1 hour.

In another bowl, stir together the ricotta, confectioners' sugar, vanilla extract, and almond extract.

Spoon ¼ cup (2 oz/60 g) of the ricotta mixture into each of 4 serving glasses. Top with ½ cup (3 oz/90 g) cherries. Repeat with another ¼ cup of the ricotta mixture and ½ cup of the cherries. Top each with the almonds. Serve right away.

Sweet Dark Cherry Clafouti

MAKES 6 SERVINGS

Unsalted butter for greasing

1 lb (500 g) dark sweet cherries, pitted

1 cup (8 fl oz/250 ml) whole milk

¼ cup (2 fl oz/60 ml) heavy (double) cream

½ cup (1½ oz/45 g) sifted cake (soft-wheat) flour

4 large eggs, at room temperature

½ cup (4 oz/125 g) granulated sugar

⅛ tsp salt

½ tsp pure almond extract

Confectioners' (icing) sugar for dusting

Position a rack in the upper third of the oven and preheat to 350°F (180°C). Butter a shallow 1½-qt (1.5-l) baking dish. Arrange the cherries in the prepared dish.

In a saucepan over medium-low heat, heat the milk and cream until small bubbles appear around the edges of the pan. Remove from the heat and vigorously whisk in the flour, a little at a time, until no lumps remain.

In a bowl, whisk together the eggs, granulated sugar, and salt until creamy. Whisk in the milk mixture and the almond extract. Pour over the cherries. Place the dish on a baking sheet. Bake until browned, 45–55 minutes. Transfer to a rack to cool. Dust with confectioners' sugar and serve warm.

SOUR CHERRIES

Smaller than sweet cherries, dark crimson colored sour cherries can be found in the market only a few weeks of summer. They are usually too sour to eat raw but are excellent when baked in pies or turnovers. They are also excellent made into preserves for a taste of summer in the other months of the year. Two well-known varieties are Morello and Montmorency.

SOUR CHERRY PIE

Preheat the oven to 425°F (220°C). Prepare and roll out Pie Dough (page 263). In a bowl, stir together ½ cup (4 oz/125 g) sugar and ¼ cup (1½ oz/45 g) all-purpose (plain) flour. Add 1 lb (500 g) pitted sour cherries to the bowl and stir to coat. Transfer to the dough-lined pan and dot with 1 Tbsp unsalted butter, cut into small pieces. Carefully transfer the second dough round over the fruit. Trim the overhang, fold the top crust edge under the bottom; press to seal and crimp decoratively. Cut slits in the top and place the pie on a baking sheet. Bake for 15 minutes. Reduce the temperature to 350°F (180°C) and continue to bake until the cherries are soft when pierced through one of the slits and a syrup has formed, 20–25 minutes. Remove from the oven and let cool for at least 15 minutes before serving. Makes 8–10 servings.

Choose fruits that give slightly to gentle pressure, emanate a flowery fragrance, and are free of bruises and blemishes. Avoid nectarines and peaches with tinges of green, as they were picked too early and may never ripen properly. Arrange them stem end down and store at room temperature. If they are soft, refrigerate them in a plastic bag for 4 to 5 days.

Nectarines & Peaches

Native to China, peaches are now grown in temperate regions of Asia, the United States and Europe. Nectarines are special variety bred from and grafted onto peach trees. A downy, velvety peel distinguishes peaches, while nectarines have a smooth skin that displays more red tones. The two fruits can be substituted for each other in recipes.

Peaches and nectarines are at their best from early to mid-summer. Both come in freestone and clingstone varieties, referring to how loosely or tightly the fruit's silken flesh holds to its large, wrinkled pit. Freestone are much easier for cutting and cooking. Both may have either yellow or white flesh. The white varieties are often more fragrant, sweeter and juicier. Peaches and nectarines are enjoyed fresh; made into pies, jams, and ice cream; and appear in sauces, glazes, and fillings for poultry and meats.

WORKING WITH NECTARINES & PEACHES

Wash peaches and nectarines under cold running water just before using them. To halve, use a small, sharp knife to cut down to the pit following the fruit's crease, then grasp the fruit in both hands and rotate the halves in opposite directions to separate. Scoop out the pit with the tip of the knife or a spoon.

BUYING PLUMS

Plums should be smooth, heavy for their size, and give gently when pressed, particularly at the blossom end. The freshest plums retain a white, powdery bloom on their peel. Avoid any that are wrinkled or overly soft. To soften hard plums, place them in a paper bag for a few days at room temperature. Store fully ripe plums in a plastic bag in the refrigerator for 3 to 5 days.

Plums

Hundreds of varieties of plums come to market during the mid- to late summer months. Both their tart-tasting peels and their juicy, translucent flesh can range in color from golden yellow to bright green to endless shades of pink, purple and scarlet. The best ones to eat fresh are large, red-skinned plums with yellow flesh, such as the popular Santa Rosa or the Burbank, North American plums named for the 19th century horticulturalist who developed over 100 different types of plums from original Japanese trees. Yellow-skinned, yellow-fleshed plums such as the Shiro are excellent for jams and conserves. The deeply purple, oval Italian plum, also known as the prune plum, holds it shape and flavor well during cooking and baking. Likewise, smaller plums such as the aptly named Greengage, the prized French plum called Mirabelle, and the pointed, bright blue Damson are ideal for highlighting in desserts, infusing in liqueurs, and boiling into jams and jellies.

WORKING WITH PLUMS

Plum skins are easy to peel if the fruits are fully ripe. If the plums are still firm and their skin clings stubbornly, cut a shallow X in the blossom end and plunge the fruit into boiling water for 1 to 2 minutes depending on the ripeness. Rinse in cold water to cool, and then carefully slip off their skins.

Nectarines with Arugula & Burrata Cheese

MAKES 6 SERVINGS

2 cups (2 oz/60 g) baby arugula (rocket) leaves

3 nectarines, halved, pitted, and cut into ½-inch (12-mm) slices

½ lb (250 g) burrata cheese

Extra-virgin olive oil for drizzling

Coarse salt and freshly ground pepper

Crusty bread for serving

Arrange the arugula on a large serving platter. Scatter the nectarine slices evenly over the top.

Place the cheese on the platter. Drizzle with olive oil and sprinkle with salt and pepper.

Serve right away with slices of crusty bread, letting diners layer the arugula, nectarines, and cheese on top of the slices.

Grilled Peaches with Honey & Black Pepper

MAKES 4 SERVINGS

¼ cup (3 oz/90 g) honey

Salt and freshly ground pepper

4 firm but ripe peaches, halved and pitted

1 Tbsp extra-virgin olive oil

Prepare a grill for direct-heat cooking over medium-high heat (page 264 or use a stovetop grill pan). Oil the grill grate.

In a small bowl, combine the honey, a pinch of salt, and 1 tsp pepper. Brush the peach halves with olive oil and place on the grill rack, cut side down. Cover the grill and cook until the peaches just begin to soften, 3–4 minutes. Turn the peaches and brush with the honey mixture. Cook until tender but not falling apart, 2–3 minutes longer. Serve right away.

Serve these peaches alongside vanilla ice cream or Greek yogurt.

Nectarine & Peach Gratin

MAKES 4 SERVINGS

Unsalted butter for greasing

2 cups (¾ lb/375 g) *each* peeled, pitted, and thinly sliced ripe peaches and nectarines, at room temperature

1½ tsp fresh lemon juice

½ tsp pure almond extract

1 cup (8 oz/250 g) sour cream

2 Tbsp whole milk

¼ cup (2 oz/60 g) granulated sugar

½ cup (3½ oz/105 g) light brown sugar, or as needed

Preheat a broiler (grill).

Butter an ovenproof 9-inch (23-cm) square baking dish. Place the fruit on the bottom of the prepared dish. Sprinkle with the lemon juice and ¼ tsp of the almond extract and toss gently.

In a large bowl, whisk together the sour cream, milk, the remaining ¼ tsp almond extract, and the granulated sugar. Spoon evenly over the fruit. Sprinkle evenly with the ½ cup brown sugar, adding more if needed to cover.

Place in the broiler 4–5 inches (10–13 cm) from the heat source and broil (grill) until the brown sugar melts, 6–8 minutes. Serve right away.

WHITE PEACHES

One of summer's most savored delights is the white peach. Fragrant and floral, white fleshed peaches have been around just as long as yellow peaches but lost popularity among farmers because their skin is more delicate and their growing season is shorter. Now enjoying a resurgence at farmers' markets, they can be used in most recipes that call for yellow peaches. Use as you would yellow peaches.

PEACH BELLINI

In a blender, purée 2 ripe white or yellow peaches, peeled, halved, and pitted, with 1 Tbsp superfine (caster) sugar until smooth. Fill each of 4 Champagne flutes evenly with the purée. Top each with chilled Champagne or Prosecco, and stir gently to blend. Serve right away garnished with thin slices of peach. Makes 4 servings.

NECTARINES WITH ARUGULA & BURRATA CHEESE

WARM PLUMS WITH HONEY & GREEK YOGURT

Warm Plums with Honey & Greek Yogurt

MAKES 4 SERVINGS

2 Tbsp honey

1 Tbsp light brown sugar

1 tsp pure vanilla extract

6 firm but ripe plums, halved, pitted, and cut into 1-inch (2.5-cm) wedges

1 Tbsp unsalted butter, cut into pieces

2 cups (16 oz/500 g) plain Greek-style yogurt

¼ cup (1 oz/30 g) pistachios, toasted and coarsely chopped

Preheat the oven to 425°F (220°C).

In a baking dish, stir together the honey, sugar, and vanilla. Add the plums and toss well with the honey mixture. Dot the plums evenly with the butter. Roast until just warm, 5–7 minutes.

Spoon a small amount of plums and a spoonful of juices from the baking dish into each of 4 serving glasses, then add ½ cup (4 oz/120 g) yogurt to each. Top with the remaining plums. Sprinkle with the pistachios and serve right away.

Stone Fruit Salad with Hazelnuts & Blue Cheese

MAKES 6 SERVINGS

2 Tbsp rice vinegar

1 tsp honey

Salt and freshly ground pepper

½ cup (4 fl oz/125 ml) extra-virgin olive oil

6 cups (¾ lb/375 g) baby arugula (rocket)

2 small firm but ripe plums, halved, pitted, and cut into ¼-inch (6-mm) slices

2 small firm but ripe apricots, halved, pitted, and cut into ¼-inch (6-mm) slices

1 firm but ripe peach, halved, pitted, and cut into ¼-inch (6-mm) slices

¼ cup (1½ oz/45 g) hazelnuts (filberts), toasted, skinned, and coarsely chopped

¼ cup (1½ oz/45 g) crumbled firm blue cheese

In a small bowl, whisk together the vinegar, honey, and a pinch each of salt and pepper. Whisking constantly, slowly add the olive oil, and continue to whisk until well combined to make a vinaigrette.

In a large bowl, gently toss together the arugula, plums, apricots, peach, and hazelnuts. Add half of the vinaigrette and toss gently, adding more as needed to lightly coat the arugula. Sprinkle with the cheese and serve right away.

Roasted Plums with Blue Cheese

MAKES 4 SERVINGS

4 plums, halved and pitted

2 tsp olive oil

3 oz (90 g) soft blue cheese, such as gorgonzola, at room temperature

4–8 thin slices whole-grain bread

Preheat the oven to 450°F (230°C).

Brush the cut side of the plums with olive oil and mound 1 tsp of cheese into each cavity. Place the plums, skin-side down, in a shallow baking dish just large enough to hold them and bake until the cheese has warmed through, about 10 minutes. Remove from the oven and let cool slightly.

Arrange the warm plums on a platter and serve with the bread slices.

APRIUMS

A relatively new fruit at the market, apriums are a cross between an apricot and plum. They differ from a pluot (page 224) in that they are ¼ plum and ¾ apricot, which makes them resemble the apricot more, though but they taste like a combination of their parent fruits. Look for apriums at the market during warm summer months.

APRIUM MUFFINS

Using a mixer, beat ½ cup (4 oz/125 g) softened unsalted butter, ¼ cup (2 oz/60 g) plus 2 Tbsp light brown sugar, and ¼ cup (2 oz/60 g) plus 2 Tbsp sugar until light and fluffy. One at a time, beat in 2 large eggs. Mix in 1 tsp pure vanilla extract. In a separate bowl, stir together 2 cups (10 oz/315 g) all-purpose (plain) flour, 2 tsp baking powder, 1 tsp baking soda (bicarbonate of soda), and ½ tsp salt. With the mixer on low speed and working in batches, add the dry ingredients alternately with 1 cup (8 fl oz/250 ml) buttermilk, mixing well after each addition. Fold in 4 pitted and diced apriums. Divide among twelve 1-cup (8-fl oz/250-ml) muffin cups lined with paper liners. Bake in a preheated 400°F (200°C) oven until a toothpick inserted into the center comes out clean, 25–28 minutes. Makes 12 servings.

Tree Fruits

Apples, pears, and other so-called tree fruits contain multiple seeds, in contrast to a single stone or pit. The seeds are typically inedible, with the exception of juicy pomegranate seeds, the prized part of the fruit. The fruits in this category have a broad range of flavors and textures. For example, apples can be tart or sweet. Pears are sweet and often very juicy. Depending on the variety, persimmons can be astringent or mild and puddinglike in texture. Quinces are so tart that they are always cooked rather than eaten raw. Figs may be the sweetest of all tree fruits.

Botanically related to roses, apples, pears, and quinces descended from wild varieties first gathered in Central Asia hundreds, even thousands, of years ago. Figs and pomegranates, members of separate families, can be traced to ancient Middle Eastern civilizations. North America has a native persimmon, but it was long ago surpassed in popularity by varieties imported from China and Japan.

The appearance of tree fruits in the market is generally the harbinger of the cool weather of fall and winter. Because figs need full days of sun to ripen properly, they are harvested in both late summer and early autumn.

Apples

Crisp, round apples are perhaps the most common tree fruit in the world. There are some 7,000 known varieties, although far fewer are widely available. Sweet, thin-skinned apples are best for eating raw, as a snack out of hand or paired with aged cheese, while tart apples are ideal for making pies, cakes, pastries, or applesauce.

Most apples are harvested from autumn to early winter. The most recognizable varieties for eating fresh include Red Delicious, sweet Golden Delicious, tart and green Granny Smith, red- and yellow-streaked Gala, and the red-marbled McIntosh. Bakers seek out varieties such as Jonathan, Cortland, Pippin, Winesap, Gravenstein and Braeburn for their sturdy texture that balance sweetness with pronounced tartness and hints of spiciness. Specialty apples are highly regional, especially heritage varieties, so it pays to ask farmers about the best ones local to your area for eating and cooking.

BUYING PEARS

Look for smooth, unblemished fruits with their stems still attached. They should be fragrant and just beginning to soften near the stem. Pears must be left at room temperature to soften and sweeten and are ready to eat when they wrinkle a little at the stem end and are slightly soft at the blossom end. Store in a plastic bag in the refrigerator for 3 to 5 days.

Pears

A perfectly ripe pear has soft, juicy flesh with a delicately floral flavor. First cultivated in Asia over 4,000 years ago, today's thousands of varieties vary in size, color, contour, texture, and flavor. Among the most familiar are the Anjou, a green, almost egg-shaped pear tinged with yellow; the Bartlett (also known as the Williams pear) with thin, light green skin; the firm, long-necked Bosc with distinctive brown russeting; the green-yellow, meltingly tender-fleshed Comice; and the tiny, red-blushed Seckel.

Sweet, fragrant pears are at their peak season during autumn and winter, a time when their freshness is especially welcome. Excellent for eating out of hand, pears also add elegance to tarts, pastries, and other winter desserts. Poached whole in wine or transformed into compote, the flavor of pears blends well with ginger, vanilla, orange peel, raisins, and warm spices such as clove, cinnamon, and ginger.

WORKING WITH PEARS

Pears can be left unpeeled for eating fresh, but be sure to peel them before cooking, as their tough skins have a slightly bitter flavor that is accentuated when cooked. When cutting pears, halve them lengthwise, then scoop out the core with a small spoon. To core whole fruit, use a spoon or melon baller to scoop out the seeds from the pear's blossom end.

Apple & Artisan Cheddar Panini

MAKES 4 SERVINGS

8 slices sourdough bread, each about ½ inch (12 mm) thick

2 Tbsp olive oil

6 oz (180 g) artisan Cheddar cheese, thinly sliced

1 red apple, cored, and cut into slices about ¼ inch (6 mm) thick

Preheat a sandwich grill or a grill pan. Place 4 bread slices on a work surface and brush 1 side of each slice with the olive oil. Layer the cheese and apple slices evenly on the unoiled side of the bread slices. Place the remaining 4 bread slices on top and brush the tops with oil. Gently press the sandwiches to compress them.

Place 1 sandwich in the grill or on the grill pan (if using a grill pan, set a heavy object such as a filled tea kettle on top of the sandwich). Cook until the bread is golden and toasted, the cheese is melted, and the apple is warmed through, 3–5 minutes. Repeat with the remaining sandwich. Serve right away.

Sautéed Apples with Pork Chops

MAKES 4 SERVINGS

4 boneless pork loin chops, about 1½ inches (4 cm) thick

Salt and freshly ground pepper

¼ cup (1½ oz/45 g) all-purpose (plain) flour

1 Tbsp unsalted butter

1 Tbsp olive oil

1 small yellow onion, diced

2 Granny Smith apples, peeled, cored, and cut into ½-inch (12-mm) wedges

1 tsp minced fresh rosemary

1 tsp honey

1 cup (8 fl oz/250 ml) chicken broth

2 Tbsp heavy (double) cream

Season the pork chops with salt and pepper. Mix the flour with a pinch of each salt and pepper. Dredge the pork chops in the flour, shaking off the excess. Melt the butter with the olive oil in a large frying pan over medium heat. Add the chops and cook until browned, 2–3 minutes per side. Set aside.

Add the onion to the pan with a pinch each of salt and pepper and sauté until soft and translucent, 4–5 minutes. Add the apples, rosemary, honey, and a pinch each of salt and pepper. Sauté until the apples are just golden in spots, 1–2 minutes. Add the broth and, using a wooden spatula, scrape up any browned bits in the pan bottom. Return the chops to the pan and reduce the heat to medium-low. Cover and cook, turning the chops once, until they are tender and register 145°F (63°C) on an instant-read thermometer, 7–10 minutes.

Transfer to a serving plate and tent with aluminum foil. Add the cream to the pan, raise the heat to high, and cook until the sauce is slightly thickened, 1–2 minutes. Pour the sauce over the chops and serve right away.

Rustic Apple Crostata

MAKES 6–8 SERVINGS

3 sweet apples, such as Fuji, peeled, cored, and thinly sliced

⅓ cup (2½ oz/75 g) light brown sugar

1 tsp cornstarch (cornflour)

½ tsp ground cinnamon

Pinch of ground nutmeg

Pinch of salt

Pastry Dough (page 263), chilled and rolled into a 16-inch (40-cm) round

1 large egg yolk beaten with 1 Tbsp heavy (double) cream

1 tsp granulated sugar mixed with ½ tsp ground cinnamon

1 Tbsp unsalted butter, cut into pieces

In a large bowl, toss together the apples, brown sugar, cornstarch, cinnamon, nutmeg, and salt.

Place the dough round on a baking sheet lined with parchment (baking) paper. Mound the apple mixture in the center of the round, leaving a border of about 3 inches (7.5 cm). Fold the dough border over onto the apples, leaving a circle of apples exposed in the center. Brush the dough with the egg mixture and then sprinkle with the cinnamon-sugar mixture. Dot the exposed fruit with the butter. Refrigerate until the dough is firm, 20–30 minutes.

Preheat the oven to 375°F (190°C). Bake the crostata until the crust is golden brown and the apples are tender and bubbling, 45–50 minutes. Slide the parchment and crostata onto a rack and let cool at least 20 minutes. Cut into wedges and serve warm or at room temperature.

APPLE & ARTISAN CHEDDAR PANINI

PEAR TARTE TATIN WITH WINTER SPICES

Pear Tarte Tatin with Winter Spices

MAKES 6–8 SERVINGS

8-by-10-inch (20-by-25-cm) rectangle of frozen puff pastry, thawed in the refrigerator

3 Tbsp unsalted butter

¼ cup (2 oz/60 g) granulated sugar

4 firm, ripe pears, peeled, halved, and cored

½ cup (4 oz/120 g) light brown sugar

2 Tbsp finely chopped crystallized ginger

1 Tbsp fresh lemon juice

¼ tsp *each* ground nutmeg and cloves

½ tsp ground cinnamon

Refrigerate the pastry dough for 15 minutes. Preheat the oven to 375°F (190°C). Using 1 Tbsp of the butter, grease a 12-inch (30-cm) round baking dish with 2-inch (5-cm) sides. Sprinkle the granulated sugar evenly over the bottom.

Place the pears, cut side up, in a tight layer in the prepared baking dish. Sprinkle with ¼ cup (2 oz/60 g) of the brown sugar. Top with the crystallized ginger and lemon juice. Cut the remaining 2 Tbsp butter into bits and dot the tops of the pears. In a small bowl, stir together the remaining ¼ cup (2 oz/60 g) brown sugar and the nutmeg, cloves, and cinnamon. Sprinkle over the pears.

On a floured work surface, roll out the pastry a little larger than the diameter of the baking dish and ¼ inch (6 mm) thick. Transfer to the dish. Tuck the edges of the pastry into the bottom of the dish to form a rim that encircles the pears. Prick the top all over with a fork.

Bake until the crust is golden brown, the pears are tender, and a thickened, golden syrup has formed in the dish, about 1 hour. Let stand for 5 minutes.

Run a knife around the inside edge of the dish to loosen the sides. Invert the tart onto a plate, dislodging and replacing any pears that may have stuck to the dish. Cut into wedges and serve warm.

Poached Pears in Riesling with Sweet Cream

MAKES 4 SERVINGS

4 firm pears such as Bosc or Anjou, peeled, halved, and cored

2½ cups (20 fl oz/625 ml) Riesling

½ cup (4 oz/125 g) granulated sugar

1 lemon zest strip, 2 inches (5 cm) long and ¾ inch (2 cm) wide

1 cup (8 fl oz/250 ml) heavy (double) cream

¼ cup (1 oz/30 g) confectioners' (icing) sugar

Place the pears in a nonreactive saucepan large enough to hold them in a single layer lying down. Add the wine, sugar, lemon zest, and 1½ cups (12 fl oz/375 ml) water. Bring to a boil over medium-high heat. Reduce the heat to medium-low, set a heatproof plate on top of the pears to keep them submerged, and simmer until a knife can be inserted easily into the center of a pear, 35–40 minutes. Remove the plate. Let the pears cool to room temperature in the liquid. Using a slotted spoon, transfer the pears to shallow bowls.

In a large bowl, whip the cream until soft peaks form, about 5 minutes. Add the confectioners' sugar and beat until stiff peaks form, 2–3 minutes more. Top the pears with the whipped cream and serve right away.

Smoked Chicken, Grilled Pear & Fontina Sandwich

MAKES 6 SERVINGS

½ cup (4 oz/125 g) unsalted butter

12 slices firm white bread, brioche, or challah

¾–1 lb (375–500 g) fontina cheese, sliced

6 slices smoked chicken

2 ripe pears, thinly sliced

In a small, heavy saucepan melt the butter over low heat. Remove from the heat and let stand briefly. Using a spoon, skim off the foam from the surface. Pour off the clear yellow liquid into a bowl. Discard the milky solids left behind in the pan.

Lay 6 slices of the bread on a work surface and top with the cheese, chicken, and pear slices. Top with the remaining bread slices.

Brush a wide frying pan or stove-top grill pan with the melted butter and warm over medium heat. Working in batches, add the sandwiches and weight with a pan lid. Cook until the bottoms are golden brown, about 4 minutes. Adding more butter as needed, turn the sandwiches, replace the lid, and cook on the second sides until golden brown and the cheese has melted, about 4 minutes more. Remove from the pan and keep warm while you cook the remaining sandwiches. Cut the sandwiches in half and serve right away.

ASIAN PEARS

Available from summer through fall, the Asian pear belongs to a species completely different from regular pears. They resemble large, pale yellow green apples. The pears have a flowery fragrance, a mildly sweet flavor, and a slightly granular texture that bursts with juice from the first bite. Asian pears are best served raw. Eat them on their own or in salads.

PEAR, HAZELNUT & DILL SALAD

Whisk together 2 Tbsp white wine vinegar, 1 tsp grainy mustard, 1 tsp honey, and a pinch each of salt and pepper. Whisk in ½ cup (4 fl oz/125 ml) extra-virgin olive oil to make a vinaigrette. Core and dice 1 Asian pear and place in a bowl. Add 6 cups (¾ oz/375 g) salad greens, ¼ cup (⅓ oz/10 g) minced fresh dill, and ¼ cup (2 oz/60 g) chopped hazelnuts (filberts). Toss with vinaigrette to lightly coat the greens. Makes 6 servings.

BUYING POMEGRANATES

Look for large, firm, deeply red fruits that boast a plump shape and smooth peel. Avoid pomegranates with dried, shrunken, browned skin. Fruits that feel heavy for their size will have the most juice in the seeds. Store pomegranates at room temperature for 1 to 2 days, or refrigerate in a plastic bag for up to 3 weeks.

Pomegranates

Since ancient times, the pomegranate has been an important food throughout the Middle East. The trees proliferate in Mediterranean climates, including Europe and California, and the seeds and juice are popular addition to the respective cuisines. Symbolic of fertility in many cultures, pomegranates derive their name from the Latin for "seeded apple." Once split open, the thick, leathery, deep red skin of this legendary fruit reveals hundreds of gem-like seeds, each surrounded by juicy, sparkling, ruby-red pulp.

Pomegranates arrive in markets during the autumn and winter months. Their seeds add sparkle and crunch when sprinkled as garnish over fruit, salads, ice cream or pastries. Its bright, fruity, sweet-sour juice appears in marinades, vinaigrettes, sauces, glazes, and drinks.

WORKING WITH POMEGRANATES

To seed a pomegranate, cut off the peel near the blossom end and remove it along with the bitter white pith. Lightly score the remaining peel into quarters from end to end. Working over a bowl, carefully break the fruit apart with your hands. Bend the peel inside out, and use your fingertips to lightly brush the seeds from the white, sectional membranes.

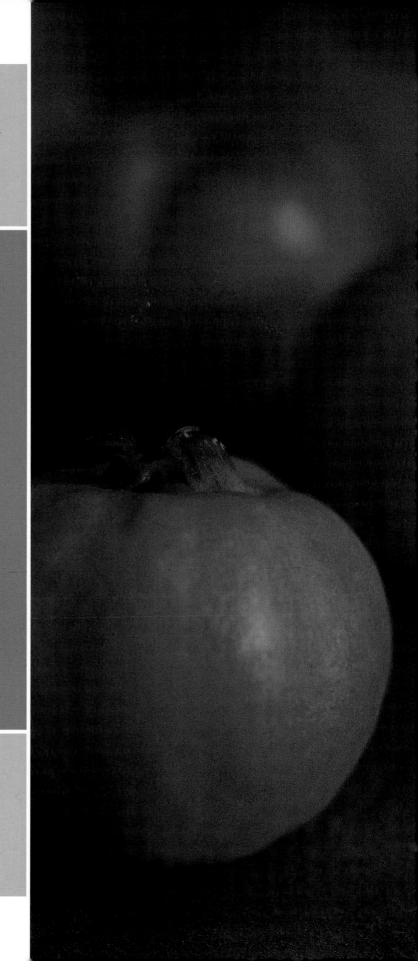

Quinces

A relative of the rose, quinces predate their close cousins apples and pears by many centuries. The fruit, also known as golden apple, is famed for a heady perfume that can fill an entire room. When raw, the fruit's hard, dry, cream-colored flesh has a powerfully astringent flavor so its not eaten raw. Once cooked, the quince softens, turns a deep rose-pink color and becomes even more flowery in fragrance.

Like other tree fruits, quinces come to market during the autumn and winter. Supported by sweet ingredients to temper its astringency, the fruit marries well with lamb, pork, poultry, and game in slow-cooked stews and roasts. Quince stars in jams and jellies and also often contributes its high-pectin setting power to other, softer fruits. Cooked down to a concentrated fruit paste, it becomes membrillo, a classic Spanish accompaniment to aged cheese.

Watercress Salad with Pomegranate & Citrus

MAKES 6 SERVINGS

2 Tbsp sherry vinegar

2 tsp minced shallot

Salt and freshly ground pepper

½ cup (4 fl oz/125 ml) extra-virgin olive oil

1 blood orange, segmented (page 264) with juice reserved

1 navel orange, segmented (page 264) with juice reserved

Seeds from 1 pomegranate

6 cups (6 oz/185 g) watercress leaves

In a bowl, stir together the vinegar, shallot, and a pinch each of salt and pepper. Whisking constantly, slowly add the olive oil until well combined to make a vinaigrette.

Add 1 Tbsp each of the juices to the vinaigrette, whisking to combine, and reserve the rest for another use.

Remove the orange segments from the juice and place in a large bowl. Add the pomegranate seeds and watercress along with half of the vinaigrette and toss to combine. Add more vinaigrette if needed to lightly coat the watercress leaves. Serve right away.

Pomegranate-Glazed Lamb Chops

MAKES 4 SERVINGS

8 lamb rib chops, frenched

Salt and freshly ground black pepper

2 tsp minced rosemary

Extra-virgin olive oil for drizzling

1 cup (8 fl oz/250 ml) fresh orange juice

½ cup (4 fl oz/125 ml) pomegranate juice

1 Tbsp pomegranate molasses

Seeds from 1 pomegranate

1 Tbsp honey

½ tsp red pepper flakes

Sprinkle the lamb chops with salt, pepper, and rosemary. Drizzle with olive oil and let stand at room temperature for 30–60 minutes or cover and refrigerate for up to 24 hours (remove the chops 30–60 minutes before grilling).

In a saucepan over high heat, bring the orange juice, pomegranate juice, molasses, pomegranate seeds, honey, and red pepper flakes to a boil. Reduce the heat to medium and cook until thickened to a syrupy consistency, 20–25 minutes to make a glaze. Divide the glaze between 2 bowls.

Prepare a grill for direct-heat cooking over high heat. Grill the lamb chops until well browned, 3–4 minutes. Turn and brush with the pomegranate glaze from one of the bowls. Continue cooking until the chops are tender and register 125°F (52°C) on an instant-read thermometer for medium-rare, or until cooked to your liking. Transfer to a platter, drizzle with the glaze from the second bowl, and season with pepper. Serve right away.

Frozen Pomegranate Semifreddo

MAKES 6–8 SERVINGS

1¼ cups (10 oz/315 g) sugar

3 large eggs

2 large egg yolks

1 tsp pure vanilla extract

Pinch of salt

2 Tbsp pomegranate molasses

¼ cup (2 fl oz/60 ml) pomegranate juice

Seeds from 1 pomegranate

2 cups (16 fl oz/500 ml) heavy (double) cream

In a heatproof bowl, combine the sugar, eggs, and egg yolks. Set the bowl over a saucepan of (but not touching) simmering water. Whisk constantly until the mixture is light and fluffy and registers 140°F (60°C) on an instant-read thermometer, about 10 minutes. Remove the bowl from over the saucepan, stir in the vanilla, salt, pomegranate molasses, pomegranate juice, and one-fourth of the pomegranate seeds. Let cool.

In a bowl, beat the cream until stiff peaks form. Gently fold the cream into the cooled egg mixture.

Line a 9-by-5-by-3-inch (23-by-13-by-7.5-cm) loaf pan with plastic wrap, leaving 1 inch (2.5 cm) of wrap hanging over each side. Transfer half of the mixture to the prepared pan, sprinkle one-third of the remaining pomegranate seeds over the top, and then transfer the rest of the egg mixture to the pan. Sprinkle with half of the remaining seeds and cover the pan with the overhanging plastic wrap. Freeze the semifreddo overnight until firm.

Remove the semifreddo from the pan, peel off the plastic, and cut into slices. Arrange on serving plates, sprinkle with the remaining pomegranate seeds, and serve right away.

POMEGRANATE-GLAZED LAMB CHOPS

HOMEMADE QUINCE PASTE WITH MANCHEGO CHEESE

Homemade Quince Paste with Manchego Cheese

MAKES 10–12 SERVINGS

2 lb (1 kg) quinces
3½–4 cups (1¾–2 lb/875 g–1 kg) sugar
1 tsp ground cinnamon
Block of Manchego cheese, shaved
Crackers for serving

Peel each quince, cut in half, and remove the core and seeds. Place the peels, cores, and seeds in a square of cheesecloth (muslin), bring the corners together, and tie securely with kitchen string.

Slice the quinces and place in a heavy nonreactive pot. Add water to cover and the cheesecloth pouch. Bring to a boil over high heat, reduce the heat to low, and cook slowly, uncovered, until the fruit is tender, 20–40 minutes. You may want to stop the cooking a few times, for 1–2 hours, to let the quinces rest and deepen their color. Add more water if the mixture begins to dry out.

Remove the cheesecloth pouch and discard. Mash the quinces with a potato masher or purée in a food processor. In a clean saucepan, combine the mashed quinces, the cooking liquid, 3½ cups (1¾ lb/875 g) of the sugar, and the cinnamon. Cook over low heat, stirring often, until thick, about 20 minutes. Taste and add more sugar if the paste seems too tart.

Ladle into hot, sterilized canning jars to within ¼ inch (6 mm) of the rims. Wipe the rims clean, cover with sterilized canning lids, and seal tightly. Process the jars in a hot-water bath for 10 minutes. Check the seals, label the jars, and store in a cool pantry for up to 1 year. (Jars that do not form a good seal should be refrigerated and used within 1 month.)

To serve, spread quince paste on top of each cheese slice or cracker. Serve right away.

Quince Teacake with Sweet Syrup

MAKES 6–8 SERVINGS

¾ cup (6 oz/185 g) light brown sugar
1 cinnamon stick, lightly crushed
Zest of 1 orange
1 Tbsp fresh orange juice
2 quinces each peeled, cored, and cut into 8 wedges
¾ cup (6 oz/185 g) unsalted butter, at room temperature, plus extra for greasing
1½ cups (7½ oz/235 g) all-purpose (plain) flour, plus extra for flouring
¾ cup (6 oz/185 g) granulated sugar
1 tsp pure vanilla extract
3 large eggs
1½ tsp baking powder
Pinch of salt
Confectioners' (icing) sugar for dusting

In a nonreactive saucepan over medium-high heat, cook the brown sugar, cinnamon stick, orange zest and juice, and 2½ cups (20 fl oz/625 ml) water until the sugar has dissolved. Add the quince wedges and bring to a boil. Reduce the heat to medium-low and simmer until tender, 45–60 minutes. Let the quince cool in the syrup then cut into ½-inch (12-mm) dice. Strain the syrup and set aside.

Preheat the oven to 325°F (165°C). Butter and flour a 9-inch (23-cm) round cake pan. In the bowl of an electric mixer, beat the butter and granulated sugar until light and fluffy, 3–4 minutes. Beat in the vanilla. Add the eggs 1 at a time, beating well after each addition. In a another bowl, combine the flour, baking powder, and a salt. Fold the flour mixture and diced quince into the butter mixture. Transfer to the prepared pan. Bake until a toothpick inserted into the center comes out clean, 35–40 minutes. Let cool on a rack for 10 minutes; unmold onto the rack and let cool.

Cut the cake into slices, drizzle each slice with the reserved syrup, and sprinkle with confectioners' sugar.

Quince Poached in Vanilla Syrup

MAKES 4 SERVINGS

2½ cups (1¼ lb/625 g) sugar
1 vanilla bean, split lengthwise
2 Tbsp fresh lemon juice
3 quinces, peeled, halved, cored, and cut into slices ½ inch (12 mm) thick
1½ tsp grated lemon zest, plus strips for garnish

In a nonreactive saucepan large enough to hold the quinces, bring the sugar, vanilla bean halves, lemon juice, and 2 cups (16 fl oz/500 ml) water to a boil over medium-high heat, stirring to dissolve the sugar. Cook, stirring often, until a light to medium-thick syrup forms, about 10 minutes.

Reduce the heat to low, add the quinces and the lemon zest, and poach the fruit, uncovered, until tender when pierced with a fork, about 20 minutes. Remove from the heat and let stand until nearly at room temperature, about 15 minutes.

Ladle the quinces into bowls or glasses with some of the syrup. Garnish with lemon zest strips and serve right away.

BUYING FIGS

Choose plump figs that are dry and soft to the touch but not wrinkled, bruised, or discolored. Fruits with a web of delicate fissures are highly prized. Extremely fragile and perishable, figs are best eaten as soon as possible after purchase. If needed, store them in the refrigerator for 1 to 2 days, arranged in a single layer on a tray lined with paper towels.

Figs

Among the world's oldest known foods, figs were used to sweeten dishes long before sugarcane was widely cultivated. Native to Western Asia, the small trees now flourish in the warm, dry climates of the Middle East, Mediterranean, and California. The soft, pear-shaped fig is, in fact, a swollen flower that carries within it many tiny seeds that are the true fruit of the tree.

Figs ripen during mid- to late summer, with some varieties lingering for a second harvest in early fall. Their skin can be purple, green, yellow, brown, or white, and their flesh ranges from pale gold to deep, rich red. Among the best-known varieties are the Adriatic, Mission (also known as Black Mission and California Black), Calimyrna, Kadota, and Smyrna. Fresh, ripe figs are best eaten out of hand but are also excellent served with cheese, grilled to accompany cured meats or savory salads, and paired with creamy desserts.

WORKING WITH FIGS

Rinse fresh figs under cold running water and gently pat dry just before serving. Over-handling will bruise the delicate fruit. The peel is edible and, unless specified in a recipe, can be left on the fruit. Use a sharp paring knife to cut figs in half lengthwise.

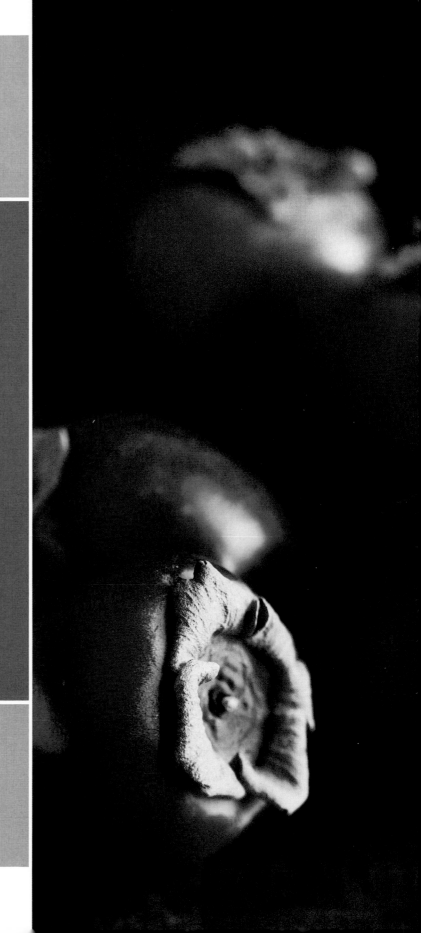

Choose plump fruits that are heavy for their size and free of blemishes. Their skin should be smooth and shiny, with no hint of yellow. Look for intact stem caps that are firm and green, not gray or brittle. Once ripe, persimmons should be eaten right away or refrigerated in a plastic bag for up to 2 days.

Persimmons

Persimmon trees display their fruit on bare branches like small and bright lanterns. Persimmons were originally cultivated in China and later carried to the West from Japan in the late 19th century. Those most familiar to us today belong to the kaki species—a word still used for the fruit in many countries.

Persimmons are in peak season from late October to late February. Two basic varieties come to markets: the heart-shaped Hachiya that must soften completely before losing its astringency and the smaller, rounder Fuyu that can be enjoyed while still firm. Crisp and sweet, Fuyu persimmons pair well with darker salad greens such as spinach, frisee, and endive. Though they require long ripening at room temperature, Hachiya persimmons reward the patient cook with a rich, sweet flavor that epitomizes the harvest season. They are delicious in cakes, puddings, quick breads, and ice creams.

WORKING WITH PERSIMMONS

Ripen Hachiya persimmons inverted on their caps until extremely soft. Unless using a food mill, Hachiyas must be peeled before cooking or puréeing. The Fuyu variety may be served with its skin on or peeled for a more delicate texture. If the persimmons are too hard to use, speed up the ripening by placing them inside a paper bag with a banana or apple.

Fig & Fromage Blanc Crostini

MAKES 6 SERVINGS

8 figs, halved lengthwise

1 Tbsp balsamic vinegar

Salt and freshly ground pepper

8 slices ciabatta bread, each ½ inch (12 mm) thick

½ cup (4 oz/125 g) fromage blanc

1 cup (1 oz/30 g) arugula (rocket) leaves

2 Tbsp extra-virgin olive oil

Preheat the oven to 400°F (200°C). Line a baking sheet with parchment (baking) paper.

Place the figs, cut side up, on the prepared sheet. Drizzle with the vinegar, then season with salt and pepper. Roast the figs until very tender, 10–15 minutes. Set aside. Leave the oven on.

Arrange the bread slices on a baking sheet and toast until lightly brown and crisp, 4–5 minutes.

Spread about 1 Tbsp of the fromage blanc on each slice of toasted bread. Top with 2 fig halves and use a fork to mash them gently. Cut each crostini in half. Top with a few arugula leaves and drizzle with olive oil. Season lightly with salt and pepper and serve right away.

Figs Simmered in Red Wine

MAKES 4 SERVINGS

2 cups (16 fl oz/500 ml) dry red wine

¼ cup (2 oz/60 g) sugar

4 peppercorns

2 whole cloves

1 cinnamon stick, lightly crushed

Pinch of grated nutmeg

8 figs, stemmed

½ cup (4 oz/125 g) crème fraîche

In a nonreactive saucepan, bring the wine, sugar, peppercorns, cloves, cinnamon stick, and nutmeg to a boil. Reduce the heat to low, add the figs, and simmer until just tender, 6–8 minutes. Using a slotted spoon, transfer the figs to a serving dish. Raise the heat to high and cook the liquid until it thickens to a syrup, 8–10 minutes.

Squeeze the bottom of each fig so it cracks open at the top. Place a spoonful of crème fraîche in each fig. Drizzle with some of the syrup. Serve right away.

Pork Medallions with Roasted Figs

MAKES 4 SERVINGS

1 pork tenderloin, about 1½ lb (750 g), cut crosswise into 4 medallions

Salt and freshly ground pepper

1 Tbsp olive oil

1 cup (8 fl oz/250 ml) hard apple cider

1 sprig fresh rosemary

2 tsp grainy mustard

6 figs, halved lengthwise

1 Tbsp unsalted butter

Preheat the oven to 400°F (200°C).

Season the pork with salt and pepper. In an ovenproof frying pan over medium-high heat, warm the olive oil. Cook the pork, turning once, until browned, 4–5 minutes total. Transfer to a plate. Add the cider, rosemary, and mustard to the pan, bring to a boil, and scrape up any browned bits from the pan bottom. Cook until the cider is reduced by half, 3–4 minutes. Return the pork to the pan, place in the oven, and cook for 6 minutes. Remove from the oven, turn the pork, and add the figs. Return to the oven and cook until the pork is tender and registers 145°F (63°C) on an instant-read thermometer, 6–8 minutes longer.

Transfer the pork and figs to a serving platter. Place the pan over medium heat and whisk in the butter to make a sauce. Spoon the sauce over the top of the pork and figs and serve right away.

PORK MEDALLIONS WITH ROASTED FIGS

PERSIMMONS WRAPPED IN SMOKED HAM

Persimmons Wrapped in Smoked Ham

MAKES 6 SERVINGS

¾ cup (6 fl oz/180 ml) balsamic vinegar

½ sprig rosemary

12 thin slices smoked ham

2 Fuyu persimmons, each cut into 12 wedges

Salt and freshly ground pepper

In a small nonreactive saucepan over medium heat, cook the balsamic vinegar and rosemary until the vinegar has reduced to ¼ cup (2 fl oz/60 ml), 15–20 minutes. Remove from the heat, discard the rosemary sprig, and let cool.

Cut each slice of ham in half. Wrap a piece around each persimmon wedge (use a toothpick to secure each ham slice, if desired). Arrange the wrapped persimmons on a serving plate, drizzle with the reduced balsamic vinegar, and season with salt and pepper. Serve right away.

Persimmon & Endive Salad

MAKES 6 SERVINGS

2 Tbsp sherry vinegar

2 tsp minced shallot

1 tsp grainy mustard

Salt and freshly ground pepper

¼ cup (2 fl oz/60 ml) extra-virgin olive oil

¼ cup (2 fl oz/60 ml) walnut oil

3 Fuyu persimmons, thinly sliced

2 heads Belgian endive (chicory/witloof), cored and cut crosswise into ½-inch (12-mm) strips

1 head radicchio, cored and cut into ½-inch (12-mm) strips

½ cup (2 oz/60 g) walnuts, toasted (page 264) and coarsely chopped

In a small bowl, stir together the vinegar, shallot, mustard, and a pinch each of salt and pepper. Whisking constantly, slowly add the olive and walnut oils until well combined to make a vinaigrette.

In a large bowl, combine the sliced persimmons, endive, radicchio, and walnuts. Add half of the vinaigrette and toss well to mix. Add more vinaigrette as needed to lightly coat the endive and radicchio. Serve right away.

Roasted Persimmon Wedges with Pistachios

MAKES 6 SERVINGS

4 Fuyu persimmons, each cut into 6 wedges

2 Tbsp extra-virgin olive oil

1 Tbsp honey

1 Tbsp minced fresh thyme

Salt and freshly ground pepper

¼ cup (1 oz/30 g) pistachios, toasted and coarsely chopped

Preheat the oven to 450°F (230°C). Line a baking sheet with parchment (baking) paper.

In a bowl, toss the persimmon wedges with the olive oil, honey, thyme, and a generous pinch each of salt and pepper. Transfer to the prepared sheet and spread out in one layer. Roast the persimmons until just tender, 12–15 minutes.

Transfer to a serving dish and sprinkle with the pistachios. Serve right away.

HACHIYA PERSIMMONS

The deep orange Hachiya persimmon must be ripened until meltingly soft before it is edible. When the fruit has ripened, the flesh is creamy and rich, with a hint of honey and pumpkin flavor. Puréed, it is a great flavoring for muffins and quick-bread batters, custards, puddings, ice creams, and pies. Available in the fall at the farmers' market.

PERSIMMON BREAD

In a stand mixer fitted with a paddle attachment, mix together ½ cup (4 oz/125 g) softened unsalted butter, ½ cup (3½ oz/105 g) light brown sugar, and ½ cup (4 oz/125 g) sugar until fluffy. Add 2 large eggs and 1 tsp pure vanilla extract and beat well. In a separate bowl, combine 1½ cups (7½ oz/235 g) all-purpose (plain) flour, 1 tsp baking soda (bicarbonate of soda), and 1 tsp salt. Add to the butter mixture and beat on low speed until combined. Stir in ½ cup (4 oz/125 g) sour cream and 1 cup (8 oz/240 g) peeled and puréed Hachiya persimmons. Transfer to a buttered 9-by-5-by-3-inch (23-by-13-by-7.5-cm) loaf pan. Bake in a 350°F (180°C) oven until a toothpick inserted into the center comes out clean, about 1 hour. Cool on a rack for 10 minutes, then unmold, and let cool completely. Makes 1 loaf.

Other Fruits

RHUBARB

GRAPES

Notable fruits found at the farmers' market that do not belong to another family are rhubarb and grapes, two very distinct produce items. Classified by botanists as a vegetable, rhubarb is commonly regarded as a fruit, though it is used in savory as well as sweet preparations. The stalks are edible only after cooking and, despite being sweetened, retain an appealing and unmistakable tartness. Whereas only one variety of rhubarb is grown for the market, many types of grapes are cultivated. Most are sweet and juicy; some can be slightly tart.

The ancestors of today's rhubarb were wild plants growing in Asia. Rhubarb eventually traveled to Europe, where it was appreciated for its medicinal qualities before it was used in the kitchen. Grapes, on the other hand, are an ancient fruit grown by the Egyptians, Greeks, and Romans. Grapes can be divided into two broad color groups: red or green. Within these general categories, grapes are distinguished from each other as those having seeds or those that are seedless.

Rhubarb usually has two growing seasons: spring and summer. Each of the many varieties of grape is harvested during a different month, but most grapes appear at the market from spring to autumn.

Rhubarb

First domesticated in China nearly 3,000 years ago, rhubarb spread west in the 18th century to Russia and Europe, where it was much desired for its many healing properties. Now rhubarb is grown mostly in cool climates. Its long, celery-like stalks range in color from pale pink to cherry red, with growing tinges of green as the plant matures. Although actually a vegetable, rhubarb is now treated much like a fruit in the kitchen. Its young stalks may be combined with other fruits, especially strawberries, which also come to market with the rhubarb during spring and early summer.

Rhubarb is usually cooked with a good dose of sugar to balance its pronounced tartness. Its delicious transformation after sweetening and cooking has earned it the nickname "pie plant." Cobbler, sorbet, relishes, and brightly flavored sauces to accompany duck or game are other classic uses for the fruit.

BUYING GRAPES

Choose grapes that are plump, firm, and colorful. Avoid grape bunches with any mold, bruises, or clusters of soft fruit that fall easily from their stems. Bloom is a naturally occurring powdery substance that covers freshly harvested grapes. Whether green or red, grapes can be stored in a plastic bag in the refrigerator for up 1 week.

Grapes

Grapes come in many sizes and colors. Their coloring ranges from sparkling silver green to deep purple black. They reflect the specific local conditions of soil and climate in which they were cultivated. Nearly 90 percent of the grapes grown for the table belong to the European species *Vitis vinifera*. Along with famous wine varietals, this group includes grapes like the red Emperor; crunchy Flame; blue-black Royal; and the oblong, green Thompson. Less familiar varieties such as the fragrant Muscat and the Muscadine are highly local specialities.

Depending on the specific variety, grapes come to market from late spring through summer to early fall. Convenient to eat, grapes are most commonly enjoyed fresh as casual snacks or as garnish on platters. They frequently add color to salads; appear in classic sauces to accompany sautéed fish, meats, and poultry; and can be added into breads or pastries.

WORKING WITH GRAPES

Rinse grapes carefully just before eating or cooking and let them drain on paper towels. For the most flavor when eating grapes fresh, bring them to room temperature. Snip large bunches into smaller clusters with kitchen shears for using as a garnish on breakfast platters or cheese trays.

Shaved Rhubarb Salad with Almonds & Cheese

MAKES 6 SERVINGS

1 Tbsp fresh orange juice

1 Tbsp white wine vinegar

Grated zest of 1 orange

Pinch of sugar

Salt and freshly ground pepper

½ cup (4 fl oz/125 ml) extra-virgin olive oil

1 stalk rhubarb

6 cups (6 oz/185 g) mixed baby spring lettuces

⅓ cup (1½ oz/45 g) slivered almonds, toasted

4 oz (125 g) fresh goat cheese

In a small bowl, stir together the orange juice, vinegar, orange zest, sugar and a pinch each of salt and pepper. Whisking constantly, slowly add the olive oil to make a vinaigrette until well combined.

Using a mandoline or very sharp knife, shave the rhubarb into paper-thin slices. Place in a bowl with the lettuces and almonds. Add half the vinaigrette and toss to combine. Add more vinaigrette if needed to lightly coat the lettuces. Crumble the goat cheese over the top and serve right away.

Pork Tenderloin with Rhubarb Chutney

MAKES 4 SERVINGS

1 cup (7 oz/220 g) light brown sugar

½ cup (4 fl oz/125 ml) cider vinegar

1 Tbsp grated lemon zest

3–4 rhubarb stalks, cut into 1-inch (2.5-cm) pieces

1 cinnamon stick

2 Tbsp minced fresh ginger

½ cup (3 oz/90 g) golden raisins (sultanas)

¼ cup (1 oz/30 g) chopped walnuts

⅛ tsp salt

1 pork tenderloin, 1–1¼ lb (500–625 g)

In a nonreactive saucepan over low heat, cook the sugar, vinegar, and lemon zest, stirring until the sugar dissolves, about 5 minutes. Add the rhubarb, cinnamon, and ginger. Raise heat to medium and cook, stirring often, until the rhubarb is soft, about 15 minutes. Remove the cinnamon stick. Add the raisins, walnuts, and salt and cook for about 3 minutes. Let cool.

Preheat the oven to 425°F (220°C). Line a small roasting pan with aluminum foil. Oil a flat roasting rack and place in the pan. Place the pork on the rack.

Roast the pork until a thermometer inserted into the thickest part registers 140–150°F (60–65°C) for medium–well done, about 40 minutes. Remove from the oven, transfer the roast to a platter, tent with foil, and let rest for 15 minutes.

Transfer the pork to a carving board and cut into slices ½ inch (12 mm) thick. Arrange on a warmed platter, top with the chutney, and serve right away.

Tangy Rhubarb–Strawberry Pie

MAKES 8 SERVINGS

Pie Dough (page 263)

1½ lb (500 g) strawberries, hulled and thickly sliced (about 3 cups/12 oz/375 g)

1½ lb (750 g) rhubarb, trimmed and cut into ¾-inch (2-cm) pieces (about 3 cups/12 oz/375 g)

1 cup (8 oz/250 g) sugar

¼ cup (1 oz/30 g) plus 1 Tbsp cornstarch (cornflour)

1 large egg white, lightly beaten with a few drops of water until slightly foamy

1 Tbsp unsalted butter, cut into small pieces

Position a rack in the lower third of the oven and preheat to 425°F (220°C).

On a lightly floured work surface, roll out the larger pastry disk into a 13-inch (33-cm) round about ⅛ inch (3 mm) thick. Transfer to a 9-inch (23-cm) pie pan, easing it into the bottom and sides. Trim the overhang to ½ inch (12 mm). Roll out the remaining pastry and transfer to a baking sheet. Place both pans in the refrigerator.

In a large bowl, toss together the strawberries, and rhubarb. In a small bowl, stir together the sugar and cornstarch until free of lumps. Add to the fruit mixture and toss to combine.

Remove the pastry from the refrigerator and brush the bottom and sides with the egg wash. Spoon the fruit mixture evenly into the dish. Dot with the butter. Place the top crust over the fruit and trim the edges to leave a ¾-inch (2-cm) overhang. Fold the edge of the top crust under the edge of the bottom crust, then crimp to seal. Cut a few vents in the top. Set the pie on a baking sheet.

Bake until the crust is golden, about 40 minutes. Transfer to a rack and let cool for at least 1 hour before serving.

TANGY RHUBARB–STRAWBERRY PIE

FOCACCIA WITH GRAPES & WALNUTS

Arugula, Blue Cheese & Grape Salad

MAKES 4–6 SERVINGS

6 cups (6 oz/185 g) arugula (rocket)

2 Tbsp extra-virgin olive oil

Salt and freshly ground pepper

1½ cups (9 oz/280 g) seedless purple grapes

1 cup (5 oz/155 g) crumbled blue cheese

Place the arugula in a large bowl. In a small bowl, whisk together the olive oil and salt and pepper to taste to make a dressing. Drizzle the dressing over the arugula and toss well. Add the grapes and blue cheese and toss again.

Divide the salad among serving plates and serve right away.

Focaccia with Grapes & Walnuts

MAKES 6 SERVINGS

¼ cup (2 fl oz/60 ml) extra-virgin olive oil, plus extra for brushing

3 fresh rosemary sprigs

½ cup (2 oz/60 g) walnuts, chopped

2 cups (10 oz/315 g) all-purpose (plain) flour, plus extra for kneading

1 Tbsp active dry yeast

¾ cup (6 fl oz/180 ml) lukewarm water

1 Tbsp aniseeds, coarsely ground

1½ tsp coarse salt

2 Tbsp sugar

1½ cups (9 oz/280 g) seedless red grapes

In a frying pan over medium heat, warm the ¼ cup (2 fl oz/60 ml) olive oil and rosemary sprigs until they sizzle. Remove from the heat. Add the walnuts and discard the rosemary. Set aside.

In a small bowl, stir together ¼ cup (1½ oz/45 g) of the flour, the yeast, and ¼ cup (2 fl oz/60 ml) of the water. Let stand until bubbles form, about 20 minutes. Add the aniseeds, ½ tsp of the salt, the sugar, the remaining ½ cup (4 fl oz/120 ml) water, and the walnuts and rosemary oil. Stir in the remaining 1¾ cups (8½ oz/270 g) flour. Turn out onto a floured work surface and knead until smooth, about 10 minutes, adding just enough flour to prevent sticking. Place in a well-oiled bowl and turn the dough to oil the top. Cover and let rise in a warm place until doubled in volume, about 1 hour.

Position a rack in the bottom third of the oven and place a pizza stone on the rack. Preheat the oven to 450°F (230°C). Punch down the dough and turn out onto a floured surface. Roll out into a large oval ½ inch (12 mm) thick. Transfer to a baking sheet. Make shallow evenly spaced indentations in the surface. Brush with olive oil. Press the grapes into the indentations and sprinkle with the remaining salt. Bake on the stone until golden and crisp 15–20 minutes.

Sautéed Chicken Breasts with Champagne Grapes

MAKES 4 SERVINGS

2 tsp unsalted butter

4 boneless, skinless, boneless chicken breast halves, each about 6 oz (185 g)

1 cup (6 oz/185 g) Champagne grapes, plus 4 small clusters for garnish

¼ cup (2 fl oz/60 ml) dry white wine

¼ cup (2 fl oz/60 ml) chicken broth

3 Tbsp minced fresh cilantro (fresh coriander)

¼ tsp freshly ground pepper

In a nonstick frying pan over medium-high heat, melt the butter. Add the chicken and cook, turning once, until lightly browned, 30–60 seconds per side. Add 1 Tbsp of the grapes and stir for a few seconds. Add the wine and broth and scrape up any browned bits from the pan bottom. Reduce the heat to low, cover tightly, and simmer just until the chicken is opaque throughout, 7–8 minutes.

Add the remaining measured grapes and all but 1 tsp of the cilantro. Stir well, cover, and cook just long enough to warm the grapes, 30–60 seconds. Season with the pepper.

Transfer the chicken to warmed plates. Top with the pan juices and grapes. Garnish with the remaining 1 tsp cilantro and the grape clusters. Serve right away.

Basil Oil

MAKES ½ CUP (4 FL OZ/125 ML)

½ cup (½ oz/15 g) fresh basil, chopped

½ cup (4 fl oz/125 ml) extra-virgin olive oil

In a blender, combine the chopped basil and olive oil and blend until combined. Transfer the basil oil to a sterilized bottle or jar. Use right away or cover tightly and store at room temperature for up to 2 days.

Green Goddess Dressing

MAKES ⅓ CUP (3 FL OZ/80 ML)

1 cup (8 oz/250 g) low-fat plain yogurt

1 cup (1½ oz/45 g) loosely packed watercress leaves and tender stems

2 Tbsp chopped fresh dill

1 green (spring) onion, including tender green tops, thinly sliced

½ tsp sugar

Salt

⅛ tsp hot-pepper sauce

In a food processor or blender, combine the yogurt, watercress, dill, green onion, sugar, ½ tsp salt, and hot-pepper sauce and process until smooth. Pour the dressing into a container with a tight-fitting lid and refrigerate for serveral hours or up to overnight. The dressing will be thin when first made, but it will thicken, and the flavors mellow, when refrigerated. Shake or stir well before serving. The dressing will keep for up to 3 days.

Sage Cream

MAKES ⅓ CUP (3 FL OZ/80 ML)

12 fresh sage leaves with stems intact, coarsely chopped

½ cup (4 fl oz/125 ml) heavy (double) cream

Combine the sage and cream in a small saucepan. Place over medium heat and cook until small bubbles appear along the edges of the pan. Remove from the heat, cover, and let stand for 20 minutes to let the flavors develop. Strain the sage pieces out of the cream and use right away.

Romesco Sauce

MAKES 1 CUP (8 FL OZ/250 ML)

1 oz (30 g) baguette chunks, crusts removed

3 Tbsp red wine vinegar

⅓ cup (1½ oz/45 g) almonds, toasted (page 264)

¼ cup (1½ oz/45 g) drained diced tomatoes

1 roasted red pepper (capsicum) (page 264), sliced

1 clove garlic

1 tsp paprika

Pinch of cayenne pepper

¼ cup (2 fl oz/60 ml) olive oil

In a bowl, combine the bread with the red wine vinegar. Put the toasted almonds in a food processor and pulse until grainy. Add the bread, tomatoes, red pepper (capsicum), garlic, paprika, and cayenne. Purée until smooth. With the motor running, pour the oil in a slow stream and process until smooth. Refrigerate for at least 1 hour.

Asian Dipping Sauce

MAKES ½ CUP (4 FL OZ/125 ML)

¼ cup (2 fl oz/60 ml) light soy sauce

2 Tbsp rice vinegar

2 tsp Asian sesame oil

2 tsp chile paste

2 tsp minced green (spring) onion

1 tsp sugar

In a small bowl, whisk together the soy sauce, vinegar, sesame oil, chile paste, green onion, and sugar until the sugar dissolves. Stir in 2 Tbsp warm water. Use right away or cover tightly and refrigerate for up to 4 days.

Tapenade

MAKES 1½ CUPS (12 OZ/375 G)

3 Tbsp capers

1½ green or black olives, such as picholine or niçoise, or a mixture of both

2 cloves garlic, chopped

6–8 anchovy fillets, rinsed

1 tsp dried thyme

⅓ cup (3 fl oz/80 ml) extra-virgin olive oil

Freshly ground pepper

If using salt-packed capers, place in a bowl with cold water to cover and soak for 20 minutes. Drain, rinse well, and drain again. Pat dry on paper towels. If using vinegar-packed capers, rinse, drain, and pat dry.

In a large mortar, combine the capers, olives, garlic, anchovies, and thyme. Using a pestle, and working in a circular motion, grind together until evenly chopped. Slowly drizzle in the olive oil while stirring constantly with the pestle until a very finely chopped spread forms. Alternatively, in a food processor combine the capers, olives, garlic, anchovies, and thyme and process until finely chopped, about 1 minute. Then, with the motor running, pour in the olive oil in a slow, steady stream and process until very finely chopped. Season to taste with pepper. Serve right away or cover tightly and refrigerate for up to 3 days.

Cooked White Rice

MAKES 4–6 SERVINGS

1 cup long-grain white rice

1½ cups (12 fl oz/375 ml) water

Place the rice in a fine-mesh sieve and rinse under cold running water until the water runs clear. Transfer the rice to a heavy saucepan and add the water. Cover the pan, place it over high heat, and bring to a boil. Reduce the heat to low and simmer, undisturbed, for about 20 minutes. Remove from the heat and let stand, covered, for 5 minutes. Fluff the rice with a fork and serve right away.

Pastry Dough

MAKES ONE 10–15 INCH (25–40 CM)
PASTRY SHELL

1¾ cups (9 oz/280 g) all-purpose
(plain) flour

1 tsp sugar

½ tsp coarse salt

½ cup (4 oz/125 g) cold unsalted butter,
cut into small pieces

3 Tbsp vegetable shortening

4–5 Tbsp ice water

Place the flour, sugar, and salt in a food
processor and process to combine. Sprinkle
in the butter pieces and add the shortening.
Pulse the mixture just until combined and
it still has a few pea-sized pieces of butter
in it. Sprinkle in 3 Tbsp of the ice water and
pulse again until the dough just comes
together when squeezed in your hand. If
the dough is still dry, add a bit more water
as needed. Turn the dough out onto a large
sheet of plastic wrap and press it into a disk.
Cover with another sheet of plastic and,
using a rolling pin, roll into a rough circle, to
the thickness required by your recipe. Chill
in the refrigerator until firm, 15–20 minutes.

Pie Dough

MAKES ONE DOUBLE-CRUST
8-INCH (20-CM) PIE SHELL

2 cups (10 oz/315 g) all-purpose
(plain) flour

1 tsp salt

½ cup (4 oz/125 g) unsalted butter, at
room temperature, cut into small pieces

5–6 Tbsp (3 fl oz/90 ml) ice water

Sift the flour into a bowl, then resift with the
salt. Pour the flour into a food processor, then
add the butter. Process until pea-sized pieces
form, 1–2 minutes. Add the ice water and
process until the dough gathers into a ball.

Remove the dough from the processor and
divide roughly in half with 1 portion slightly
larger than the other. Prepare as directed in

the recipe or do the following: on a floured
work surface, roll out the larger portion
into a round about 10 inches (25 cm) in
diameter and ⅛ inch (3 mm) thick. Drape
the round over the rolling pin and carefully
transfer to an 8-inch (20-cm) pie pan. Trim
the overhang to ½ inch (12 mm).

On a floured work surface, roll out the
remaining dough portion into a round about
9 inches (23 cm) in diameter and ⅛ inch
(3 mm) thick. Place the round on a baking
sheet and refrigerate until ready to use.

Cornmeal Shortcake

MAKES ONE 8-INCH (20-CM) ROUND
OR SIX 2-INCH (5-CM) SQUARES

1½ cups (7½ oz/235 g) unbleached
all-purpose (plain) flour

½ cup (2½ oz/75 g) yellow cornmeal

1 Tbsp baking powder

1 Tbsp sugar

½ tsp salt

2 Tbsp chilled unsalted butter,
cut into small pieces

1 cup (11 fl oz/340 ml) heavy
double cream

Preheat the oven to 425°F (220°C). Line a
baking sheet with parchment (baking) paper.

In a bowl, stir together the flour, cornmeal,
baking powder, sugar, and salt. Cut in the
butter with a pastry blender until the mixture
resembles coarse meal. Add the cream
gradually, stirring until the mixture begins
to come together. Knead briefly in the bowl
until a soft, moist dough comes together into
a ball. Turn the dough onto a lightly floured
work surface and knead gently 3 or 4 times.
Pat the dough into a round about 8-inches
(20-cm) in diameter (to make individual
shortcakes, shape the dough into a 5½-by-
12-inch/14-by-30-cm rectangle and cut
into 6 equal squares) and transfer to
a baking sheet.

Bake until risen and golden brown, about
20 minutes. Serve as directed in the recipe.

Cobbler Crust

MAKES CRUST FOR A 2-QT (2-L) COBBLER

1 cup (5 oz/155 g) all-purpose (plain) flour

¼ cup (2 oz/60 g) sugar

1 tsp baking powder

½ tsp salt

¼ cup (2 oz/60 g) chilled unsalted
butter, cut into small pieces

⅓ cup (3 fl oz/80 ml) whole milk

In a bowl, combine the flour, sugar, baking
powder, and salt. Toss with a fork to blend.
Using a pastry blender, cut in the butter until
the mixture resembles coarse crumbs. Add the
milk and stir until a stiff dough forms.

Turn the dough out onto a floured work
surface and knead quickly into a ball. It will
be sticky. Wrap in plastic wrap and refrigerate
for 1 hour. Flour the work surface and, using
a rolling pin or your fingers, spread out the
dough into a round ½ inch (12 mm) thick.
Cut out 8 equal sized rounds. Set aside
until ready for use.

Crisp Topping

MAKES 3 CUPS (15 OZ/470 G)

¾ cup (4 oz/125 g) almonds,
toasted (page 264)

1½ cups (7½ oz/235 g) all-purpose
(plain) flour

⅔ cup (5 oz/155 g) granulated sugar

½ cup (3½ oz/105 g) firmly packed
brown sugar

1 tsp ground cinnamon

½ tsp ground ginger

Salt

½ cup (4 oz/125 g) chilled unsalted
butter, cut into small pieces

In a bowl, stir together the almonds, flour,
granulated sugar, brown sugar, cinnamon,
ginger, and a pinch of salt. Add the butter
and, using a pastry blender, cut in until the
mixture resembles coarse cornmeal. Set
aside until ready to use.

TECHNIQUES

Roasting Peppers

Roast the pepper (capsicum) over the flame of a gas burner or in a preheated broiler (grill), turning with tongs as needed, until the skin is blistered and charred black on all sides, about 10–15 minutes.

Slip the pepper into a paper bag and fold over the top of the bag to create a closed environment. The steam created by the hot pepper will soften the flesh and skin and also allow the skin to be easily removed.

Remove the stem and discard. Slit the pepper open, then remove and discard the seeds and ribs. Place the pepper on a cutting board and remove the blackened skin with a paring knife or your fingers. Do not rinse.

Zesting Citrus

Scrub the fruit well to remove any wax. Gently pull a citrus zester over the surface to produce fine shreds of colored zest. Or push the fruit against the fine rasps of a handheld grater or the razor-edged holes of a Microplane grater. Do not grate the bitter white pith beneath the zest. If you also need to use the juice of the lemon, remove the zest before juicing.

Segmenting Citrus

Cut a slice from the top and bottom of the citrus to reveal the flesh. Stand the fruit upright and slice downward to remove the peel and white pith. Holding the fruit in one hand, cut along either side of each segment to release it from the membrane, letting the segments drop into a bowl. When all the segments have been removed, squeeze the remaining membrane over the bowl to extract all the juice. Repeat with the remaining fruits. Remove the citrus segments and place them in a large bowl.

Blanching Vegetables

Bring a large saucepan of salted water to a boil. Add the vegetables and blanch until tender-crisp, about 5 minutes for stalky vegetables such as asparagus, green beans, or carrots and 10 minutes for heavy, denser vegetables such as potatoes. Transfer to a colander and rinse under cold running water until cool. Transfer to paper towels to drain.

Toasting Nuts

Position a rack in the middle of the oven and preheat to 325°F (165°C). Spread the nuts in a single layer on a rimmed baking sheet or a pie pan. Toast, stirring occasionally, until the nuts are fragrant and their color deepens, 5 to 20 minutes, depending on the type of nut and the size of the pieces. For example, sliced (flaked) almonds will toast quickly while the hazelnuts (filberts) will take much longer.

Toasting Seeds

Place the seeds in a dry, heavy frying pan over medium heat and warm until they are fragrant and just begin to change color, shaking the pan as necessary to prevent scorching. This should take only a few minutes. Pour onto a plate, let cool, then grind in a spice grinder or with a mortar and pestle.

Hard-Boiling Eggs

Fill a saucepan with salted water and bring to a full boil over high heat. Gently lower 1 or more eggs into the water and reduce the heat to low. Simmer for 8 minutes.

Transfer the eggs to a bowl filled with ice and water to stop the cooking. After a few minutes, remove the eggs from the water and hit them against a counter to crack, then peel away and discard the shells.

Paring Tough Stalks

Tough stalks such as asparagus or broccoli may be peeled to help them cook through. Use a small, sharp paring knife or a sturdy, sharp vegetable peeler to peel off just enough of the thick outer skin to reveal the tender flesh beneath.

Direct-heat Grilling

Charcoal grill Using long-handled tongs, arrange ignited coals into 3 heat zones: one 2 or 3 layers deep in one-third of the fire bed, another that is 1 or 2 layers deep in another third of the fire bed, and leaving the final third of the fire bed free of coals. When the coals are covered with a layer of white ash, place the food on the grill grate directly over the first layer of coals, which should be the hottest. Move the food to another area of the grill if the heat seems too high, the food appears to be cooking too fast, or if flare-ups occur.

Gas grill Turn on all the heat elements as high as they will go. Close the grill cover and let the grill heat for 10–20 minutes before using. When you're ready to cook, turn one of the heat elements off. Place the food on the grill grate directly over the hottest part of the grill. Turn down the heat as needed to adjust the grill temperature, or move the food to the cool zone if flare-ups occur.

INDEX